Basel Abbas & Ruanne Abou-Rahme
John Akomfrah
Rana Begum
Joseph Beuys
Anna Brownsted
Candoco Dance Company & Laila Diallo
Alice Channer
Nathan Coley
Edmund de Waal
Jeremy Deller
eL Seed
Jamie Fobert
Helen Frankenthaler
Naum Gabo
Regina José Galindo
Anya Gallaccio
Henri Gaudier-Brzeska
Barbara Hepworth
Callum Innes
Mary Kelly
Idris Khan
Issam Kourbaj
Linder
Richard Long
Melanie Manchot
Julie Mehretu
Gustav Metzger
Oscar Murillo
Ben Nicholson
Harold Offeh
Cornelia Parker
Vicken Parsons
Katie Paterson
Zoran Popović
Khadija Saye
Emma Smith
Caroline Walker
Kate Whitley

**Edited by Sarah Lowndes
and Andrew Nairne**

**Exhibition curated by Andrew Nairne
Assisted by Guy Haywood**

Actions.
The image of the world can be different

Kettle's Yard
University of Cambridge
2018

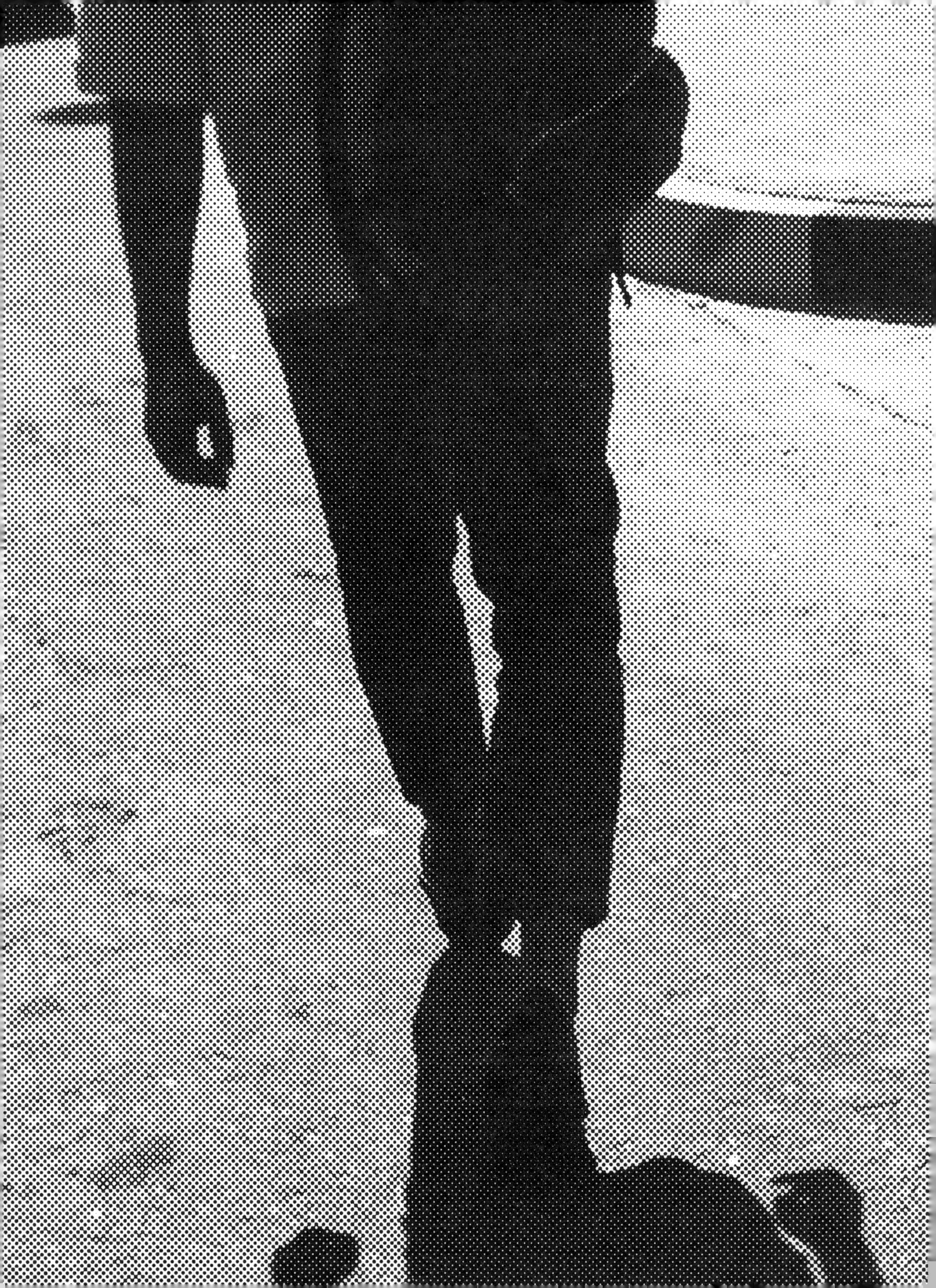

Preface
Andrew Nairne

Inspired by the visionary artist Naum Gabo, *Actions. The image of the world can be different* reflects the energising diversity of art now and seeks to reassert the potential of art as a poetic, social and political force in the world.

The exhibition celebrates the opening of the new Kettle's Yard. Presenting the work of thirty-eight artists, it aims to show the potential of our new galleries and education spaces, complementing the uniqueness of the Kettle's Yard House and collection. These new spaces have been superbly designed by Jamie Fobert Architects. They are a further sensitive and imaginative extension from the original cottages, converted by Jim Ede in 1957, the year he opened Kettle's Yard. The first dramatic extension to the cottages, designed by Leslie Martin and David Owers, opened in May 1970 with a dazzling concert by Jacqueline du Pré and Daniel Barenboim. Martin and Owers' renowned architectural achievement doubled the area available for the collection, enabled concerts to be held and included a sequence of three small galleries. Over the following two decades, a series of further extensions were completed, each time increasing the space available for temporary exhibitions.

In 2004 an opportunity arose to enlarge Kettle's Yard significantly. Michael Harrison, the Director for nearly twenty years, had both the vision to imagine the potential of creating new spaces for education and the determination to raise the funding needed. Education was at the heart of Jim Ede's conception of Kettle's Yard, but for many years the room used for working with schools, community groups and for practical workshops was by necessity a small converted gallery. The new Education Wing, with its three generous spaces, will transform the role Kettle's Yard can play in the life of the community and the University.

Finally, in 2012, it was decided to encompass redesigning the galleries as part of a single holistic project, to include a new welcome area, shop and café.

Over the thirteen years it has taken to reach this moment, many organisations and hundreds of people, including many artists, have given generously of their time, advice and support. Thank you to everyone. Substantial grants from the Heritage Lottery Fund and Arts Council England have, at different stages, enabled the ambition and scope of the project to grow. Their confidence in our vision for Kettle's Yard as a place where the heritage of the House is given life by exhibitions and activities, has been vital and encouraged others to donate. We owe a particular debt of gratitude to Anne Lonsdale, Chair of the Kettle's Yard Committee, to Paul Zuckerman and Alex van Someren, the Chairs of our two successive Development Groups and to Michael Harrison. I would also like to single out my colleagues Summar Hipworth and Cherie Evans who, consecutively, have managed the many challenges of a major building project from preparation to completion. Our considerable thanks of course to our colleagues in the University, especially within Estate Management, who have given their expertise and continuing support.

As I write in November 2017, *Actions* is an exhibition in the making. In New York, one of the paintings in progress in Julie Mehretu's studio will come to Cambridge. Idris Khan and Rana Begum are making new work for specific spaces: in the new Sackler Gallery and St Peter's Church next to Kettle's Yard. We are delighted that, with additional support from Arts Council England, we have been able to commission new work from Khan, Begum, Cornelia Parker, Melanie Manchot and other artists. Manchot's project has involved a group of Bangladeshi women who live in Cambridge collaborating with the artist on a series of images made in iconic places in the city, including King's College and the Cambridge Union Debating Chamber. Most of the contemporary art which visitors will encounter is being exhibited for the first time, including new work by Vicken Parsons, Oscar Murillo and Linder.

As well as artists who have not previously exhibited at Kettle's Yard, *Actions* includes artists from the collection, artists whose work we have shown in the past and artists we are collaborating with on future exhibitions. They span different generations across the twentieth and twenty-first centuries, starting their lives in many places around the globe. As Sarah Lowndes reveals in her *Actions* timeline, the exhibition is a coming together of an astonishing array of diverse voices. They are singing many songs, yet they are all making art with purpose. Their actions as artists exemplify Gabo's belief that "the image of the world can be different".

Actions is a changing exhibition. The Cambridge-based Syrian artist Issam Kourbaj will make a repeated action each day. There will be new performances by Regina José Galindo, Harold Offeh, Emma Smith, Anna Brownsted and Candoco Dance Company, as well as talks, discussions and activities for all. Until 2 April work by all thirty-eight artists will be on display. Then for the final four weeks we will display paintings by Caroline Walker in Gallery 2 and present John Akomfrah's two-screen film *Auto Da Fé* (2016) in the Sackler Gallery. Walker is making a series of new works with the assistance of the London-based charity Women for Refugee Women. Our particular thanks to Natasha Walter and Samantha Hudson for their assistance. Akomfrah's award-winning film explores historic and contemporary migration as a consequence of religious persecution. Our deepest gratitude to all the artists in *Actions*, for their commitment to the exhibition, this book and the many events involving their participation. It has been a privilege for us to work with so many outstanding artists. Our sincere thanks also to the numerous individuals, galleries and artists' estates who have helped us in so many ways to realise the exhibition. At Kettle's Yard, Guy Haywood, Assistant Curator has been an outstanding colleague, working on every aspect of the project, as has Jennifer Powell, Head of Collection and Programme. *Actions* is among the most ambitious exhibitions Kettle's Yard has undertaken. My heartfelt thanks are due to everyone in the team for their hard work and inspiration.

This book would not have been possible without the ideas, insights and written contributions of Sarah Lowndes, who has been an exceptional co-editor. Our thanks also to Paul Goodwin for taking up our invitation to respond to Sarah Lowndes' letter, in an contemporary dialogue echoing the exchange between Naum Gabo and Herbert Read. The book has been beautifully designed by A Practice for Everyday Life.

The scale and form of *Actions*, with work displayed across the whole of Kettle's Yard including in the House, the new lift, on T-shirts and online, as well as in the city, is for us in many ways an experimental project. Its research-led nature, involving close dialogue with artists and the juxtaposition of modern art from the collection with new art, reflects our role as part of the University of Cambridge. We hope the new conversations which arise from *Actions* about the value and purpose of art, about what art can do, will be a catalyst for continuing research and experiment across our future programme. Our new Edlis Neeson Research Space offers opportunities to connect communities with artists and the collection and to open up research as a shared project of learning and discovery in which every visitor can participate.

In 1970 Jim Ede wrote of Kettle's Yard that "it could, if funds were forthcoming, one day become a centre of international interest, mounting exhibitions of such an order that people the world over would need to visit them". I believe, that with *Actions* and our future programme, we can say this day has arrived. In a letter to a student Ede also wrote "Do come in as often as you like – the place is only alive when used". Kettle's Yard has always been about life and art, and people and art. On behalf of all the outstanding staff over the past thirteen years who have contributed so much to create the new Kettle's Yard – welcome.

An exchange of letters between Naum Gabo and Herbert Read (1944)

Dear Herbert,

It is now more than a year and a half since *Horizon* asked me to write an article about my own work. At that time I lightheartedly promised to do it and only later did it dawn on me that I had engaged myself in an adventure full of peril. When an artist ventures to write about himself and about his work he is heading straight into a minefield where his first mistakes will be the end of him.

Many artists have walked innocently enough into that trap and done themselves more harm than good. Not that their works have actually suffered, but the misunderstandings and misinterpretations unloosed by their words were so confusing that it would have been better had they kept silent.

On the other hand, looking back on the destiny of many works of art in their historical array, and having in view their relation to their own time and people as well as to posterity, I have come to the conclusion that a work of art, restricted to what the artist has put in it, is only a part of itself. It only attains full stature with what people and time make of it.

I realise in making such a statement I may already have struck a mine – in fact I even sense the distant reverberations of explosions in many artistic camps, friend's and foe's.

I will therefore not walk one step further in this dangerous field without help and guidance from someone who knows the ground and who cares enough about my work and the idea it stands for. After all, my art, as all visual art is, is by nature mute. Had the painter or sculptor been able to say in words what he wanted to express with pictorial and spatial means, I do not think there would have been so many pictures and sculptures for the public to look at and for the students of art to explain.

Here is where you come in. You know more than I ever will what the public ought to know in order to judge in fairness about my work. You know both my creed and my work; could you, would you, lend me a hand and lead me through this field to safety?

Ever since I began my constructions, and this is now more than a quarter of a century ago, I have been persistently asked innumerable questions, some of which are constantly recurring up till the present day.

Such as, 'Why do I call my work "Constructive"? Why abstract?'

'If I refuse to look to Nature for my forms, where do I get my forms from?'

'What do my works contribute to society in general, and to our time in particular?'

I have often tried to answer these questions. So have you and others. Some people were satisfied, but in general the confusion is still there, and the questions still persistently recur.

I am afraid that my ultimate answer will always lie in the work itself, but I cannot help feeling that I have no right to neglect them entirely and in the following notes there may be some clue to an answer for these queries.

(1) My works are what people call 'Abstract'. You know how incorrect this is, still, it is true they have no visible association with the external aspects of the world. But this abstractedness is not the reason why I call my work 'Constructive'; and 'Abstract' is not the core of the Constructive Idea which I profess. This idea means more to me. It involves the whole complex of human relation to life. It is a mode of thinking, acting, perceiving and living. The Constructive philosophy recognizes only one stream in our existence – life (you may call it creation, it is the same). Any thing or action which enhances life, propels it and adds to it something in the direction of growth, expansion and development, is Constructive. The 'how' is of secondary importance.

Therefore, to be Constructive in art does not necessarily mean to be abstract at all costs: Phidias, Leonardo da Vinci, Shakespeare, Newton, Pushkin, to name a few, – all were Constructive for their time but, it would be inconsistent with the Constructive Idea to accept their way of perception and reaction to the world as an eternal and absolute measure. There is no place in a Constructive philosophy for eternal and absolute truths. All truths and values are our own constructions, subject to the changes of time and space as well as to the deliberate choice of life in its striving towards perfection. I have often used the word 'perfection' and ever so often been mistaken for an ecclesiastic evangelist, which I am not. I never meant 'perfection' in the sense of the superlative for good. 'Perfection', in the Constructivist sense, is not a state but a process; not an ultimate goal but a direction. We cannot achieve perfection by stabilizing it –

we can achieve it only by being in its stream; just as we cannot catch a train by riding in it, but once in it we can increase its speed or stop it altogether; and to be in the train is what the Constructive idea is striving for.

It may be asked: what has it all to do with art in general and with Constructive art in particular? The answer is – it has to do with art more than with all other activities of the human spirit. I believe art to be the most immediate and most effective of all means of communication between human beings. Art as a mental action is un-ambiguous – it does not deceive – it cannot deceive, since it is not concerned with truths. We never ask a tree whether it says the truth, being green, being fragrant. We should never search in a wok of art for truth – it is verity itself.

The way in which art perceives the world is sensuous (you may call it intuitive); the way it acts in response to this perception is spontaneous, irrational and factual (you may call it creative), and this is the way of life itself. This way alone brings to us ultimate results, makes history, and moulds life in the form as we know it.

Unless and until we adopt this way of reacting to the world in all our spiritual activities (science above all included) all our achievements will rest on sand.

Unless and until we have learned to carry our morality, our science, our knowledge, our culture, with the ease we carry our heart and brain and the blood in our veins, we will have no morality, no science, no knowledge, no culture.

To this end we have to construct these activities on the foundation and in the spirit of art.

I have chosen the absoluteness and exactitude of my lines, shapes and forms in the conviction that they are the most immediate medium for my communication to others of the rhythms and the state of mind I would wish the world to be in. This is not only in the material world surrounding us but also in the mental and spiritual world we carry within us.

I think that the image they invoke is the image of good – not of evil; the image of order – not of chaos; the image of life – not of death. And that is all the content of my constructions amounts to. I should think that this is equally all that the constructive idea is driving at.

(2) Again I am repeatedly and annoyingly asked – where then do I get my forms from?

The artist as a rule is particularly sensitive to such intrusion in this jealously guarded depth of his mind – but, I do not see any harm in breaking the rule. I could easily tell where I get the crude content of my forms from, provided my words be taken not metaphorically but literally.

I find them everywhere around me, where and when I want to see them. I see them, if I put my mind to it, in a torn piece of cloud carried away by the wind. I see them in the green thicket of leaves and trees. I can find them in the naked stones on hills and roads. I may discern them in a steamy trail of smoke from a passing train or on the surface of a shabby wall. I can see them often even on the blank paper of my working-table. I look and find them in the bends of waves on the sea between the open-work of foaming crests; their apparition may be sudden, it may come and vanish in a second, but when they are over they leave me with the image of eternity's duration. I can tell you more (poetic though it may sound, it is nevertheless plain reality): sometimes a falling star, cleaving the dark, traces the breath of night on my window glass, and in that instantaneous flash I might see the very line for which I searched in vain for months and months.

These are the wells from which I draw the crude content of my forms. Of course, I don't take them as they come; the image of my perception needs an order and this order is my construction. I claim the right to do it because this is what we all do in our mental world; this is what science does, what philosophy does, what life does. We all construct the image of the world as we wish it to be, and this spiritual world of ours will always be what and how we make it. It is Mankind alone that is shaping it in certain order out of a mass of incoherent and inimical realities. This is what it means to me to be Constructive.

(3) I may be in error in presuming that these maxims are simple to explain and easy to understand. I cannot judge, but I know for certain that for me it is much more difficult to prove the social justification for my work at this time.

A world at war, it seems to me, may have the right to reject my work as irrelevant to its immediate needs. I can say but little in my defence. I can only beg to be believed that I suffer with the world in all the misfortunes which are now fallen upon us. Day and night I carry the horror and pain of the human race with me. Will I be allowed to ask the leaders of the masses engaged in a mortal struggle of sheer survival: '...Must I, ought I, to keep and carry this horror through my art to the people?' – the people in the burned cities and scorched villages, the people in trenches, people in the ashes of their homes, the blinded shadows of human beings from the ruins and gibbets of devastated continents... What can *I* tell *them* about pain and horror that they do not know?'

The human race is ill; dangerously, mortally ill – I offer my blood and flesh, for what it is worth, to help them; my life, if it is needed. But what is the worth of a single life – we all have learned to kill with ease and the road of death is made smooth and facile. The venom of hate has become our daily bread and only nurture. Am I to be blamed when I confess that I cannot find inspiration for my art in that stage of death and desolation.

I am offering in my art what comfort I can to alleviate the pains and convulsions of our time. I try to keep our despair from assuming such proportions that nothing will remain in our devastated life to prompt us to live. I try to guard in my work the image of the morrow we left behind us in our memories and foregone aspirations and to remind us that the image of the world can be different. It may be that I don't succeed in that at all, but I would not accept blame for trying it.

Constructive art as a whole and my work as part of it, has still a long way to go to overcome the atmosphere of controversy that surrounds it. It has been and still is deliberately kept from the masses on the grounds that the masses would not understand it, and that it is not the kind of art the masses need. It is always very difficult to argue with anybody on such obscure grounds as this; the simplest and fairest thing to do would be to allow the masses to make their own judgement about this art. I am prepared to challenge any of the representatives of public opinion and put at their disposal any work of mine they choose to be placed where it belongs – namely, where the masses come and go and live and work. I would submit to any judgement the masses would freely pronounce about it. Would any leader of the masses ever accept my challenge – I wonder!

Meanwhile I can do nothing but leave my work to the few and selected ones to judge and discriminate.

Yours as ever,
GABO.

Dear Gabo,

It was unnecessary to apologize for the way you explain the constructive idea in art; like all artists who feel and think deeply about their work, you have said things which no critic could say for you, and said them with an eloquence which he might well envy. Certainly I myself could not improve on your statement, either by refinement or addition. All I can do, in this brief reply to your letter, is to anticipate some of the misunderstandings to which your words might be open.

You have done two things. You have shown why your art is called and rightly called 'constructive'; and you have tackled the problem of 'communication' – the most difficult problem which the artist in a democratic society has to face.

It is unfortunate that there are many sensitive and intelligent lovers of art, with no overriding prejudice against the modern movement as such, who yet fail to respond to so-called 'abstract' art. They find themselves unable to distinguish between a formal arrangement of line and colour which they rightly regard as merely 'decorative': and a constructed object which has a formal life and independence, which exists with an organic vitality all of its own.

It seems to me that we shall have to search rather deeply for the true explanation for this phenomenon. Our modern civilization has to a large extent lost the sense of form – or, to be more exact, the faculty of immediately apprehending formal values. Even in music, where this faculty is absolutely indispensable, a great many listeners get on very comfortably without it, allowing their senses to be flooded formlessly and indiscriminately by the *flow* of sound. Here, where I personally am incompetent, it is possible to see the enormity of the failure: form, in music, is for me a unity only dimly realized, in some few preludes and fugues of Bach, for example. Knowing my limitations in this art, it is easier for me to sympathize with those lovers of art who but dimly apprehend the formal unity of one of your constructions. They see lines meeting and crossing, radiating from certain points, planes intersecting – and there they stop, perhaps secretly longing for the colour and opacity which you have denied them – for colour is something that their atrophied senses may still be able to appreciate.

Why do they stop at that point? My dear Gabo, if we could confidently answer that question we should be close to the secret of the failure of our civilization. We are up against one of the fundamental inhibitions of our society – an inhibition which affects more segments of life than this aesthetic one we are discussing. It affects, most fatally, as I think you realize, our relations with one another – the simple exchange of sympathy and affection, the *reciprocity* which is the secret of social happiness. It is as though a vizor had fallen in front of our eyes, blocking some essential channel of communication. I am speaking in metaphors, but actually I believe that we are dealing with a physiological displacement. Since the triumph of scholasticism in the Middle Ages, the educated classes in Europe have been subjected to an intellectual discipline which has over-developed certain areas of the brain, at the expense of others. I can give you the scientific formula for the process: 'The specialized area represented in the forebrain or neo-pallium, and its connections with adjacent special senses, supersedes and tends in its functions even to exclude the reactions which, through the diencephalon, mediate the function expressive of man's organism as a total process.'[1] And this physiologist, who is also a psychologist, then points out that, 'this enormous disproportion of function now directed toward the cortical or neopallial segment, due to the preponderant use of the symbol, has made far-reaching and unsuspected encroachments upon the primary feelings and sensations of man as a total organism.' And this is the point which you, as well as I, try to make. You say, 'the way in which art perceives the world is sensuous... the way it acts in response to this perception is spontaneous, irrational and factual... and this is the way of life itself'. Yes, indeed; but it is not the way of life in this time of Armageddon, which is a time of prejudice, of calculated hated, of deliberate destruction. For even war, in our 'scientific' civilization, has lost its spontaneity.

I only introduce these larger aspects to show that the problem is not limited to the field of art: we are not opposed merely by a few stupid academicians or jealous rivals: we are fighting a mass neurosis which has its roots in the historical developments of the past five centuries. It would therefore be foolish to be very optimistic about our immediate success.

This brings me to the only other comment I wish to make. You betray a social conscience. As a Russian who has experienced in person the terrors and exaltations, the high hopes and frustrations of the greatest social revolution of modern times, you might reasonably have taken refuge in some escapist philosophy. But you still retain a faith in the masses, and you are even confident that these masses would understand and appreciate your constructive art, if allowed a free and unbiased contact with it. To a degree you are perhaps right: I have always found that simple unsophisticated people have a more natural, serious and sound reaction to abstract art than the neurotic climbers who cling desperately to some rung of the social or educational ladder. But do not ask for the 'judgement' of the masses. That is to encourage the very attitude of intellectual detachment which we are most anxious to avoid. Erect your constructions in public places by all means; but then wait and see... The metaphor of the catalyst has been overworked in modern criticism, but it is a very useful one. You must not expect a direct reaction from a work of art in modern society: but dropped like a foreign substance into that agitated sea, it might, without losing either its identity or its purity, effect a transformation both rich and strange.

Yours ever,

H.R.

Published originally in *Horizon*, Vol. X, No. 53 (July 1944).

[1] Trigant Burrow, M.D., Ph.D., *The Biology of Human Conflict* (New York: Macmillan Company, 1937), 117.

Introduction
Andrew Nairne

Every exhibition has its own story. A few years ago I came across the first monograph on the work of Naum Gabo, an artist in the Kettle's Yard collection. It was published in 1957. As you might expect, given its subject, it is a beautifully constructed book. It includes a fold-out facsimile of the Realistic Manifesto wall poster originally pasted up in the streets of Moscow in 1920 and a pair of Perspex spectacles for viewing stereoscopic images of Gabo's sculptures. The book also has a remarkable exchange of letters between Gabo and the writer and critic Herbert Read, originally published in *Horizon* magazine in July 1944.

Gabo's letter addresses questions he is frequently asked, including: "What do my works contribute to society in general, and to our time in particular?" In an especially moving section, he accepts that his art may be perceived as "irrelevant" to the immediate needs of a world at war. However, his letter makes a profound case for the value of not only his art but all art, which can be encompassed by his conception of "the Constructive Idea":

> *"It involves the whole complex of human relation to life. It is a mode of thinking, acting, perceiving and living. The Constructive philosophy recognises only one stream in our existence – life (you may call it creation, it is the same). Any thing or action which enhances life, propels it and adds to it something in the direction of growth, expansion and development, is Constructive. The 'how' is of secondary importance."*

When we began discussing how we could best celebrate the opening of the new Kettle's Yard, I remembered Gabo's visionary letter, and in particular the following sentence: "I try to guard in my work the image of the morrow we left behind us in our memories and foregone aspirations and to remind us that the image of the world can be different."

Borrowed for an exhibition in the twenty-first century, Gabo's appeal on behalf of his own art and the artists of his time is still relevant today. The visual arts, in all forms, have the capacity to change our view of the world and so influence how we individually and collectively act and engage with life.

Jim Ede, who created Kettle's Yard, shared this belief in the purpose and value of art and the interaction between art and life. Ede describes meeting Gabo in his book *A Way of Life* (1984):

> *"I had become friends with Naum Gabo and his brother (Antoine) Pevsner in Paris around 1923 or 1924. I had found them in a garret in the sky – they were making a model for a construction perhaps 40 cm high which they hoped to have placed in the Champs Élysées, but then it would be 100m high. It would be in perpetual movement. I don't think this was ever made."*

Today, through the generosity of others, Kettle's Yard has a number of Gabo's works in the collection. The most exceptional perhaps is *Linear Construction in Space No.1*, made in St Ives in Cornwall around the time Gabo composed his letter. This beautiful and pioneering sculpture, a harmony of space and light distilled through Perspex and nylon threads, usually sits on the black Steinway piano in the Kettle's Yard House. For *Actions* it will be among the first works encountered by visitors in the new galleries.

If Gabo's vision, his ambition for what art can do, is the inspiration for the exhibition, we also knew we wanted to make an exhibition which would reflect the energising diversity of art now, include commissioned new work and continue long-standing creative partnerships with our local communities.

Actions would be our headline title, a definition of art making as something with conscious purpose, though this could take a thousand different forms. What the artists in *Actions* have in common, then, is a connected and generative quality about their work, expressing the 'Constructive Idea' for us, now.

Actions goes beyond the visual arts and includes the architect of the new Kettle's Yard, a composer, a dance company and a choreographer. The aim is to create a gathering of artistic expressions, to see what happens when a myriad of diverse voices come together. The selection is both carefully determined and, we hope, surprising, working with artists we know well and with others who we have only recently discovered. Of the latter, Khadija Saye, who died in the Grenfell Tower fire in June 2017, was just setting out on her career when we invited her to participate in *Actions.* Following in Jim Ede's footsteps, Kettle's Yard has always sought to support emerging artists. It is our privilege to be able to exhibit these deeply felt and luminous photographs for the first time in the UK, following their display at the Venice Biennale.

In a television interview late in life the avant-garde Latvian theatre director and writer Asja Lācis (1891–1979), said "we have no right to be satisfied with anything, even if things go well. On the contrary, we have to do better. And continuously search for the new, the contemporary." The art in *Actions* offers much to aesthetically enjoy and love, but this essential strength is allied to insight about the present moment; the desire to contribute to and animate contemporary discourse, whether cultural, social, political, or economic. Above all, taking its cue from Gabo, *Actions* seeks to reassert the potential of art as a potent force in a troubled world.

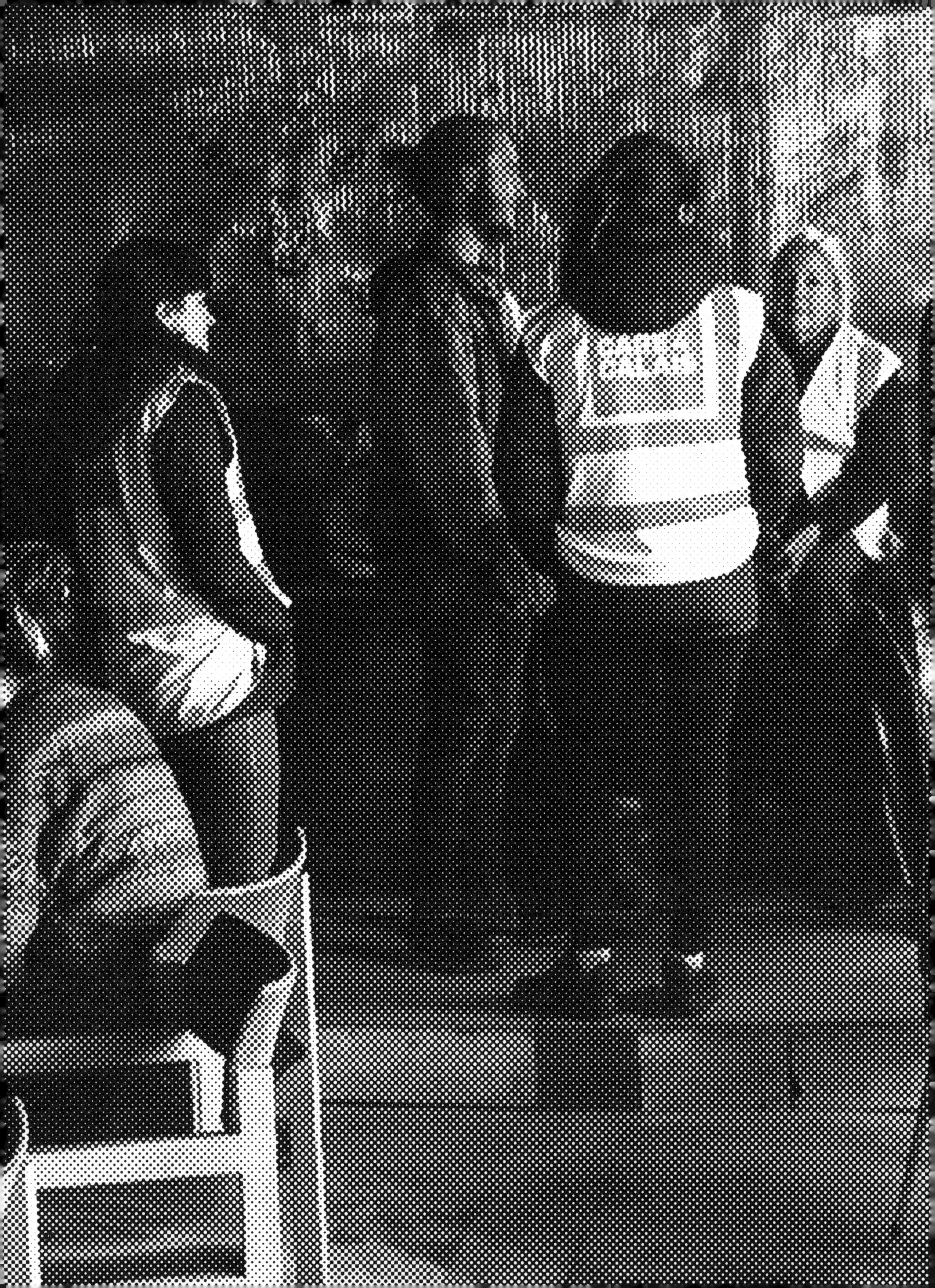

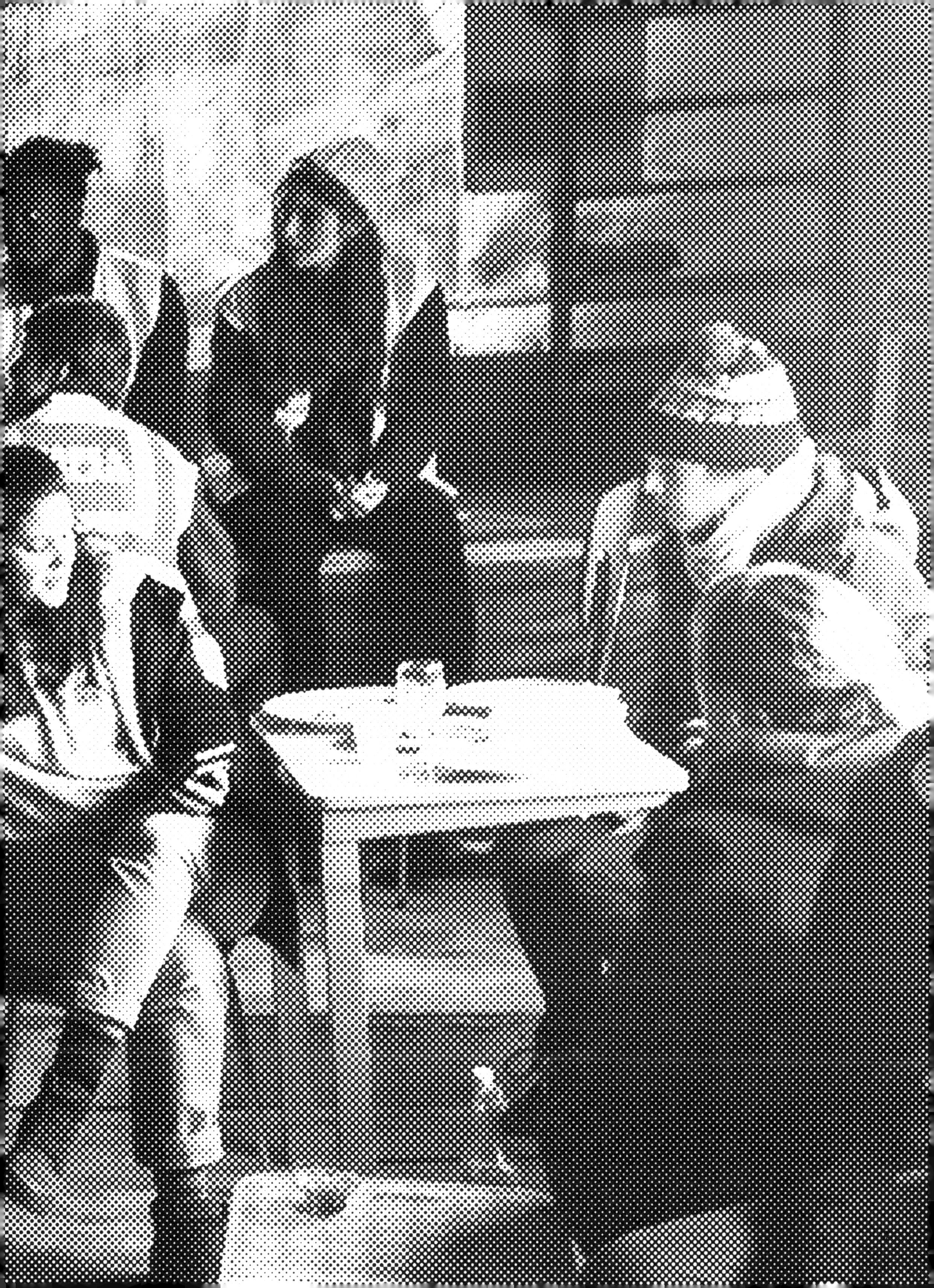

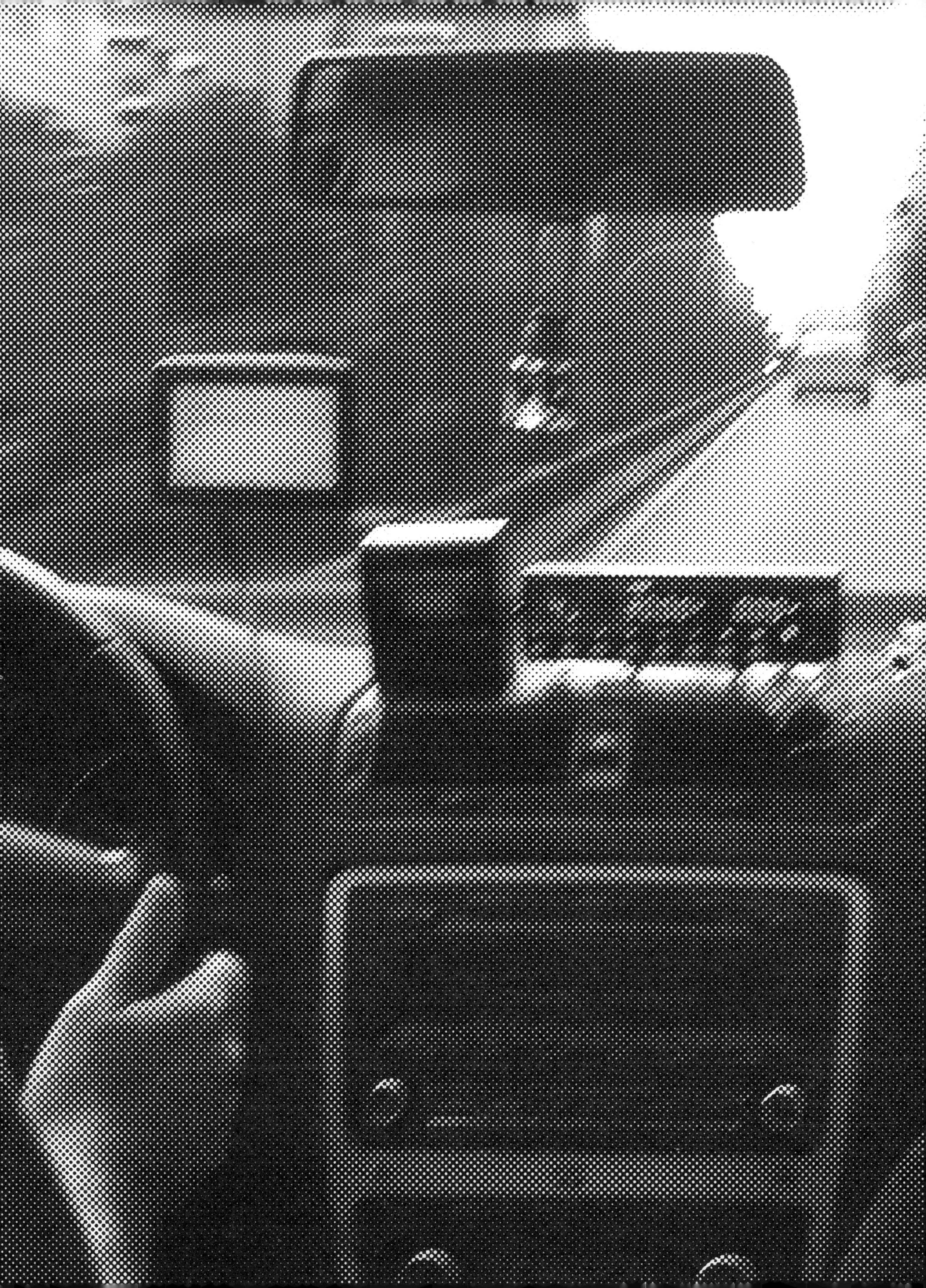

10/2–2/4/18

"We never ask a tree whether it says the truth, being green, being fragrant. We should never search in a work of art for truth – it is verity itself."

Naum Gabo

Basel Abbas & Ruanne Abou-Rahme

Born in Nicosia, Cyprus and Boston, USA, 1983
Live and work in Ramallah and New York

Basel Abbas and Ruanne Abou-Rahme make expanded film and sound works that use poetry, images and artefacts as means to explore geopolitical issues affecting the people in their Palestinian homelands and beyond. *And Yet My Mask Is Powerful* (2016) takes its script from American poet Adrienne Rich's *The Wreck* (1971), which follows the journey of a diver into the inky depths of the ocean and along the edges of consciousness. The poem explores the desire to encounter history directly in order to re-understand the past and present situation; "*the thing I came for, the wreck and not the story of the wreck, the thing itself and not the myth*". Rich's words are sampled by Abbas and Abou-Rahme who overlay imagery of a group of young Palestinians exploring their people's abandoned villages within Israeli territory, pushing through wild vegetation and past forgotten crumbling buildings. At once depopulated sites of conflict and upheaval, through the fresh eyes of these young explorers (whose masks are recreations of Neolithic antiquities from the area), they now appear as sites of renewed energy that are alive with non-human life, whose inaccessibility has given way to flora and fauna that reclaim the land, and time, as their own.

Abbas and Abou-Rahme's dense, research-driven projects often gestate over a number of years. A wide range of source material collected from field trips and the internet is excavated, reconstructed and activated, allowing for new layers of narrative and ways of understanding the relationship between history, memory, imagination and reality. Their projects often culminate in immersive visual and sonic landscapes that overwhelm the senses and encourage deep engagement from the viewer. The wider research for *And Yet My Mask Is Powerful* has been compiled into a new publication of the same name, published in 2017 by Printed Matter, New York. **GH**

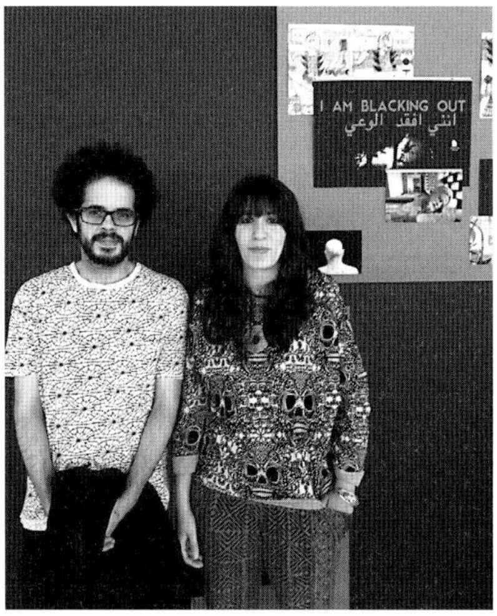

I came to see the damage that was done and the treasures that prevail.
Adrienne Rich, *Diving into the Wreck*, 1973

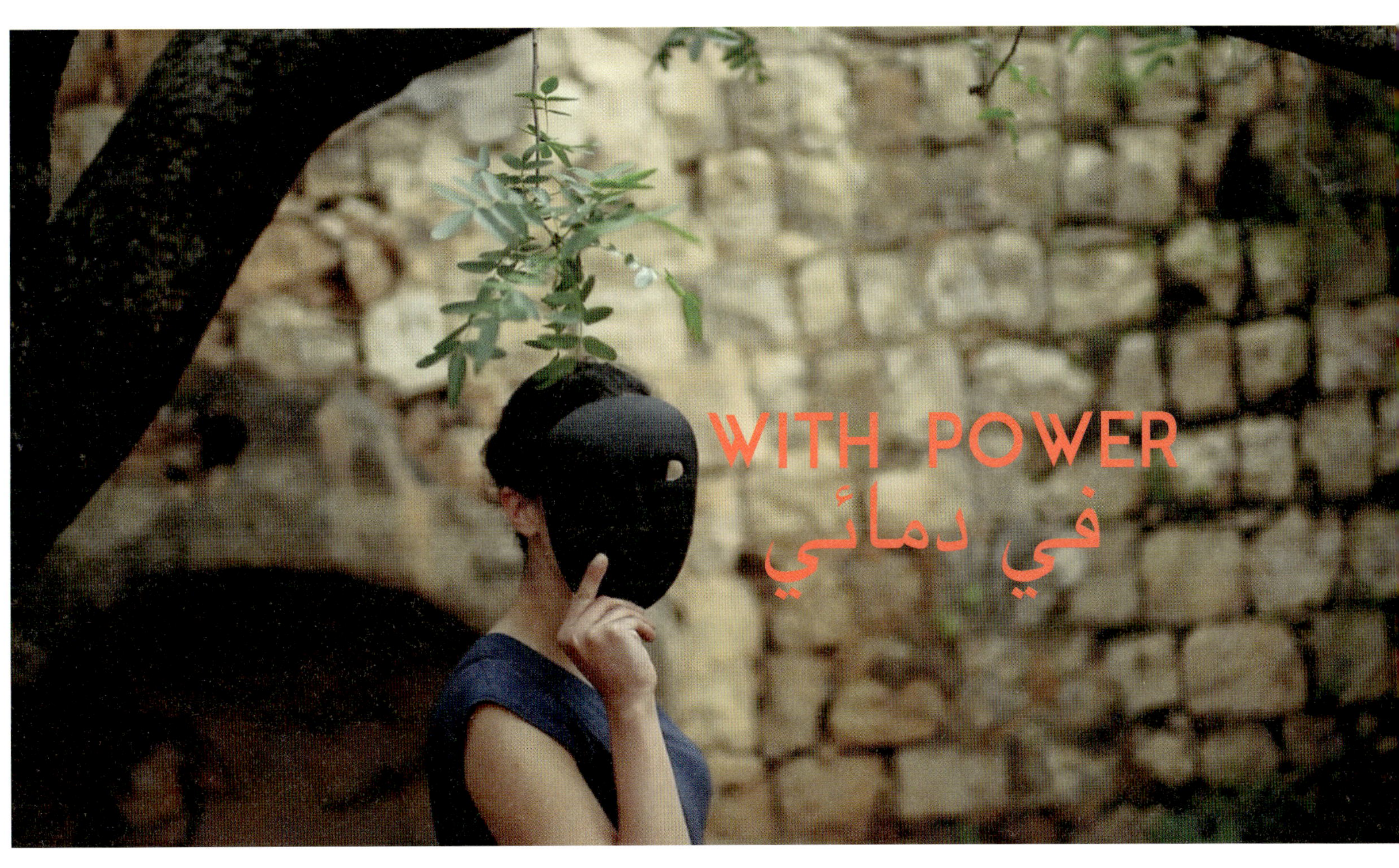

And Yet My Mask Is Powerful, 2016
Single-channel HD video, two-channel sound,
8 minutes 44 seconds

John Akomfrah

Born in Accra, Ghana, 1957
Lives and works in London

John Akomfrah is an artist and filmmaker who is known for his rich, deeply moving films that interrogate issues around migration, identity, colonialism and collective memory. *Auto Da Fé* (2016), which translates as Acts of Faith, is a feature-length film presented as a diptych in the second part of *Actions*. It charts eight migratory episodes across the last four centuries, from the flight of Sephardic Jews from Brazil to Barbados in 1654 right up to the most recent and ongoing movement of people from Mosul in Iraq, reaffirming humanity's continuing struggle with inequality and intolerance, and the individual instinct for survival. In this film Akomfrah moves away from the montage techniques that characterised his previous works such as *Vertigo Sea* (2015) and *The Unfinished Conversation* (2013), where archive documentary footage and found imagery were brought together to explore a particular issue. Instead he calls upon a cast of voiceless characters in historically accurate period dress to navigate us through a series of melancholic landscapes, each of which are dominated by the presence of the sea. Through the lens of history, Akomfrah explores the plight of those seaborne refugees in the twenty-first century, forced to take desperate measures to escape, left with little choice but to navigate so closely around death.

Akomfrah is a founding member of the influential Black Audio Film Collective which in the 1980s produced films exploring Black British identity and culture. In 1998, he formed Smoking Dog Films with long-time collaborators David Lawson and Lina Gopaul. His films are regularly presented across multiple screens where contrasting or tangential imagery is presented simultaneously, allowing opportunities for new associations and understanding to arise through the act of viewing. **GH**

After the Portuguese caravels, the slave ships, sharks and bodies in the water, "the men with eyes as heavy as anchors" arrive in Derek Walcott's poem The Sea Is History *(1980). Within a line and without record, the men are buried under the sea, in "that grey vault" where the West's memory of its own vast cruelties is lost to the amnesic tides. For John Akomfrah, such histories are held just under the surface of the waves, in the global subconscious. An archivist of the "grey vault", Akomfrah sees in the sea the same turbulence and drifts of identity that he finds in the found footage he uses in his films.*
Holly Corfield Carr, "John Akomfrah", 2016

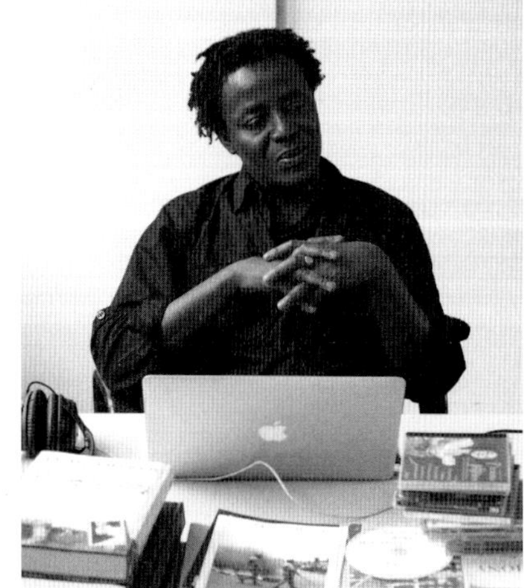

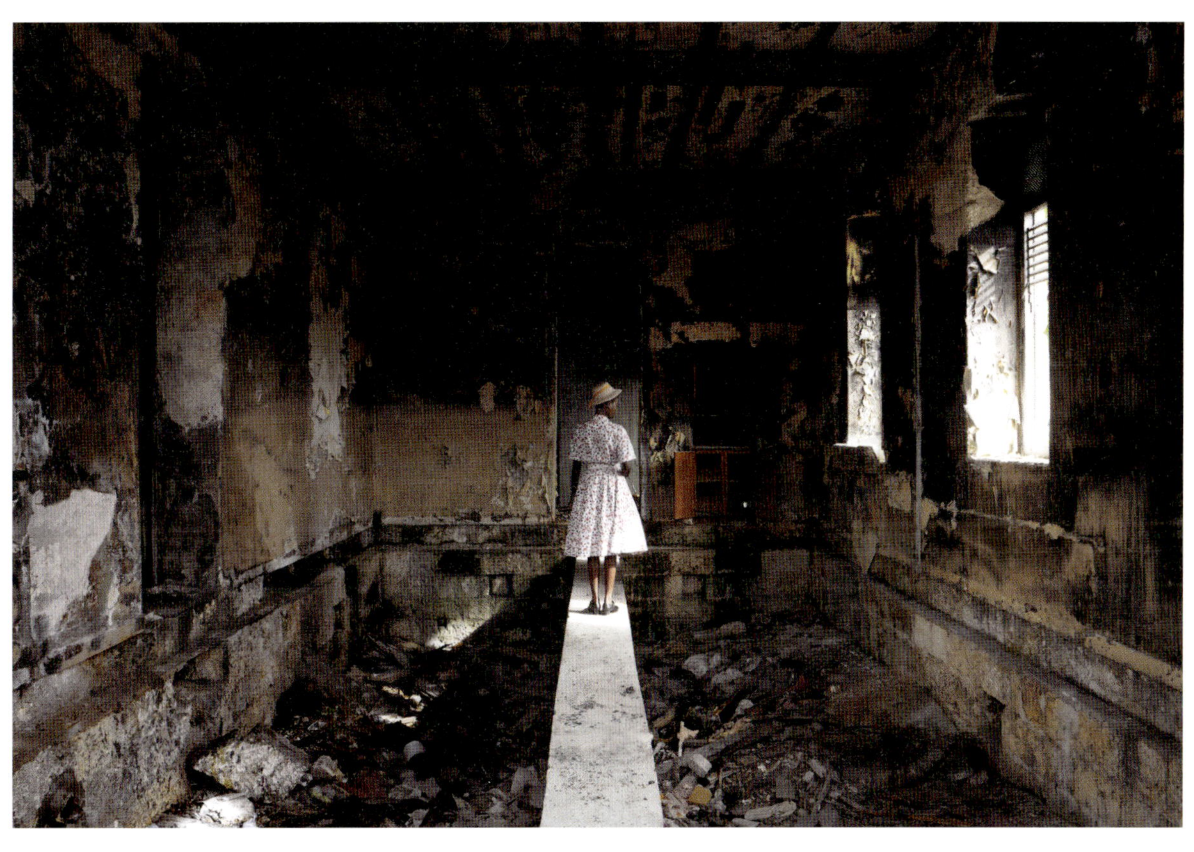

Untitled, 2016
C-print mounted on Dibond
1016 × 1524 mm

Rana Begum

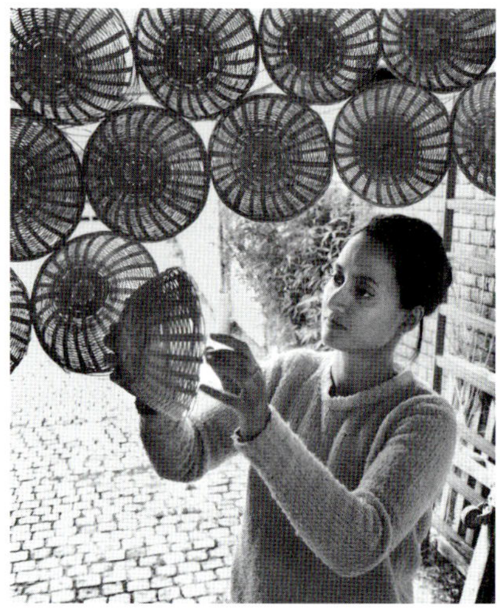

Born in Sylhet, Bangladesh, 1977
Lives and works in London

For *Actions*, Rana Begum has created a new site-specific installation in St Peter's Church, adjacent to Kettle's Yard. Begum's installation in Cambridge is the third iteration of her series of works made using hundreds of interconnected baskets, but the first time she has made a large-scale sculpture with baskets in the UK. Begum first began using baskets in her work in 2014, when she presented the installation *No. 473* at the Dhaka Art Summit in Bangladesh: an immersive sculpture comprised of nearly a thousand locally hand-woven bamboo baskets, connected to form a wave-like multi-domed structure, that spectators could walk beneath, gradually experiencing shifting patterns of light and shade. The work drew upon her childhood memories of experiments with basket weaving in her village as well as the time spent reading the Qur'an at a local mosque, where the dappled morning light, sound of the water fountain and the mesmeric recitation created an atmosphere of peaceful concentration. Begum observed that this work "really brought to life an ambition that has always been there in the back of my mind – to create a space which captures light and is calm and meditative." Later in 2014 Begum made a second immersive form *No. 545* at Galeri Manâ in Istanbul, also constructed with locally made baskets, but this time black in colour: creating more strikingly geometric contrasts between the black woven forms and the surrounding bright light of the exhibition space.

Begum's practice synthesises the disciplines of sculpture, painting and architecture in constructions which are often rendered using powder-coated industrial metals such as mild and galvanised steel and extruded aluminium. The vivid hues and patterning of Begum's works are influenced both by the road signs, hazard markings and advertising signage of London, where she lives and works, and by her early childhood in Bangladesh, where she absorbed the intricate forms, bright colours and repetition found in Islamic art and architecture. Begum's work is activated by the motion and perception of the viewer, as for example in her *Fold* series of painted metal reliefs and free-standing sculptures, which invite the viewer to contemplate the shifting colours of folded and painted irregular metal polygons. The modular nature of built structure also recurs throughout Begum's practice, as for example in the hypnotic repeating chevrons of *No. 700 Reflectors* (2016), rendered using 30,000 reflectors, animating 50 metres of a new square at King's Cross, London. **SL**

Of course, Begum's childhood memories inform her practice, but most texts gloss over the influence of British Art or North-American minimalist artists such as Agnes Martin and Donald Judd on her thinking, focusing instead on sacred geometry tied to Islamic influences. Truth, order, simplicity, and harmony are as important to Begum's work as they were to the minimalist artists before her, but Begum also cites teachings from the Qur'an regarding honesty when talking about her artistic decisions to let materials speak for themselves. When natural light hits the surface of Begum's sculptures, and the viewer moves through the space, new colours begin to materialise and dance as light and matter collide.

Diana Campbell Betancourt, "From Bangladesh to Britain and Back", 2017

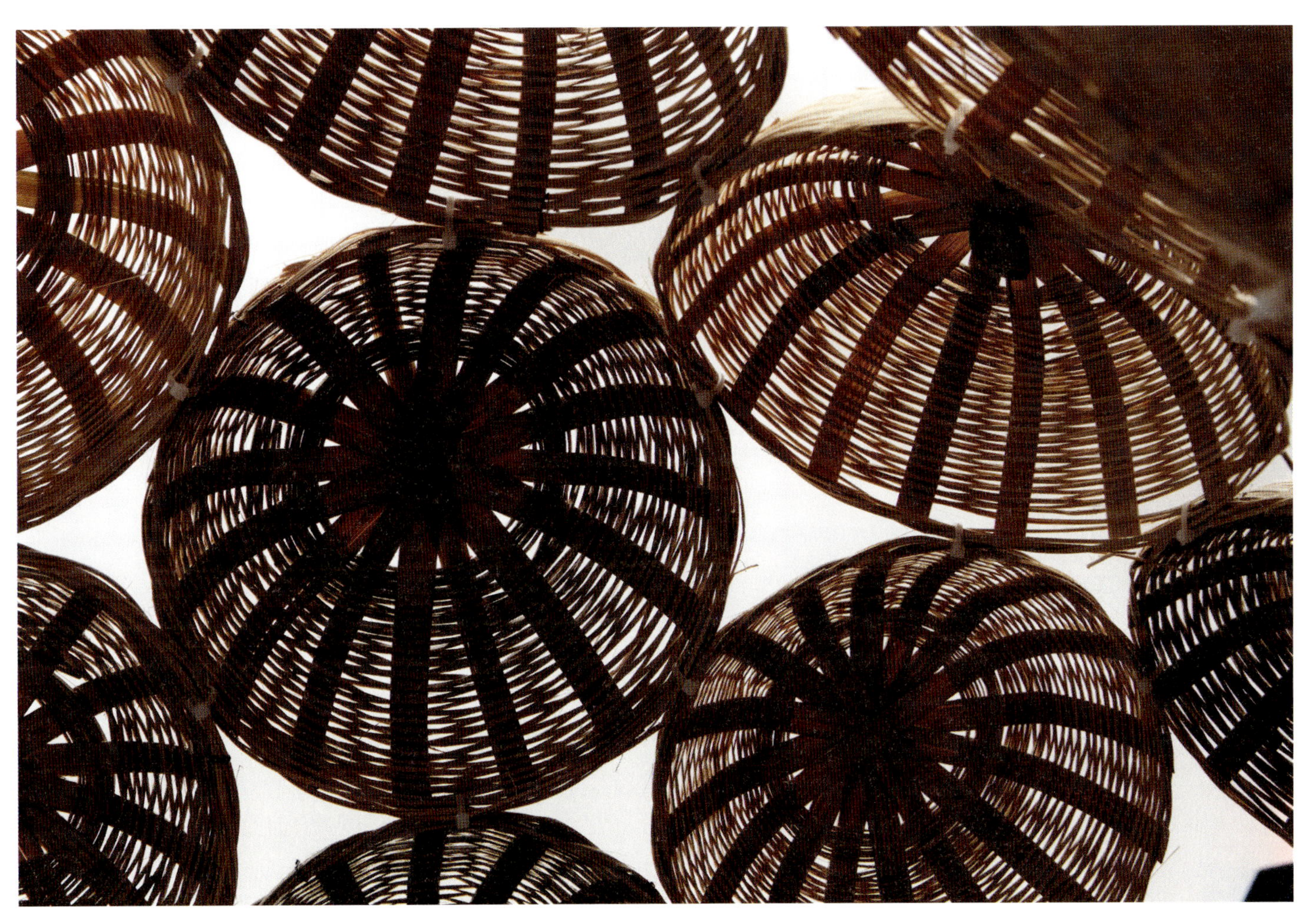

No. 764 Baskets, 2017–18
Handmade bamboo baskets
Dimensions variable

Joseph Beuys

This is one of the most powerful artworks of the twentieth century. I have often wondered how so many people who were not present at the performance are still drawn to the encounter and instinctively relate to the warmth and optimism of its meaning. A generation later these images are still as iconic and challenging as ever, and I am thrilled that a new readership will have the chance to identify with nature's powerful languages, the scapegoat and outsider, with love for other forms of life, and above all, respect for them.
Caroline Tisdall, preface to the second edition of *Coyote*, 2008

Born in Krefeld, Germany 1921
Died in Düsseldorf, Germany 1986
Lived and worked in Düsseldorf

Joseph Beuys' practice hinged on two central aspects: his commitment to widening access to and understanding of visual art, and his ritualistic and shamanistic performances, such as his infamous action *I Like America and America Likes Me* (1974). Beuys flew to New York, where he was met by an ambulance at the airport, placed on a stretcher wrapped in a felt blanket and taken to a straw-filled room in the René Block Gallery, where a live coyote was waiting. Beuys' action addressed the damage done by white settlers to the American continent and its native cultures (symbolised by the coyote) while also serving to register his opposition to the hegemony of American art and American military actions in Vietnam. Beuys shared the space with the coyote, for eight hours a day over the course of three days, either lying on his stretcher swathed in the felt blanket, or standing up using the blanket as a cloak and interacting with the animal in various symbolic ways, such as gesturing with the hook of a shepherd's staff, striking a large triangle or tossing his leather gloves to the animal. Every day, fifty new copies of the *Wall Street Journal* were introduced into the space, which the coyote acknowledged by urinating on them. At the end of the three days, Beuys embraced the coyote and was taken to the airport, again in an ambulance, leaving America without ever having set foot on its soil.

Beuys was a Fluxus artist, staging happenings and performances, but was also a sculptor, installation artist, graphic artist, art theorist, pedagogue and one of the founders of the Green Party. Beuys' practice revolved around the interrelationship of art, society and politics and he continues to exert significant aesthetic influence over the contemporary art scene, from his use of low cost, everyday materials such as fat, felt, wax, honey, batteries and pocket torches, to the ideas he promoted, notably his concept of 'social sculpture', which he used to describe meaning that is generated between people involved in a variety of discourses. Between 1961 and 1962, Beuys was Professor of Monumental Sculpture at the Staatliche Kunstakademie in Düsseldorf, where his students included Sigmar Polke, Blinky Palermo, Jörg Immendorf and Anselm Kiefer. Beuys professed "teaching is my greatest work of art", however his attempt to implement unrestricted admission to his class ultimately led to his dismissal in 1972. Thereafter, Beuys remained committed to his view that "every human being is an artist" and in April 1973 he founded the Free International University in his Düsseldorf studio as a non-profit, organizational place of research, work and communication. **SL**

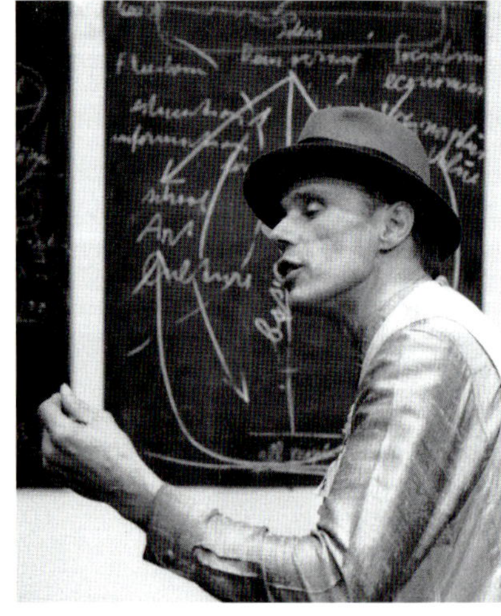

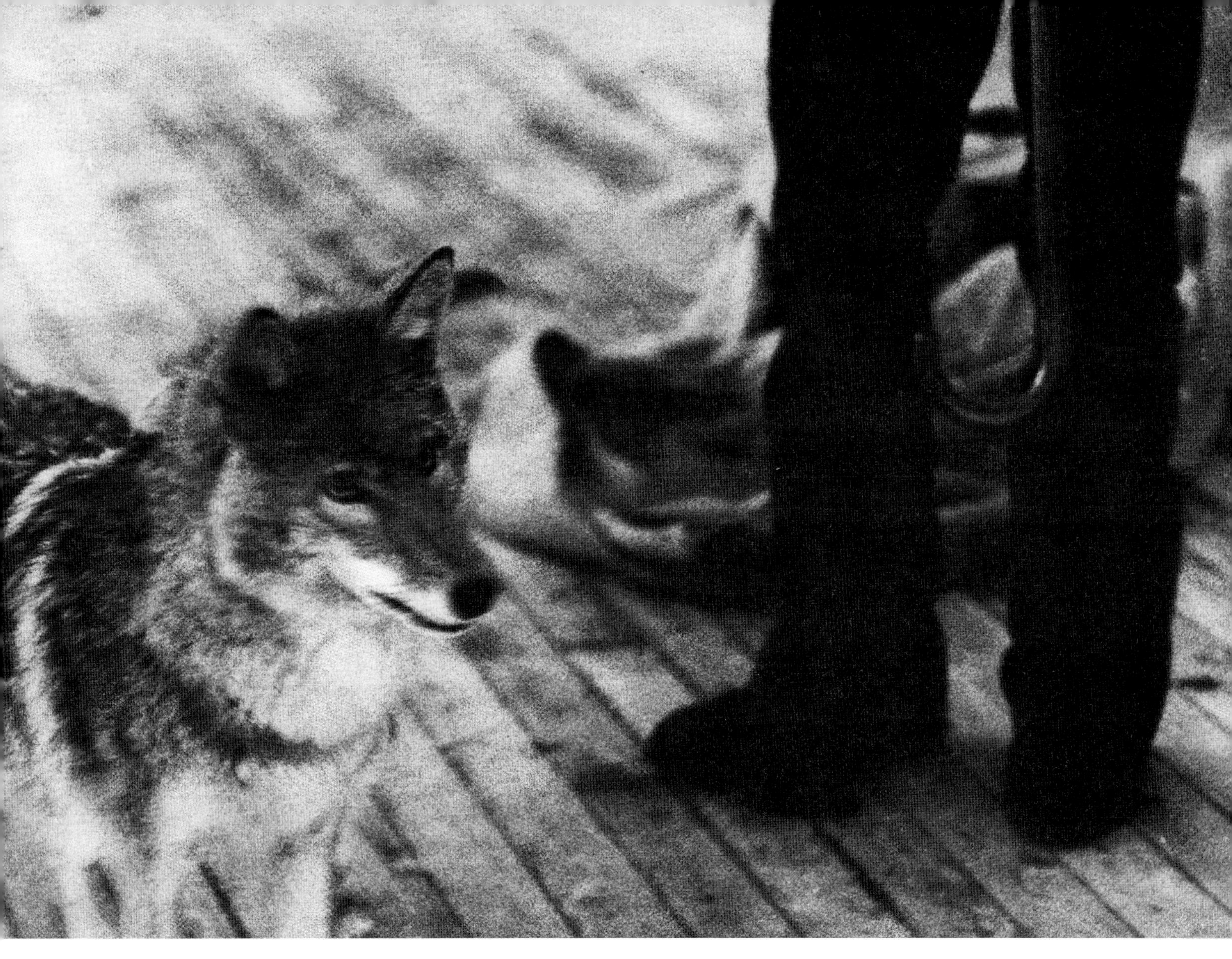

I Like America and America Likes Me, 1974
Film, 38 minutes, black and white
Director: Helmut Wietz

Anna Brownsted

Anna Brownsted constructs encounters that are simultaneously familiar yet unexpected. Her work interrupts our sense of the everyday by offering an invitation: to sit, to listen, to notice. During her meticulously realised experiences anything feels possible. It is here that her work can be found – between what's real and what's imaginary – and the extent to which these boundaries can actively be blurred, pushed or tested.
Harriet Loffler, 2017

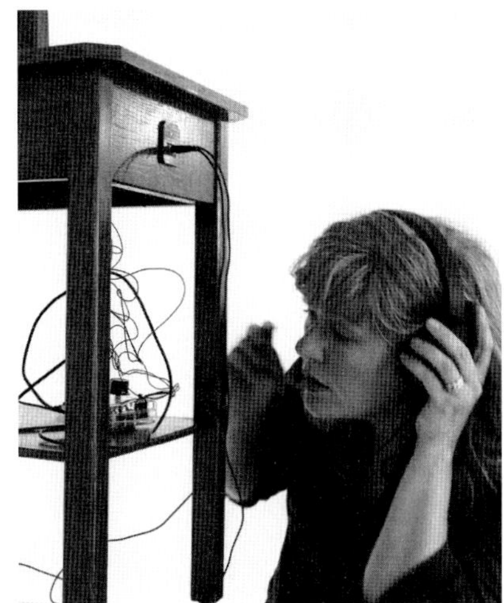

Born in Dallas, USA, 1974
Lives and works in Cambridge

Anna Brownsted's work in *Actions* was first shown in a year-long online exhibition, commissioned by Fermynwoods Contemporary Art in 2016. Shot in a single eight-hour session just after the election of Donald Trump as the forty-fifth US President, *Diplomat* is a sequence of 100 films (one for every day of a president's first one hundred days in office), showing the artist repeatedly playing a recording of John F. Kennedy's famous inaugural address of 1961. The record, warped through heat damage, was produced by a company called Diplomat and released shortly after Kennedy's assassination in 1963. Each time the record is played the needle jumps unpredictably so that every film looks and sounds different. The turntable is filmed so we see its shadow in what appears to be late afternoon sunlight, reflecting perhaps the poignancy of our knowledge that Kennedy's time in office and ability to effect change, was to be cut short. The repetition of Brownsted's action and the distant but still powerful idealism of Kennedy's address collapse the past into the contemporary moment. Using the lens of history, in itself unresolved, *Diplomat* lays bare the contested and traumatic present.

Originally trained in theatre, Brownsted works with sound, text, installation and performance, often exploring the space between fiction and reality. *We Have Only This* presented at the Cambridge Junction in 2015 was an audio promenade, designed for individuals: a journey through the building marked by unsettling live encounters. In another work in the same year Brownsted questioned the banality of the signage boards at Anglia Ruskin University, with its 'Collaborative Zone' and 'Corporate Suite', adding fictional locations such as 'The Rat Race', 'Hidden Agenda' and 'Last Chance Saloon'. In a new film, called *Prop Cues*, a pair of vintage silver gloves resting on a chair flutter in a breeze. By creating an indefinite loop and running the film forward and backwards, Brownsted conjures a sense, true of all her work, of fragile beauty and immediacy. **AN**

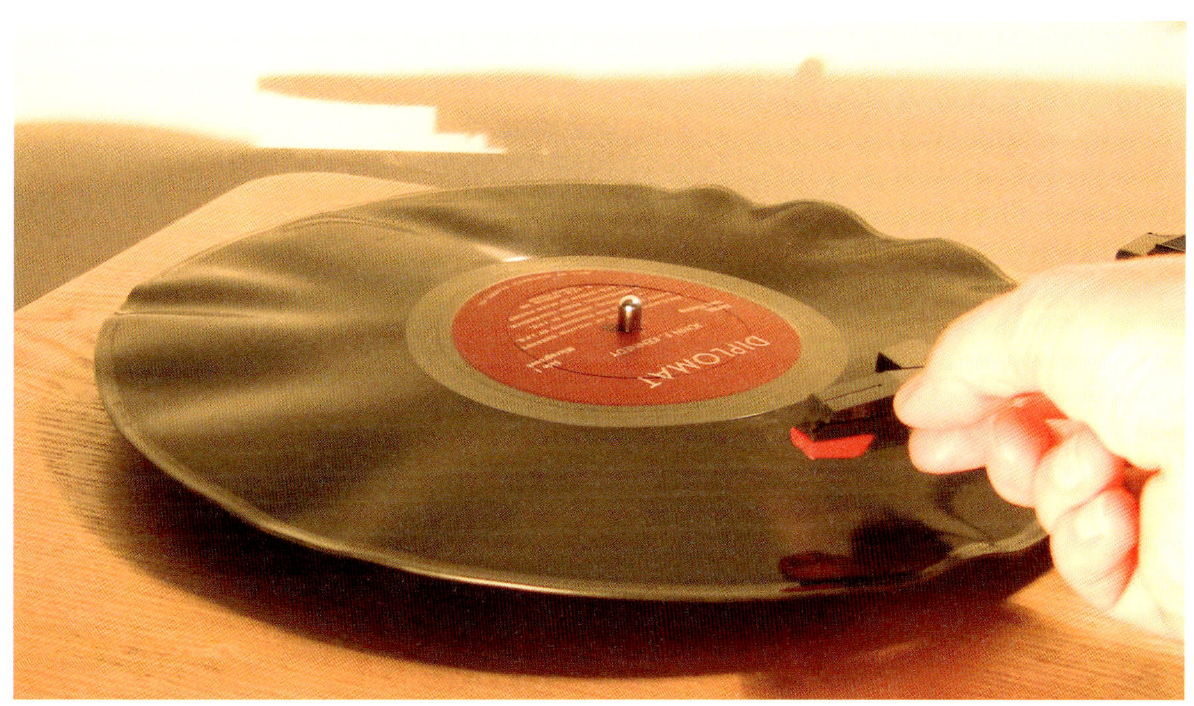

Diplomat, 2016
One hundred digital videos
333 minutes total running time.

Candoco Dance Company & Laila Diallo

Candoco Dance Company supports choreographers who question their own practice and engage with pushing the boundaries of the art form and how it is presented on stage. The company's ambitions are driven by our belief that diversity is inherently exciting and most likely to lead to the next great idea ... we must ensure there is room for different bodies, perspectives and experiences within dance.
Ellie Douglas-Allan, Learning Producer, Candoco Dance Company, 2017

I make dance because it seems to me that movement, people moving and the experience of watching people move and the joining in the dance can move us. It can move us deeply. To action, to tears, to thought. It can take us to a place of solace or respite, a place of escape or one of connection.
Laila Diallo

Candoco Dance Company
Founded in London, 1991

Laila Diallo
Born in Québec, Canada, 1976
Lives and works in Bristol

Actions brings together for the first time the choreographer and dancer Laila Diallo and Candoco Dance Company – the leading dance company of disabled and non-disabled dancers. Diallo's revelatory choreographic work and interdisciplinary practice closely resonates with Candoco's ongoing interest in presenting work that pushes the boundaries of what dance looks like and what it can do. Diallo's piece, performed as part of *Actions*, meanders through the old and new spaces at Kettle's Yard provoking conversations between bodies, space, architecture and the other artworks displayed in the exhibition. The new work has been made with dancers Anne-Gaëlle Thiriot and Kathleen Hawkins and celebrates their bodies and the sometimes unexpected or unfamiliar images that are created through them.

After dancing with Wayne McGregor's Random Dance for eight years, Diallo has come to prominence for her choreographic work. She was an Associate Artist at the Royal Opera House between 2009 and 2012 and since 2005 she has been creating dance works that have toured across the UK and internationally. Diallo's process of making is not predetermined or prescriptive. She embraces openness and experiment, often beginning with a research question or source that is explored through movement and the bodies of the dancers, and always in a very close dialogue with them. Diallo has suggested that her ambition is to make works that explore how dance can provoke and move us, how it can make us dream or ground us on earth and reveal something of the human condition.

Celeste Dandeker-Arnold and Adam Benjamin founded Candoco Dance Company in 1991 and it grew quickly into the first company of its kind in the UK. Candoco commissions and produces work by exceptional choreographers for the core company of seven dancers, which tours nationally and internationally. Since 2002 the company's productions have reached over twenty-five countries. Its extensive education programme provides access to the highest quality of dance to everyone, and this programme has pioneered increased access to vocational dance training for disabled dance students. Candoco Dance Company has unquestionably expanded the dance landscape encouraging both mainstream and disability sectors to think outside of accepted norms. It continually inspires its audiences through groundbreaking productions. Diallo's work with Candoco for *Actions* offers new possibilities of what 'image of the world' dance can communicate whilst broadening perceptions of art and ability. **JP**

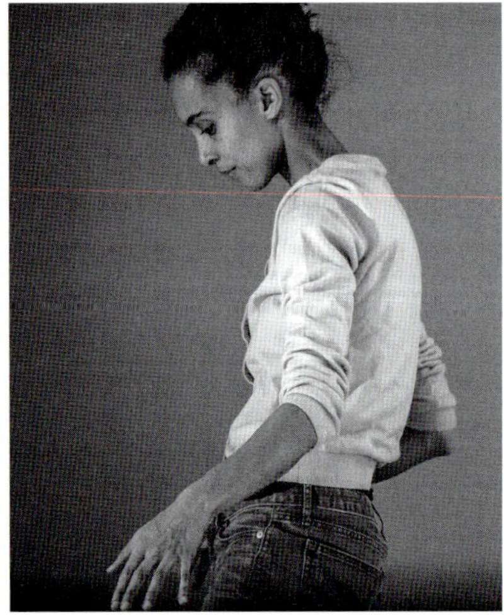

Laila Diallo in *Edge and Shore* (2015)

Turning 20, Candoco Dance Company (2011)

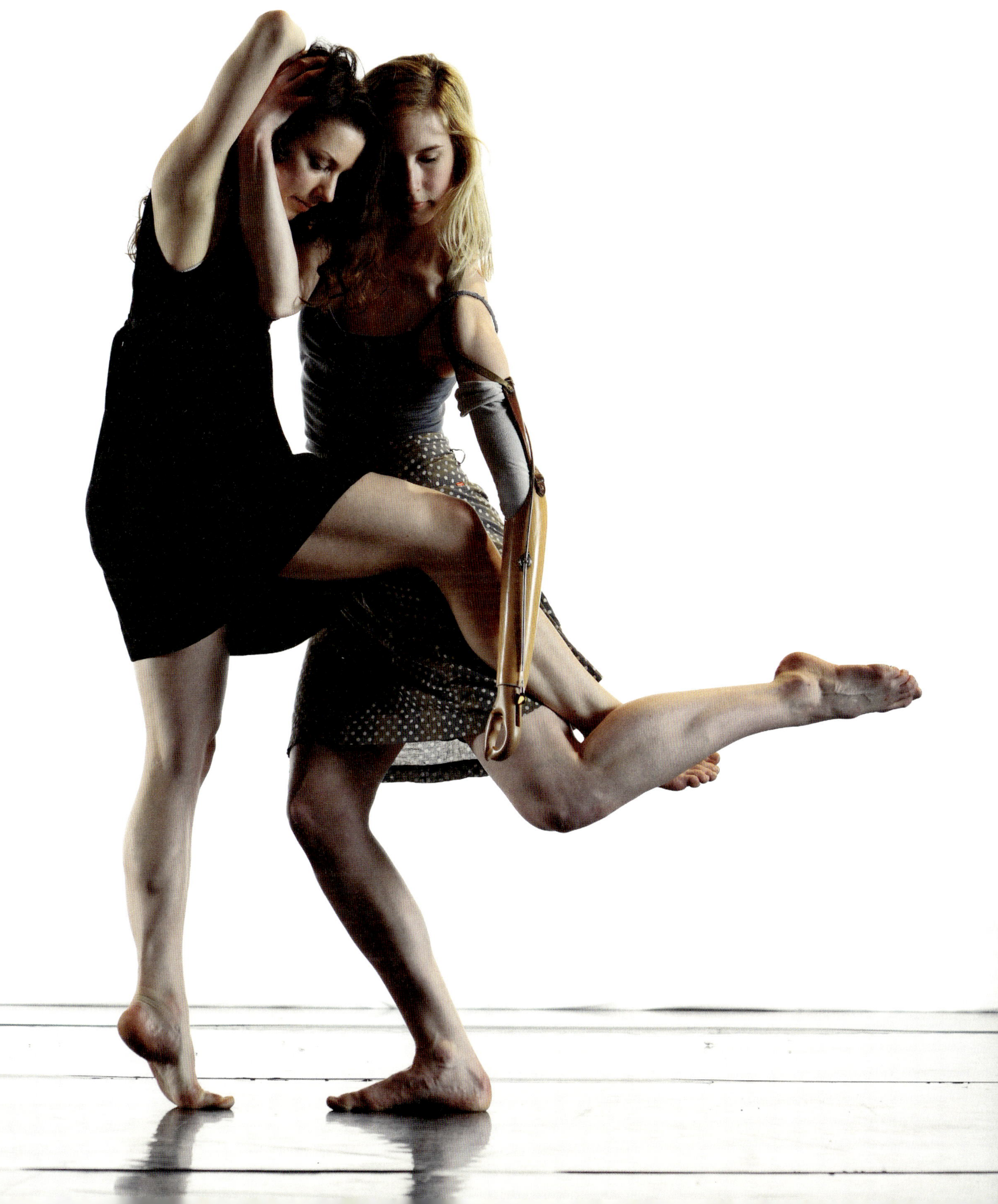

Alice Channer

Born in Oxford, 1977
Lives and works in London

Alice Channer describes the photograph shown on this page as a "co-authored portrait" in which material, form and artist are interdependent. A deeply held respect for materials and processes of production runs throughout Channer's sculptural practice. For *Actions*, she has cast in aluminium (and from wax) two slender upright forms that stand in the centre of the gallery. The outer surface of the aluminium is imprinted with the textures of American Apparel maxi dresses that Channer moulds in silicone, casts in wax and hooks over the thigh of a shop dummy to create a curved base. At the top of each sculpture there is an eyelet resembling that of a needle. The inner surfaces are, by contrast, highly polished and reflective. Standing at just above head height, and dependent on a body and garment in their production, a conversation between our own bodies and these sculptures feels inevitable and urgent. This dialogue is heightened, as we are encouraged to walk in between and amongst them through their placement in the gallery space. Channer has spoken about awkward confusions between organic and inorganic matter and between embodied and disembodied forms in her works. This is nowhere better felt than in these two forms. Her collective title for the works is *Stalagmites*. Channer borrows this from the towering geological structures that grow upwards from the floor of caves and which are characterised by their rounded tips. Stalagmites depend upon their environment to propagate and there are many interdependencies on which Channer's sculptures also rest: body, material, foundry, floor, space, viewer and each other.

Channer's London-based studio is full of wonderful contradictions: maxi dresses and other garments are tucked away in boxes ready for use; natural forms including mussel shells are found in their untouched state and dipped, or fully cast, in highly polished metals; images from American *Vogue* magazine are pinned to the wall, and a huge wax bone-like form lies ready for casting, its footprint drawn out on the floor of the studio with the help of 3D computer imaging. *Stalagmites* (2017) relates to earlier works by the artist such as *Hot Springs* (2014) in which vertical forms are combined with puddles of mirrored steel and compressed garments resembling oil spills. Channer is acutely aware of working in a period of unprecedented environmental change, but she also exploits the materials of her time; these are often man-made and depend upon industrial processes of production. Her work boldly pushes forward dialogues between sculpture, material and the body, in our rapidly changing world. **JP**

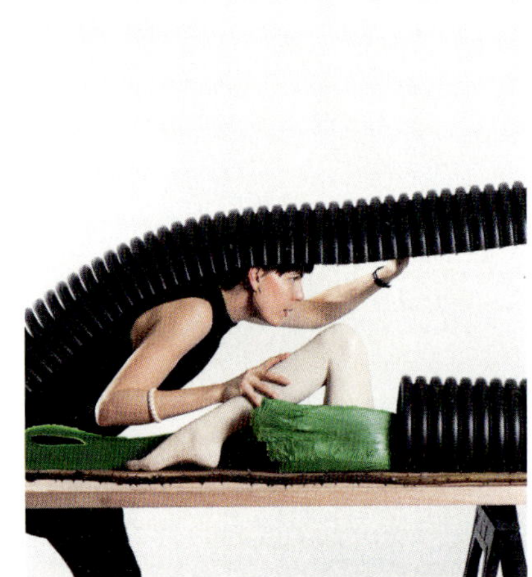

The twenty-first century needs objects that are vulnerable, uncertain, other, alien. To navigate climate change, mass extinctions and extreme and rapid human-made changes in community, society, geology, politics, biology and economy, we need new kinds of objects. They must be confidently doubtful, awkward as well as elegant, h o r i z o n t a l as well as vertical, soft as well as hard. Objects like these might show us new kinds of embodiment – how to mutate, adapt, change state, survive, prosper.
Alice Channer, *Art in America*, 2015

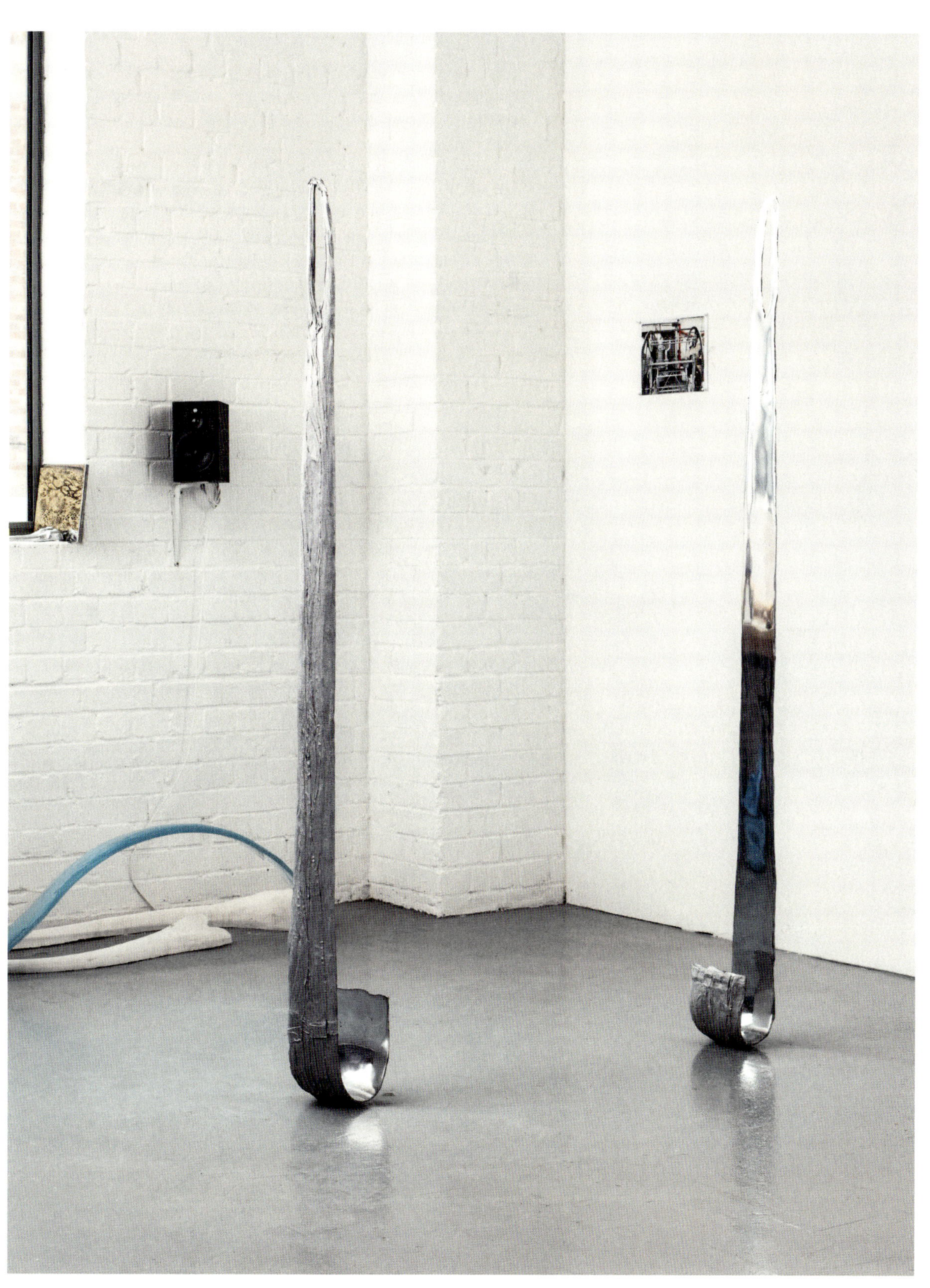

Stalagmites, 2017
Cast and mirror polished aluminium
1800 × 165 × 1200 mm

Nathan Coley

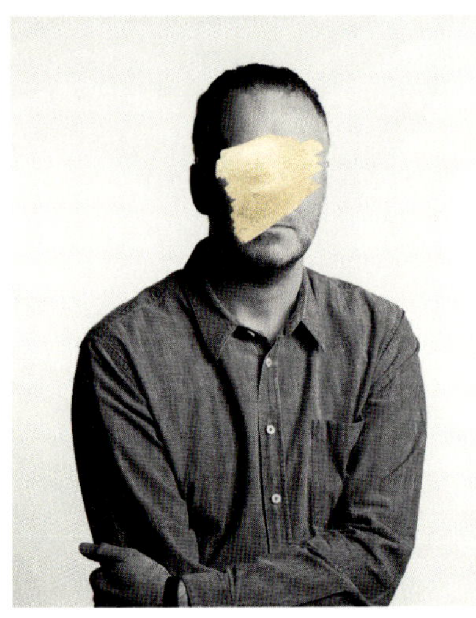

Born in Glasgow, 1967
Lives and works in Glasgow

Nathan Coley's work for *Actions* is unmissable. Coley has made an illuminated text which has been installed in St Peter's churchyard, next to Kettle's Yard. Nine metres wide by two metres high, the text, made of white lightbulbs on a large scaffolding construction, reads: THE SAME FOR EVERYONE.

It is a new edition of a major work Coley made for Aarhus European Capital of Culture 2017. Coley placed ten sculptures with the same message in different locations across central Denmark. Critical to Coley's work and to his light sculptures is that the text is 'found', that it already exists. *The Same for Everyone* comes from a hand-painted sign he found on a building plot in the self-build community Friland, in which everyone constructs their own houses. The sign in Danish read *ens for alle*. While this may simply have been a practical message, re-presented by the artist as 'the same for everyone' the words become especially powerful in a Danish context. Denmark prides itself on being a highly egalitarian country. Yet, the four words can be read in many different ways. Is this an empowering, idealistic message, or a deeply questioning one, or even perhaps an authoritarian order? Coley's structures and white lights, simultaneously hot and cold, seductive and alienating, are reminiscent of fairground signs suggesting celebration. In contrast, the messages they convey are unexplained, anonymous and enigmatic.

The new edition for *Actions* has the words laid out in a single line, floating above the churchyard, not far from St Peter's Church. The structure sits among the trees facing the new Kettle's Yard. For Coley and surely for us, that the message is located here in a churchyard in Cambridge becomes critical. Is this a biblical message? Or could it be a dry prediction, with graves beneath, of equality in death: a twenty-first Century memento mori? Sited towards the north of the city, not far from the housing estates of Arbury and King's Hedges, is this a proposition powerfully questioning the life and educational inequalities to be found in Cambridge? Or perhaps whether an institution like Kettle's Yard can ever be, or should be, the same for everyone?

Working in many different media for the past twenty-five years, Coley creates compelling structures and situations which explore how the familiar environment of architecture and place are coded, reflecting and conditioning social relations. In his work, Coley seems to step forward and then walk away. His illuminated sculptures, for which he is perhaps best known, blow apart the niceties of consensus and force us to think again. **AN**

Ultimately, the reading of Nathan Coley's work differs from viewer to viewer, which only adds to the fascinating dichotomy between boldness of statement and intangibility of meaning. The questions and doubts are ours; the artist does not directly interrogate us. Interpreting Coley's work says more about the viewer; it is a mirror reflecting our own associations and biases back at us.

Neil Lebeter, "The Same for Everyone", 2017

The Same for Everyone, 2017
Illuminated text on scaffolding
Dimensions variable
Originally commissioned as part of Aarhus 2017 – European Capital of Culture

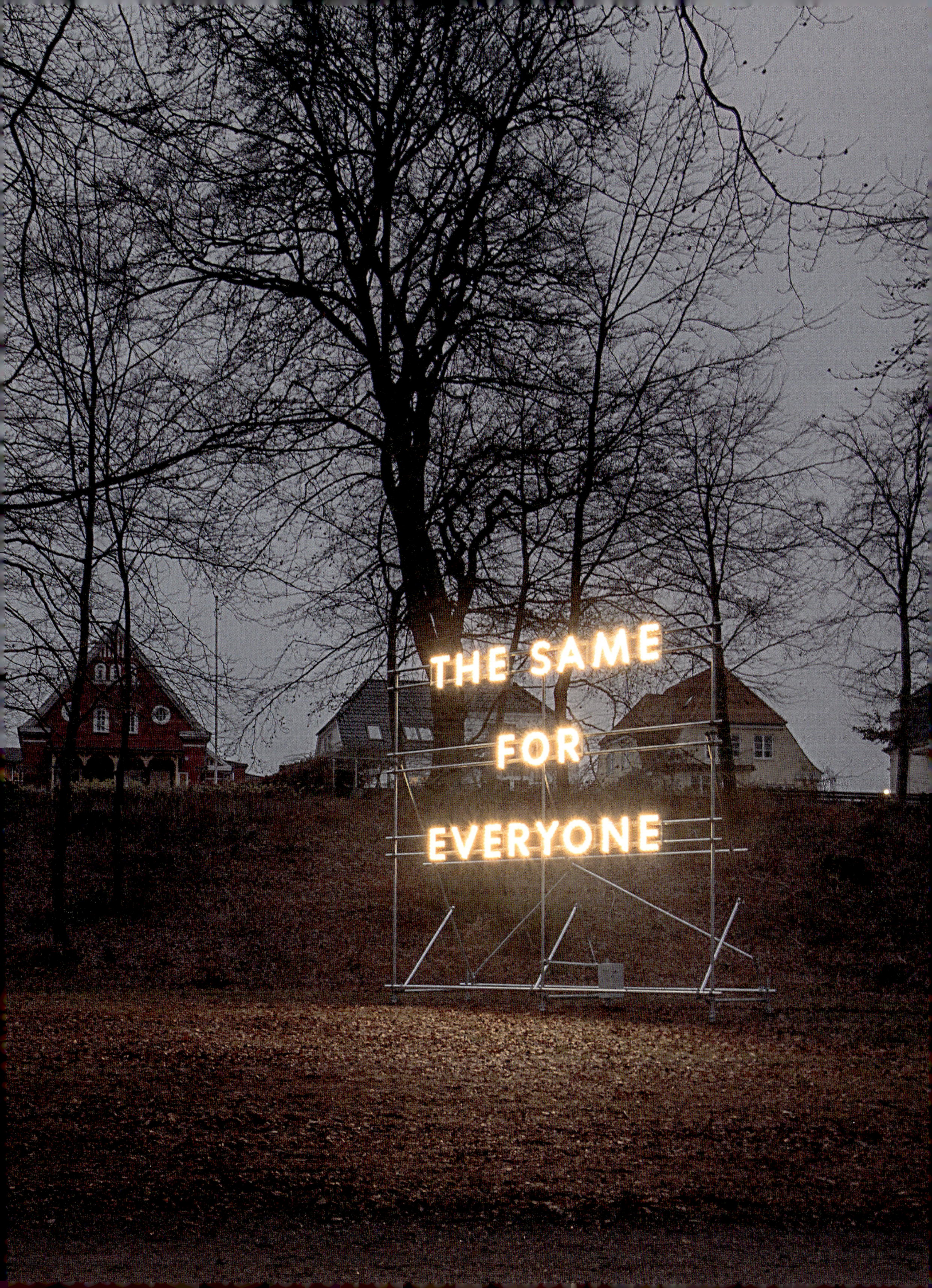
THE SAME
FOR
EVERYONE

Edmund de Waal

Born in Nottingham, 1964
Lives and works in London

In the Kettle's Yard House two glazed vitrines by Edmund de Waal occupy a space between the upper and lower levels of the 1970 extension. The vitrines are small and black, visible but unobtrusive, as if waiting to be found. *letters from Paris II* and *letters from Paris III*, both made in 2017, draw you into their worlds. Both vitrines contain a plain porcelain vessel, the colour of charcoal. The first also contains, partially hidden behind the vessel, a piece of silver and a gilded porcelain tile. In the second vitrine two Cor-Ten steel blocks stand in front and to the side of the vessel. De Waal has written of his vessels, "I am making nothing grander than a cylinder. Barely a vessel. More a sketch of a pot, the merest impression of my hand – each vessel is a breath and I am counting time."

These compositions of objects, poetic and open ended, mirror the care Jim Ede took with the selection and precise placing of every artwork and object, including pebbles and shells, within the Kettle's Yard House. For de Waal, as for Ede, all objects have the potential to make us look and feel more intently, as we recall or imagine their histories of use, or how their current physical state reflects their creation. De Waal's vitrines, with their evocative title and the play of light and shadow around objects both exposed and hidden from view, seem both energised and still.

De Waal has known Kettle's Yard since he was a student at Cambridge studying English in the mid 1980s. It has remained a touchstone for him in the development of his work. In 2007, he made a landmark solo exhibition at Kettle's Yard of new installations both in the gallery and in the House, with arrangements of pots on shelves and inside cupboards. The success of his family memoir, *The Hare with Amber Eyes* (2010), compounded de Waal's dual life as a writer and artist. Each pursuit, as he acknowledges, shapes the other; a relationship he explores most profoundly in his subsequent book, *The White Road* (2015), on his journey into an obsession with porcelain and white itself. His use of translucent vitrines, in which vessels appear as blurred shapes, such as in *another hour, I-VI* (2017), reflect de Waal's acute recognition of the limitations of history and memory. **AN**

A vitrine is a kind of page. It holds objects and spaces in a parallel way to the placing of words and pauses on a piece of paper. These two small dark works, letters from Paris, are a gentle nod to the iterative life of letters coming and going from Paris to Jim Ede and back again. Kettle's Yard is full of overheard conversations between people, books and art, and these works are part of this continuum.
Edmund de Waal, 2017

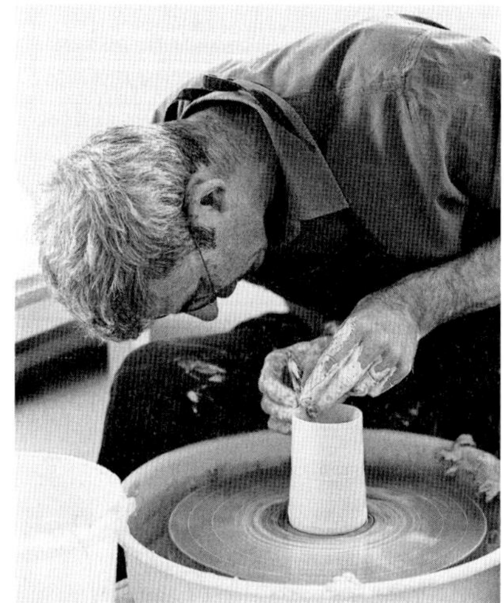

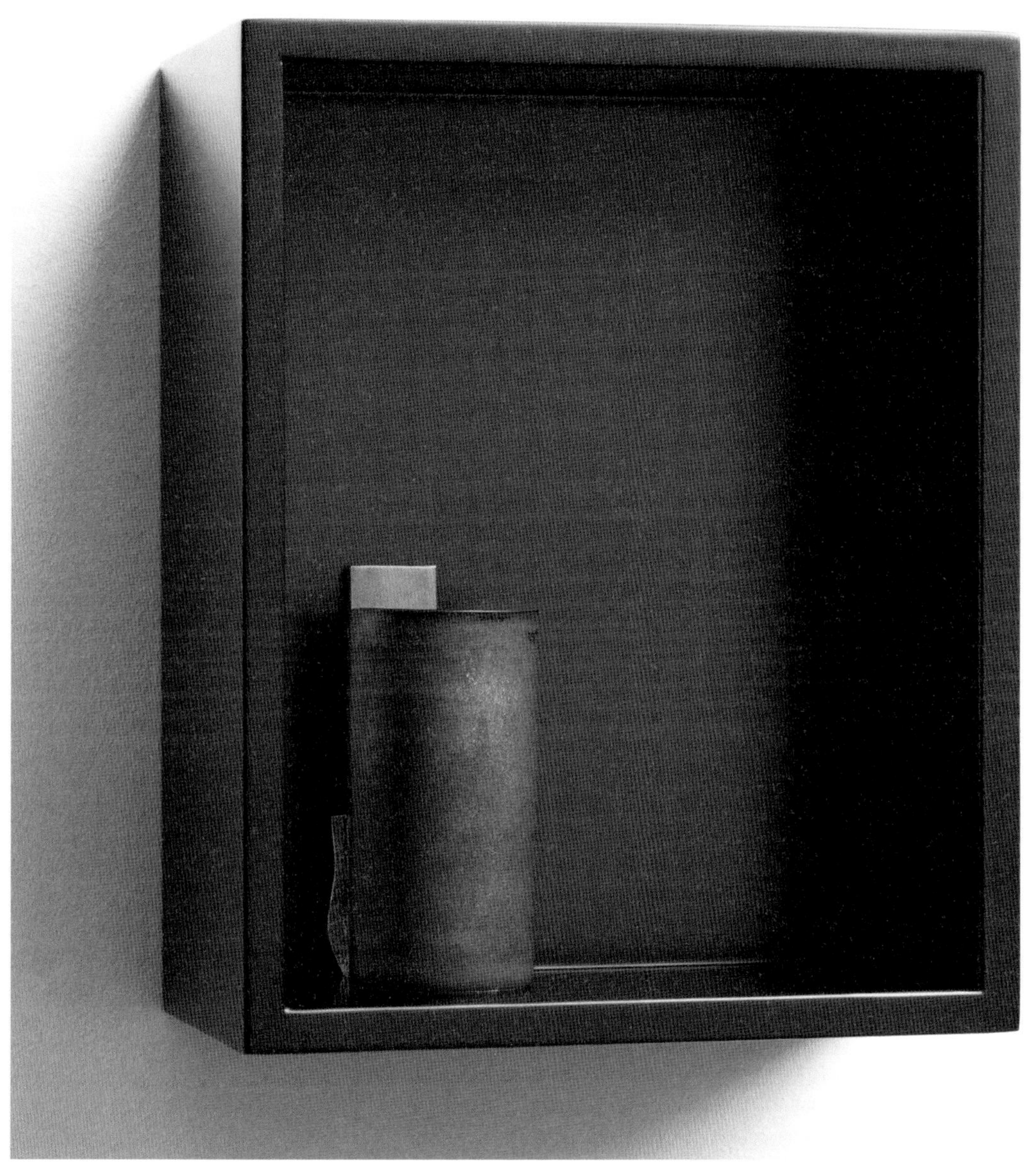

Letters from Paris, II, 2017
Porcelain vessel, gilded porcelain tile and
silver piece in an aluminium and Plexiglas vitrine
170 × 210 × 100 mm

Jeremy Deller

Artists are given some sort of freedom to act in a certain way that no one else really can do. I'm quite interested in pushing certain boundaries. In fact I'd like to do it more. I gave a talk in a prison once, I talked about art and crime and how artists and criminals actually are very similar in some ways, because they're both trying to test the boundaries of acceptability, of social behaviour, but also... they're contained in these very secure, well-lit places, that are usually quite clean and can be quite sterile.

Jeremy Deller, *The Song is Bigger than the Band. A Conversation. The Infinitely Variable Ideal of the Popular*, 2016

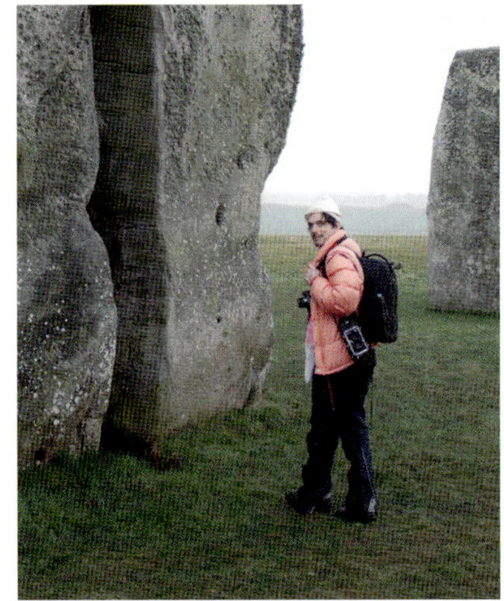

Born in London, 1966
Lives and works in London

Jeremy Deller's work for *Actions* is not found on the walls of the gallery. It circulates through all of the spaces at Kettle's Yard, from beside a Barbara Hepworth sculpture in the House, into the café and even the office kitchen. Deller has designed a new T-shirt to be worn by members of staff in the House and galleries for the duration of the exhibition, seizing the infrastructure of the organisation as a site for display and conversation. Deller's socially engaged works regularly manifest away from the neutrality of the gallery's white walls and take on a number of guises – from film, fly-posters or clothing to a life-size Stonehenge bouncy castle or a live performance with a brass band. Whatever the form, his ideas typically mine a particular situation in the British cultural and political landscape and present us with a provocation, observing our society with a critical eye, through the lens of culture.

Deller's position as an artist is often catalytic, using the umbrella of visual art to bring people together to explore ideas and histories in temporal situations that, even after decades of progressive practice beyond modernism, challenge our ideas around what art can be. In *The Battle of Orgreave* (2001), he wanted to recreate riotous scenes that he had witnessed on television as a teenager, of the notorious miners' strike of 1984 that culminated in violent clashes between workers and police, taking place at the height of Margaret Thatcher's divisive government. Deller was captivated by what he saw, believing the scenes to resemble something closer to civil war rather than a political dispute over labour. In a work of similarly ambitious scale, in 2016 he instigated an event involving over a thousand men clad in First World War army uniforms, who appeared unannounced at locations across Britain. Marking the centenary of the Battle of the Somme, the figures said nothing, rather gathering silently and dispersing on foot into train stations, onto public transport or through shopping centres, occasionally breaking into renditions of "We're here because we're here", a poignant First World War song that repeats that phrase to the tune of *Auld Lang Syne*. In this poignant work Deller again deliberately sidestepped the boundaries of the sites we traditionally associate with experiencing art: indeed, this project avoided the label of 'art' entirely until his involvement was revealed after the event. Deller wanted instead to reach "everyday British life... to avoid heritage places – churches, war memorials. I wanted to take it to the public." **GH**

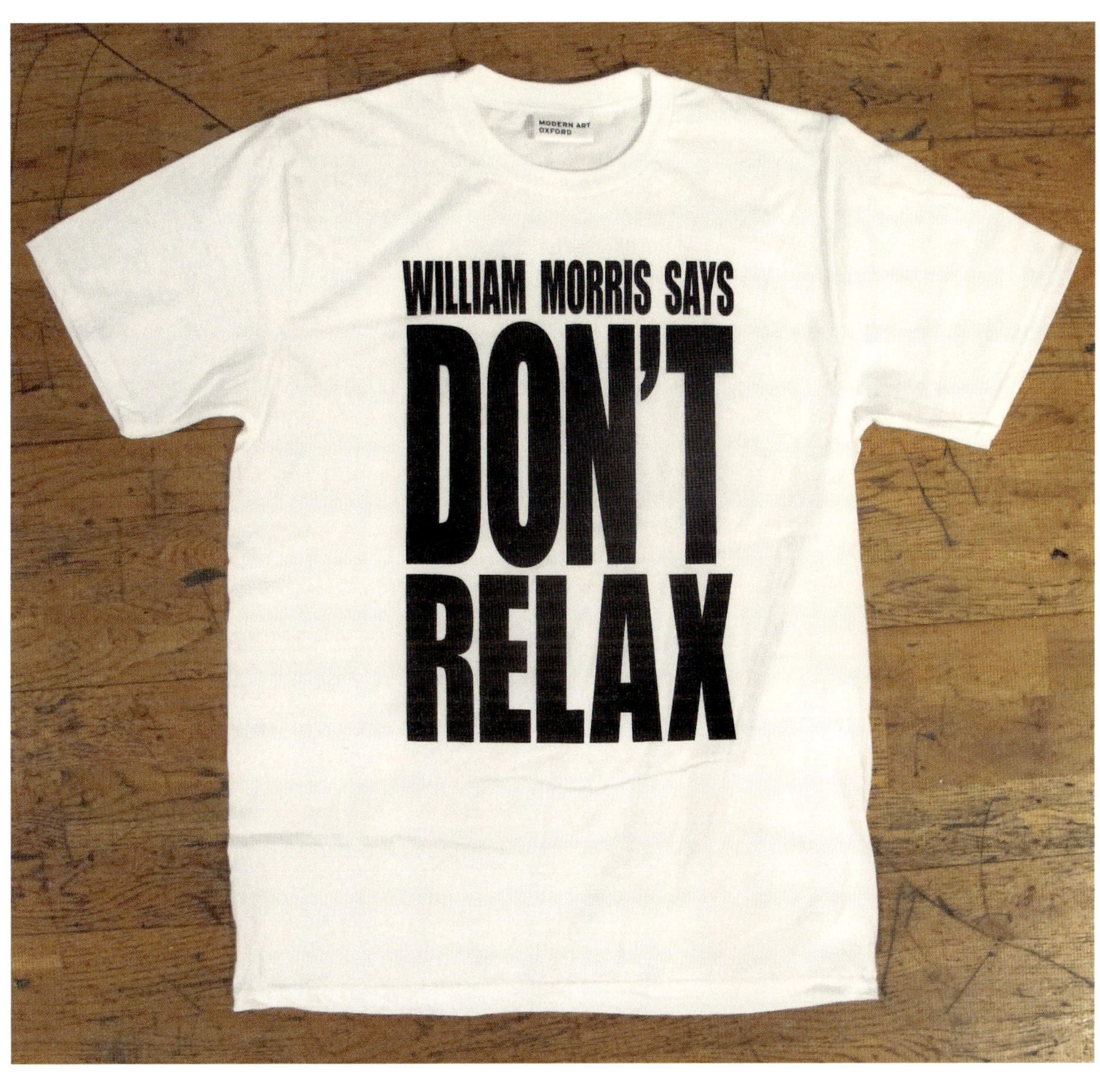

William Morris Says Don't Relax, 2014
T-shirt

eL Seed

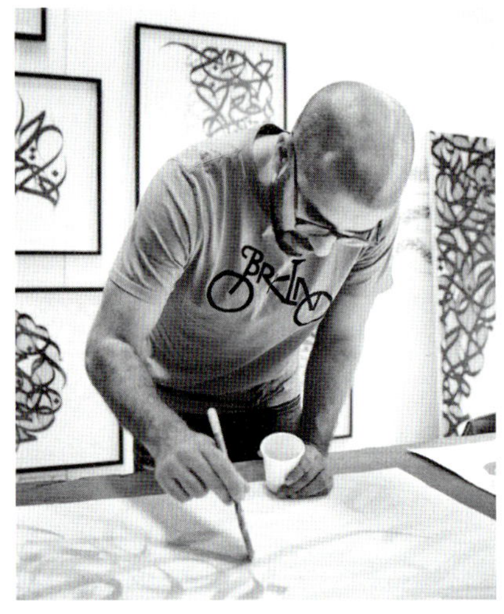

Bringing people, future generations, together through Arabic calligraphy is what I do. Writing messages is the essence of my artwork. What is funny, actually, is that even Arabic-speaking people really need to focus a lot to decipher what I'm writing. You don't need to know the meaning to feel the piece. I think that Arabic script touches your soul before it reaches your eyes. There is a beauty in it that you don't need to translate.
eL Seed, Transcript of talk given at TED2015, 2015

Born in Paris, 1981
Lives and works in Paris

For *Actions*, eL Seed has realised a new site-specific mural working with the community partners of Kettle's Yard in north Cambridge. In recent years the artist has often worked collaboratively with communities to realise his large-scale wall paintings, most notably in 2016, when he conceived of an ambitious mural to honour the historic garbage collectors of the Manshiyat Naser neighbourhood in the suburbs of Cairo. eL Seed explained, "The Zaraeeb (which means the pig breeders), have developed one of the most efficient and highly profitable systems on a global level. Still, the place is perceived as dirty, marginalized and segregated because of their association with the trash." eL Seed worked with a team of assistants and in cooperation with local residents to complete the enormous anamorphic mural, painted using white, black, orange, yellow and turquoise paint across the exteriors of fifty buildings. The mural can only be viewed in totality from the vantage point of the nearby sacred site, Muqattam Mountain, which is also the location of the 20,000 capacity St Simon cave church, which was carved by the Zaraeeb in the 1970s to create a Coptic Christian place of worship for their community within the majority Muslim country of Egypt. From the viewpoint overlooking the village, el Seed's vast fragmented mural coalesces into a sun-like mandala inscribed with a looping calligraphic quote from fourth-century Coptic bishop Saint Athanasius of Alexandria, which reads: "Anyone who wants to see the sunlight clearly needs to wipe his eyes first." Documentation of *Perception* forms part of the *Actions* exhibition.

eL Seed was born in the Parisian suburb of Le Chesnay to Tunisian parents. In his late teens, he became more interested in his cultural heritage and learned to read and write Arabic, an endeavour which had a profound impact on his artistic practice. Aged sixteen, he adopted the pseudonym eL Seed, inspired by French dramatist Pierre Corneille's five-act tragicomedy *Le Cid* (1638). Like Corneille's central protagonist, eL Seed dedicated himself to a life in the service of art and social justice. He began his career on a modest scale, drawing on and spray-painting walls in the streets of Paris. In recent years, eL Seed has used the vehicle of street art to promote peace, unity and greater social tolerance in communities riven by inequality such as the favelas of Rio de Janeiro and the slums of Capetown. eL Seed realises his dramatic and colourful murals in a style he calls "calligraffiti", which is a blend of the ancient art form of calligraphy with stylistic elements derived from both classic Wild Style and contemporary graffiti forms. His bold murals typically feature quotations from inspirational texts rendered in Arabic script, as a central motivation of eL Seed's artistic practice is challenging preconceptions of Arabic culture. **SL**

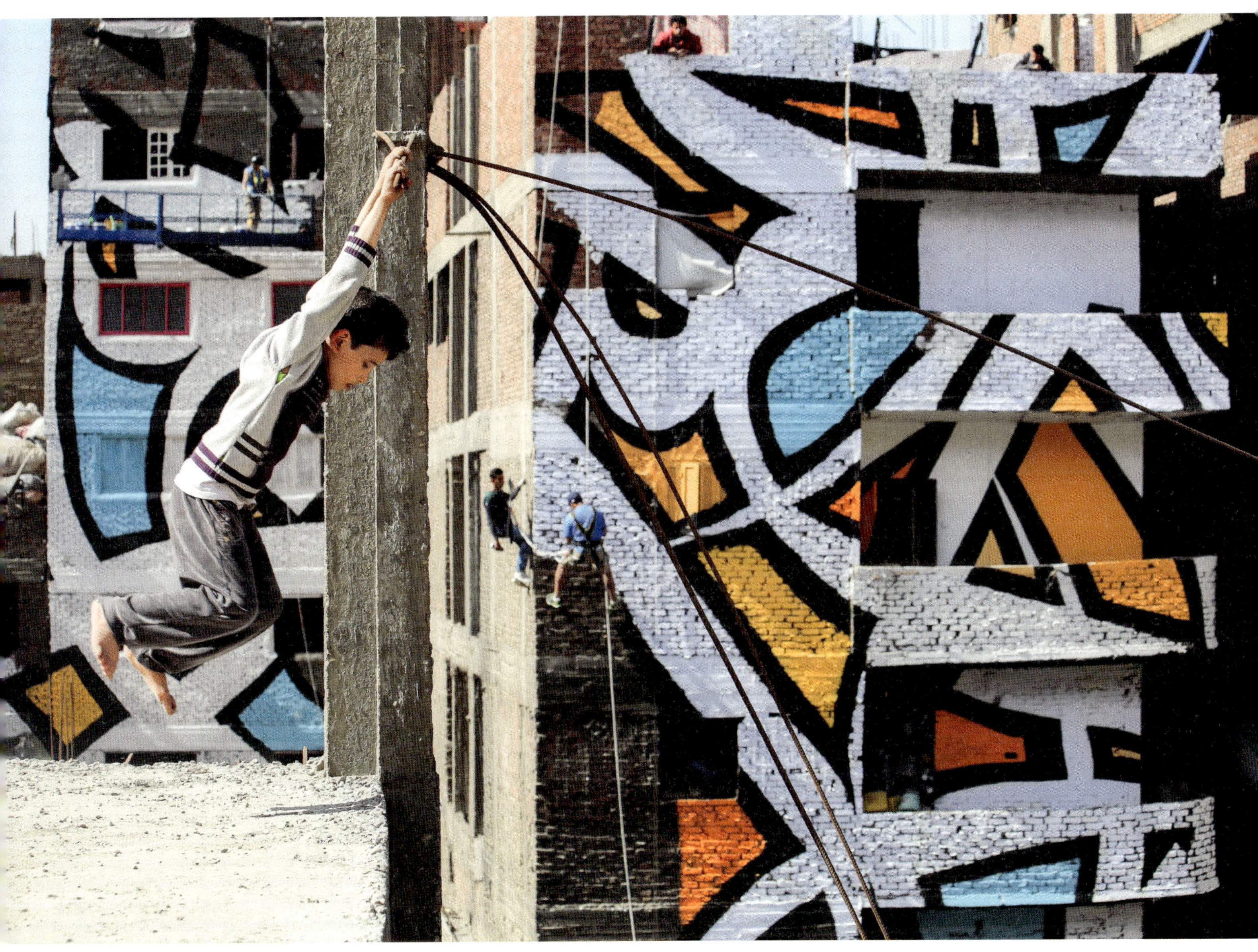

Documentation of *Perception*, 2016

Jamie Fobert

The new galleries created by Jamie Fobert at Kettle's Yard allow for the direct experience of light and volume.
Antony Gormley, in correspondence with Kettle's Yard, 2017

Jamie Fobert Architects
Founded in London, 1996

Walking around the new, and as yet still empty, spaces at Kettle's Yard in the winter of 2017 is an intensely physical experience. Space, light and volume are acutely felt. These characteristics, as well as a careful choice of materials, create close conversations between the original Kettle's Yard House and 1970 extension and Jamie Fobert Architects' extraordinary new spaces for 2018.

Founded in 1996, Jamie Fobert Architects (JFA) is a close team of innovative architects led by Canadian-born, London-based Jamie Fobert. JFA's work with Kettle's Yard began in 2004 as a project for an Education Wing under the Directorship of Michael Harrison (shown in the adjacent sketch). The project was extended to encompass the gallery spaces and public spaces by the current Director Andrew Nairne in 2012. Fobert has described his process as that of working 'in' architecture. Through his archival research and conversations with David Owers, who collaborated with Sir Leslie Martin to create the 1970 extension to the 1957 House, Fobert further developed his deeply held respect for the original site at Kettle's Yard. This, combined with his commitment to innovative architecture that considers the future inhabitants of the spaces that he designs, underpins the Kettle's Yard project. Fobert's architecture looks attentively to the past, but also propels Kettle's Yard forwards into a future full of new and exciting possibilities.

As a practice, JFA works across residential, retail and the arts sectors. They have most recently extended spaces at Tate St Ives and continue to work with the Charleston Barns. Through each of these projects, Fobert's close connections to, and interest in, the visual arts are visible. At Kettle's Yard, a number of subtle motifs from the Martin and Owers extension offer points of connection that affirm the sense of a site that is now one: Martin's roof lights have been adapted in Gallery 2; the double height of the Clore Learning Studio takes its spatial cue from the 1970 extension; original brickwork has been revealed and extended; the lateral movements on which Martin's architecture was predicated have been restored by the structure of the new spaces. However, the spaces also feel fresh and new. A majestic concrete slab in the Clore Learning Studio guides visitors down to a space for educational activities that are now placed physically at the heart of Kettle's Yard. Elsewhere, a beautiful black steel staircase leads up to the Edlis Neeson Research Space and Ede Room. Fobert has suggested that his purposefully wide internal connecting spaces promote moments of rest and meeting; this sensibility was shared by Kettle's Yard's creator Jim Ede, who encouraged visitors to his home to take time out of their busy lives to enjoy the artwork and objects that surrounded them and to have conversations. One of the drawings adjacent is a sketch for the welcome area and desk. This area, as well as the patinated black bronze canopy and the façade on Castle Street, have been closely considered formally and materially to promote the welcoming experience and ethos of openness to all, which is at the very heart of Kettle's Yard. **JP**

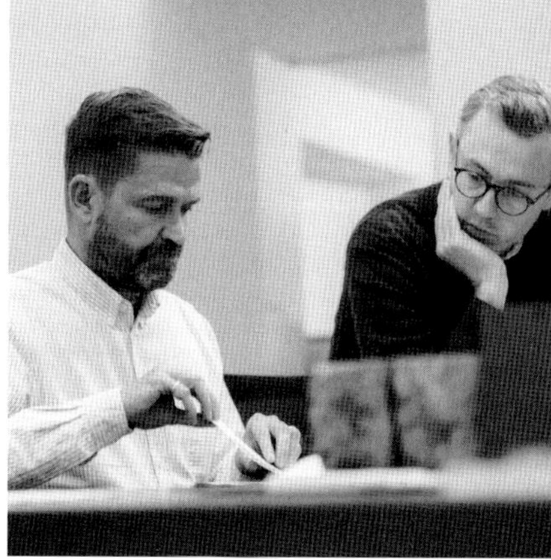

Jamie Fobert (left), with Oliver Bindloss, project architect

Above
Early sketch of learning room at Kettle's Yard, 2004
Pen and colour wash on tracing paper
220 × 150 mm

Below
Plan, elevation and sketch of welcome desk at Kettle's Yard, 2016
Pen and ink on tracing paper
300 × 300 mm

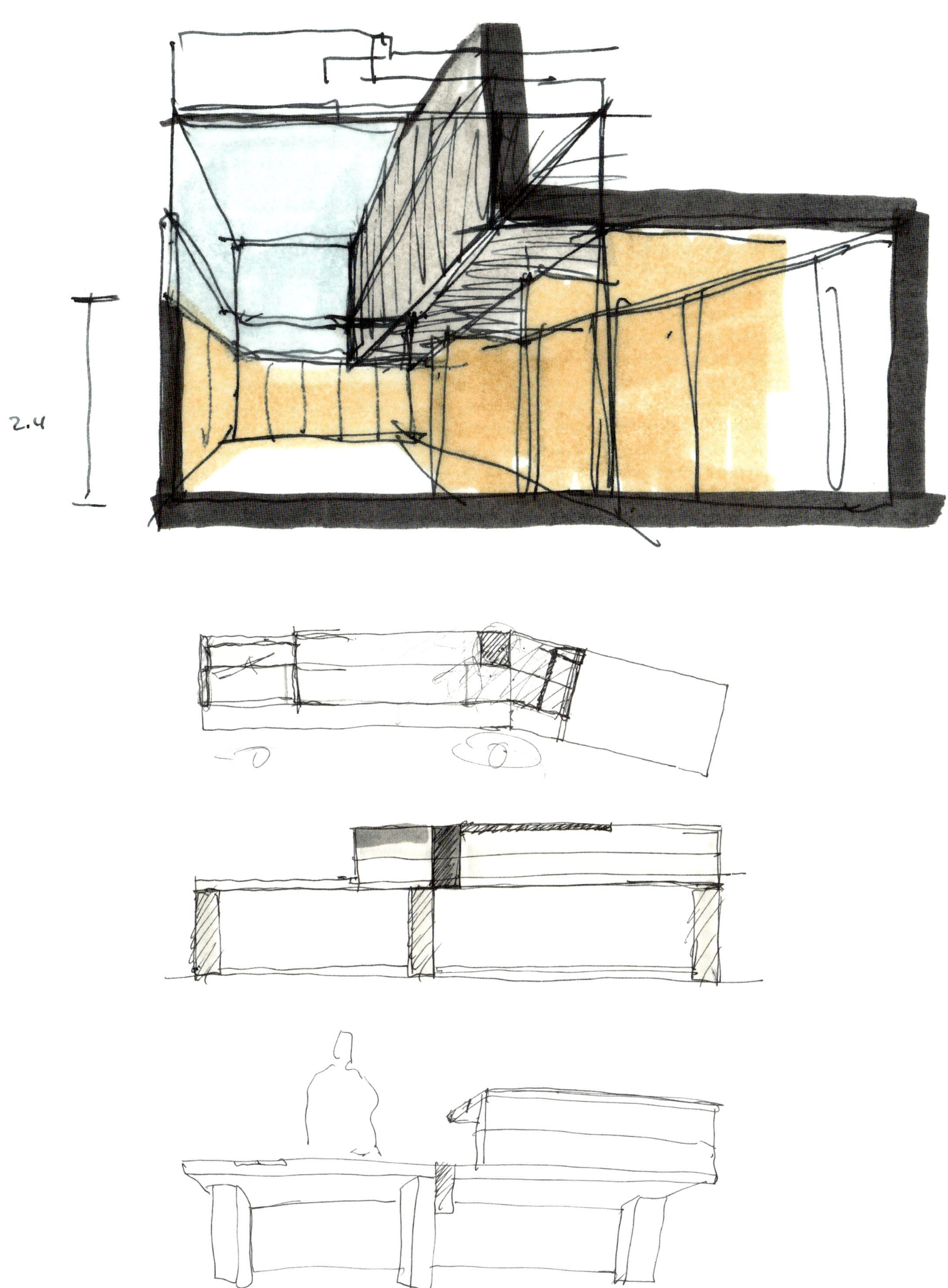
2.4

Helen Frankenthaler

There are no rules. That is how art is born, how breakthroughs happen. Go against the rules or ignore the rules. That is what invention is about.
Helen Frankenthaler, 1994

Born in New York, 1928
Died in Darien, Connecticut, 2011
Lived and worked in New York

Helen Frankenthaler's painting *Untitled* (1960–61) is a characteristically bold experiment on paper. It combines thin washes of oil paint in primary colours, which leak, bleed and burst on the page. The result is an abstract composition that is full of movement and life. Free from any under drawing or preparatory work, the painting is improvised and choreographed directly and through the artist's decisive action.

This work was made between 1960 and 1961, when Frankenthaler was midway through her long career. It is easy to overlook the double signature that appears on *Untitled*: one is positioned at the bottom corner and the other barely visible under the flash of red paint just off-centre. This suggests that Frankenthaler trialled the work in different orientations, further emphasising the freedom with which she approached the composition. *Untitled* is likely to have been executed in thinned oil paint which produces a halo-like effect at its edges; this is evident in many of Frankethaler's works on paper and canvas in oil, which was her favoured medium until around 1963 when she began to experiment with acrylic paint. Frankenthaler's abstract paintings of all scales have a strong emotive power. This painting is principally abstract, with a large area of sweeping blue brushwork that might evoke the dynamism of a roaring sea. As the curator Bryan Robertson commented in 1969, on the occasion of Frankenthaler's major retrospective at the Whitechapel Art Gallery, London: "Each painting is an immediate experience, lived wholly in the present." Robertson generously bequeathed this work to Kettle's Yard.

Frankenthaler was born in New York and this city remained her home. She was active in the developing New York School and in the 1950s had been initially influenced by artists including Jackson Pollock. Her first solo exhibition was held in 1951. Her groundbreaking technique of 'colour-stain' or 'soak-stain' involved a direct connection between the hand and the raw unprimed canvas. She applied thin washes of oil paint usually working directly on her studio floor and on a monumental scale, moving around all sides of her canvases. Her paint was diluted with turpentine to the point at which it could achieve the fluidity and translucency that she desired. Describing her methods of applying paint in an interview of 1985 with *Architectural Digest*, she stated that "I often pour it, making it more or less liquid as I go along, or I can use sponges, or a wet or dry brush – any number of means. The point is to get down on the canvas what I need." Frankenthaler's use of large expanses of colour influenced Colour Field painters such as Kenneth Noland and Morris Louis. Frankenthaler succeeded in a New York art world whose networks were still primarily dominated by male artists and critics. She was a pioneering painter with a palpable appetite for experimentation that pushed painting forwards. **JP**

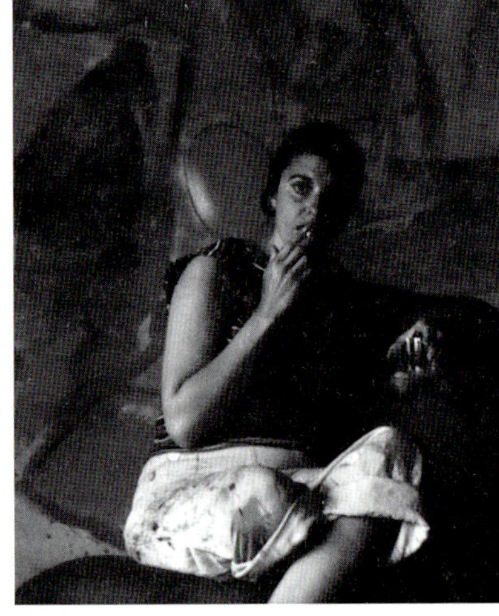

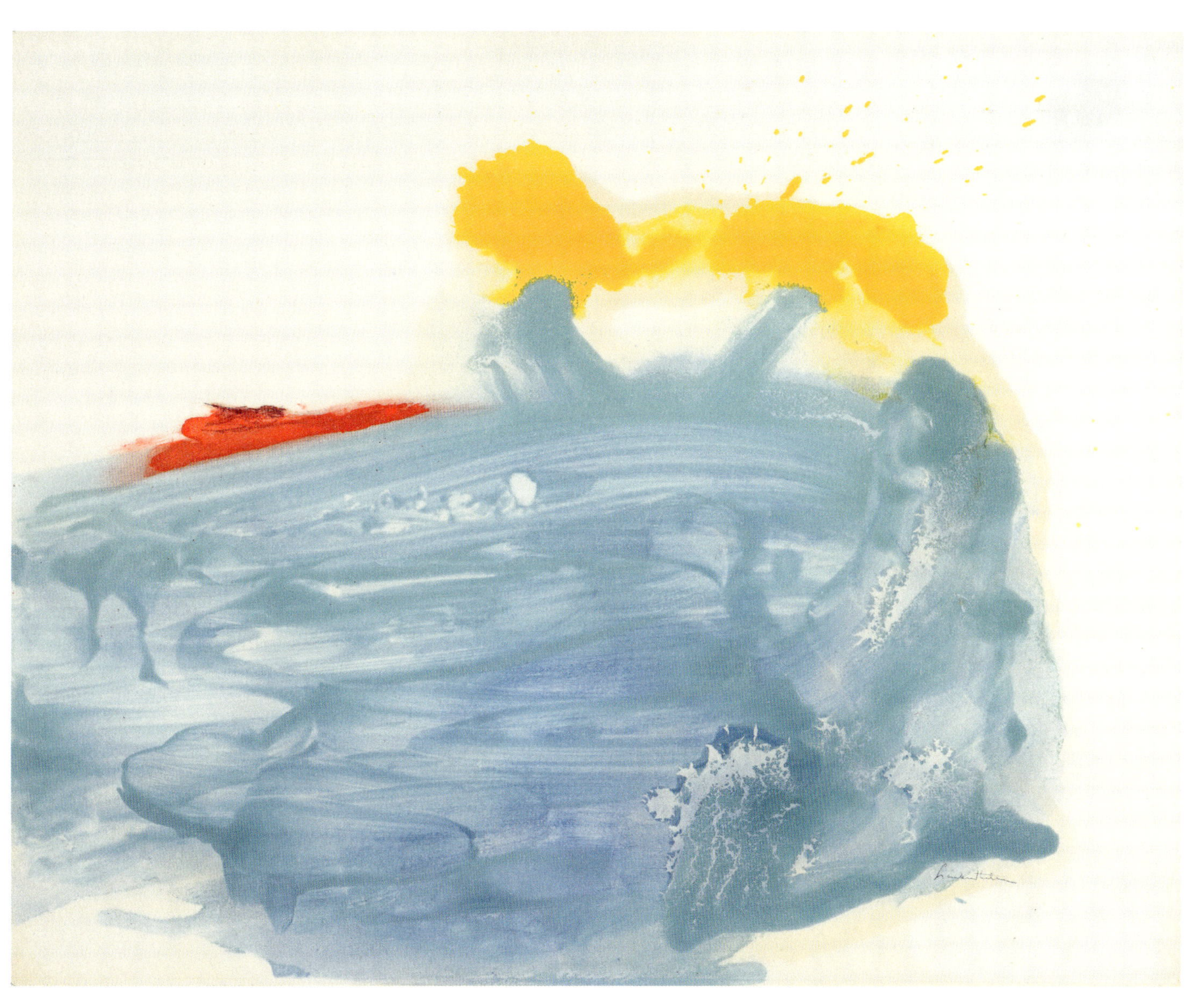

Untitled, c.1960–61
Oil on paper
5800 × 7300 mm

Naum Gabo

Born in Bryansk, Russia, 1890
Died in Waterbury, Connecticut, USA, 1977
Lived and worked in Moscow; Paris; London; St Ives, England and USA

Naum Gabo's pioneering sculpture *Linear Construction in Space No. 1* consists of a rectangular, transparent Perspex frame, around which nylon threads are tightly wound in close proximity to create an oval void. Made in Cornwall between 1944 and 1945, Gabo used two new synthetic materials which account for the work's shimmering appearance. As Natalia Sidlina has noted: "Perspex and nylon have very specific properties: the former collects pockets of light like a prism, while the latter absorbs it evenly along the whole length of its threads, thus employing the light to develop a new way of defining form in sculpture". Gabo produced seventeen versions of *Linear Construction in Space No. 1* of which the one at Kettle's Yard is thought to be the fifth. The first one Gabo made he dedicated to the Russian liberation of Leningrad. He saw his small-scale constructions as models for much larger monuments which could play a dynamic role in society as public works of art.

The appearance of Gabo's sculptures may also have been influenced by an interest in mathematical models and the work of Henry Moore and Barbara Hepworth, who were also experimenting with opening up volume and with stringing. During the war, Gabo was part of a community of artists in the St Ives area, which included Hepworth and Ben Nicholson. It was during this time, in 1944, that Gabo published his letter (the inspiration for the *Actions* exhibition) setting out his thoughts on the value and purpose of art to the writer and critic Herbert Read.

Gabo's *Linear Construction in Space No. 2* was conceived in 1949 and continued the artist's fascination with light and space and the idea of dematerialization in sculpture. Sometimes suspended vertically and so able to gently rotate and sway, Gabo's new construction encompassed the concepts of time and movement found in other works throughout his career.

Having studied medicine and natural sciences and later engineering between 1912 and 1914, and with a strong interest in the new physics, Gabo wanted to develop an art that was as radical and visionary as developments in science. Gabo became a leading exponent of Constructivist art, with its formal emphasis on structure and abstraction, and co-edited with Ben Nicholson and Leslie Martin the influential book *Circle*, published in 1937. From 1936 to 1946 Gabo and his family lived in London and then Cornwall, before emigrating to the United States in 1946. His later career allowed Gabo to realise a number of large-scale sculptures around the world. **AN**

Why, may I ask, is not the contemporary artist to be permitted to search for and bring forward an image of the world more in accordance with the achievements of our developed mind, even if it is different from the image presented in the paintings and sculptures of our predecessors?
Naum Gabo, "On Constructive Realism", 1948

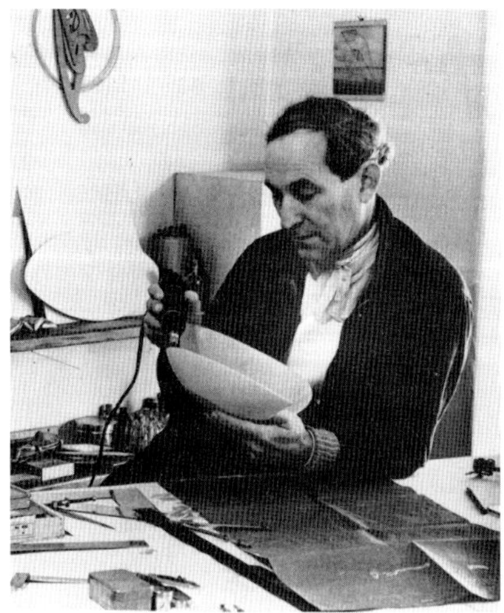

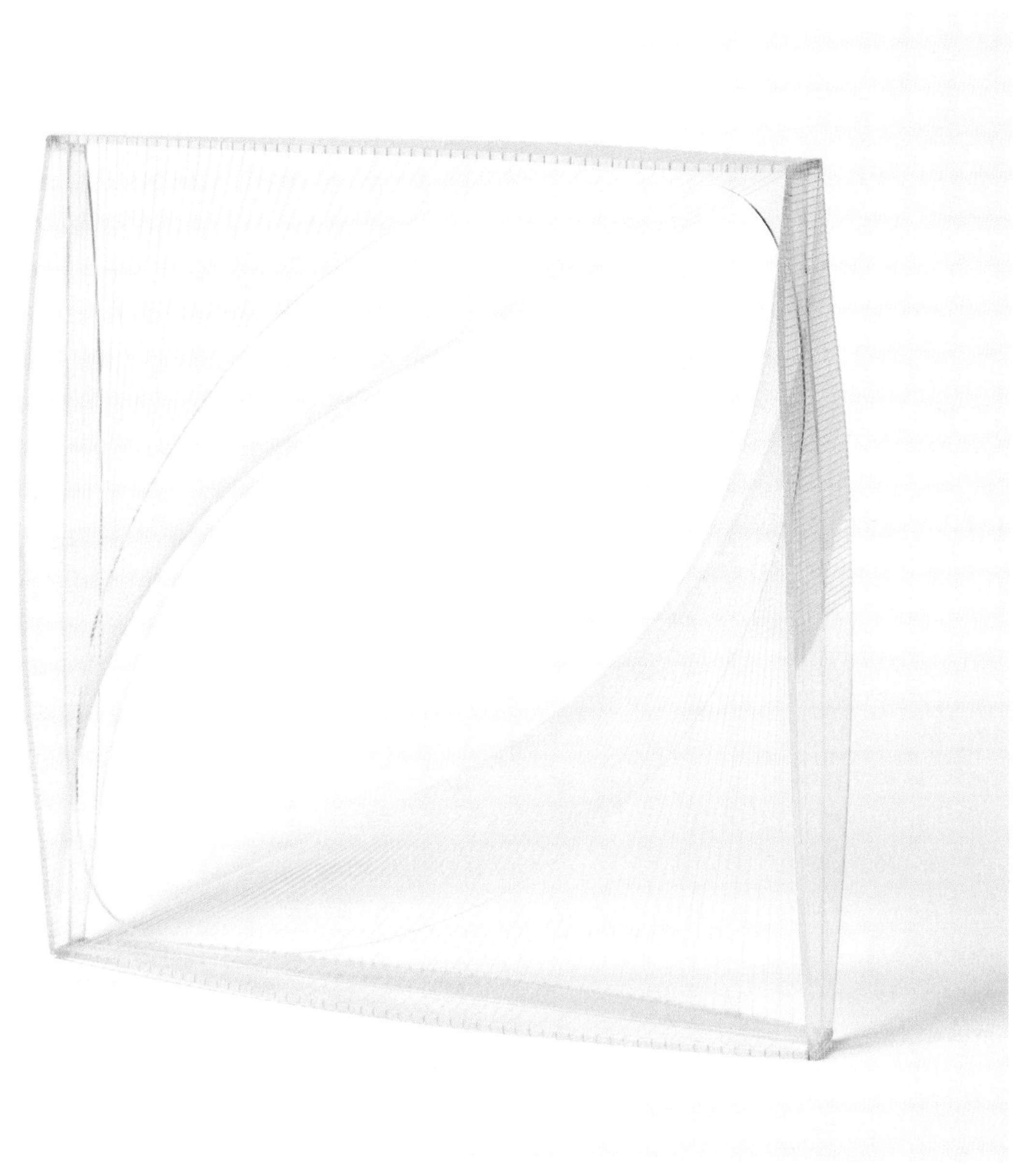

Linear Construction in Space No. 1, 1944–45
Perspex and nylon thread
304 × 304 × 62 mm

Regina José Galindo

Who do not have faces, but arms.
Who do not have names, but numbers.
Eduardo Galeano, *Los Nadies/The Nobodies*, 1989

Born in Guatemala City, 1974
Lives and works in Guatemala City

Regina José Galindo has made two new performance works for *Actions*. The *Monument to the Invisibles*, staged on the manicured lawn of a Cambridge College, is performed by Galindo and six volunteers, each positioned at points around the lawn, standing on plinths 3.5 metres high, but concealed beneath shrouds of white fabric. *Monument to the Invisibles*, in common with Galindo's other performance works, expresses the trauma that is repressed in her homeland of Guatemala, a place that the artist has described as "a country without memory". In another performance, Galindo used a small room in the Kettle's Yard House, not usually accessible by the public, to enact a work reflecting on the experience of migration.

In the gallery, a film of Galindo's durational performance work *Tierra* (2013) is shown. *Tierra* was made by the artist in response to the charges of genocide and crimes against humanity made during the 2012 trial of José Efraín Ríos Montt, a former President of Guatemala. Montt was accused of the mass murder of innocent citizens and disposing of their bodies in a vast grave dug by a bulldozer: he was subsequently acquitted of this, and all other charges. *Tierra* opens with an image of the artist standing naked in a green field, a bucolic scene which is literally destroyed by the arrival of an earth-moving machine, which excavates a yawning pit around the artist, who stands, motionless and silent, on a grassy plinth that grows ever smaller.

Galindo's socially and politically motivated practice has often made reference to the legacy of the Guatemalan Civil War (1960–96). Between 1998 and 2000, Galindo first developed her work as a poet alongside other artists including Jessica Lagunas and Aníbal López, writing the pieces that became part of her book *Personal and Intransmisible* (2000) and which led to her first visceral and disturbing performances. A constant in Galindo's performances is the artist's display of her own vulnerability, a method she describes as enacting "an empathetic bridge" between her exposed body and the consciousness of the audience. For *Piel* (*Skin*) (2001), Galindo shaved off all the hair on her body, and then left the space of the Venice Biennale to walk naked for ninety minutes through the city streets. The practice of walking recurred in one of Galindo's most celebrated works, *Quién puede borrar las huellas? (Who Can Erase the Traces?)* (2003), a work made to convey her rage at the news that José Efraín Ríos Montt was being permitted to run for president. Galindo dressed in black and then walked barefoot through the streets of Guatemala City, from the Constitutional Court to the National Palace, carrying a basin filled with fresh human blood, bought from a medical laboratory, into which she periodically dipped her feet. **SL**

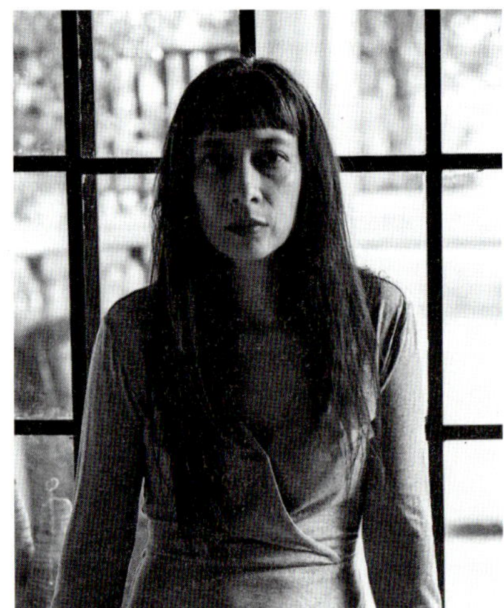

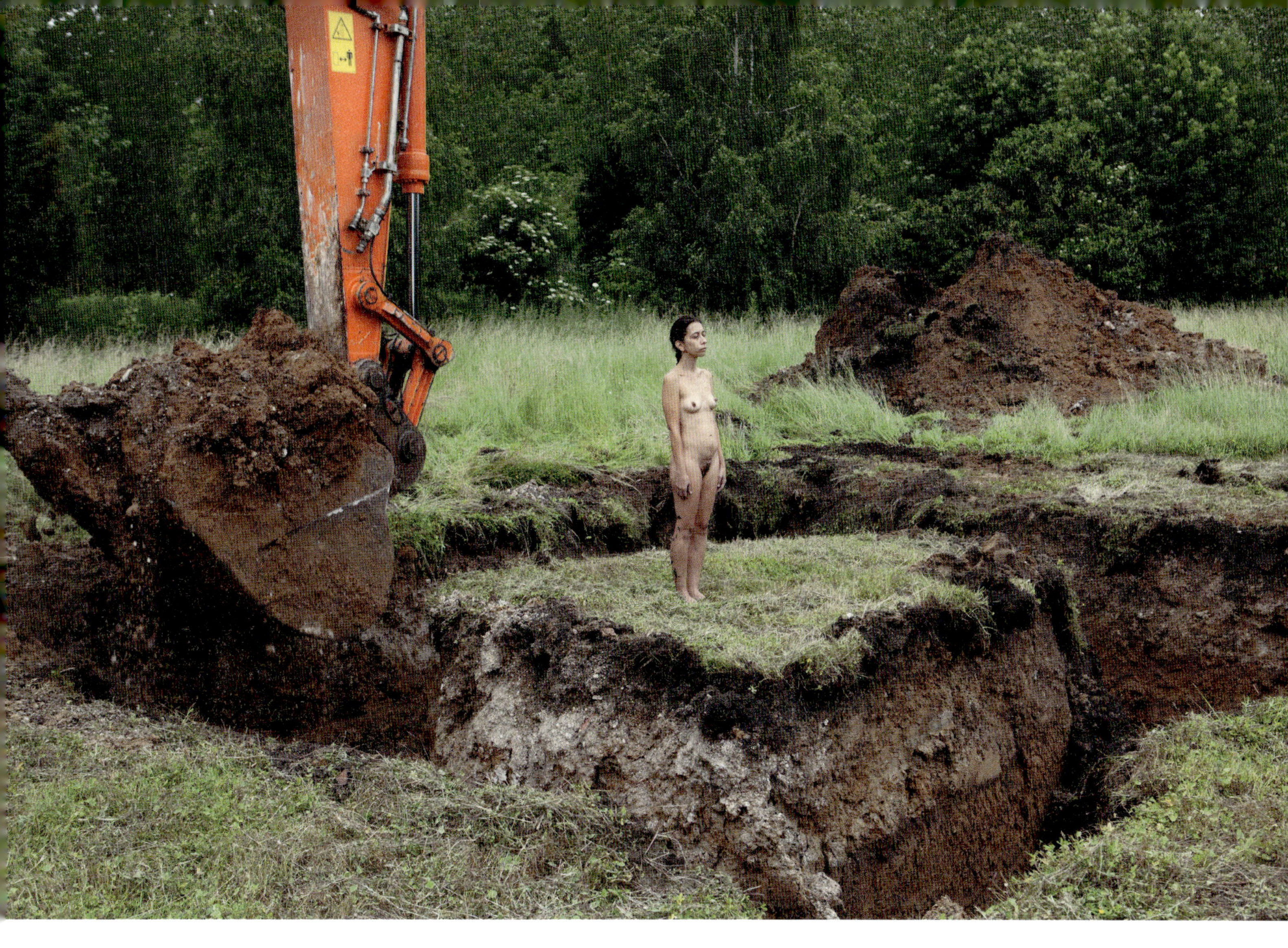

Tierra, 2013
Digital video with sound
33 minutes 30 seconds

Anya Gallaccio

Born in Paisley, Scotland, 1963
Lives and works in San Diego and London

Anya Gallaccio's recent series of dirt drawings called *Untitled, Imagined Dirt Landscapes* (2016) are rendered using marbling techniques to imprint traces of dirt and mixed mineral watercolour on paper. Dirt is a material that Gallaccio has worked with numerous times, drawing out the connotative and associative potential of the found media through "natural readymades" in which the artist both sets up a situation but also allows chance operations to unfold. The dirt used for this new series of works was collected by the artist during a road trip across the desert landscapes of Death Valley, the Grand Canyon, Sedona in Arizona and a meteor crater in Arizona. Since 2008, Gallaccio has lived in California, where the experience of being confronted by a different kind of landscape has affected the direction of her work. Gallaccio's practice has long addressed the relationship between craft, site and content, but unlike other artists known for working with and in the natural landscape, such as Robert Smithson and Richard Long, Gallaccio is attracted equally to stable or hard materials such as rocks, minerals and metals and also to materials that disintegrate, such as salt, ice, chocolate, flowers and fruit.

Gallaccio came to prominence as part of the *Freeze* generation of artists who graduated from Goldsmiths in the late 1980s, and quickly attracted critical acclaim for her works using flowers, such as *Preserve Beauty* (1991–2003) and *Head Over Heals* (1995), both made using gerbera daisies which gave audiences an experience either of fresh floral display or malodorous rot, depending on the timing of their visit. Gallaccio is also well known for visually stunning and emotive works such as *Two Sisters* (1998), a 6-metre high, 2.5-metre diameter and 70-tonne column of chalk bonded by plaster installed on the silt bed of the Minerva Basin, Hull, which was commissioned by Locus+. The work was modified by the tidal flow of the River Humber until it eroded and collapsed. Gallaccio has also worked with harder materials to realise permanent sculptural works, such as the 3-square metre sunken grotto lined with amethyst *The Light Pours Out of Me* (2012) located at Jupiter Artland sculpture park in a private estate outside Edinburgh. Recently, Gallaccio reincarnated a dead tree in *Untitled, Ghost tree* (2016), a work commissioned for the reopening of the Whitworth in Manchester – the work was a full scale stainless steel structure, inspired by a tree felled during the renovation of the museum. The 'ghost tree' was fabricated in polished stainless steel, the reflective surface mirroring the surrounding trees and making the object both an absence and a presence, connecting with Gallaccio's long-term project of using sculptural forms to engage with ideas of place, time, life, death, beauty, decay and renewal. **SL**

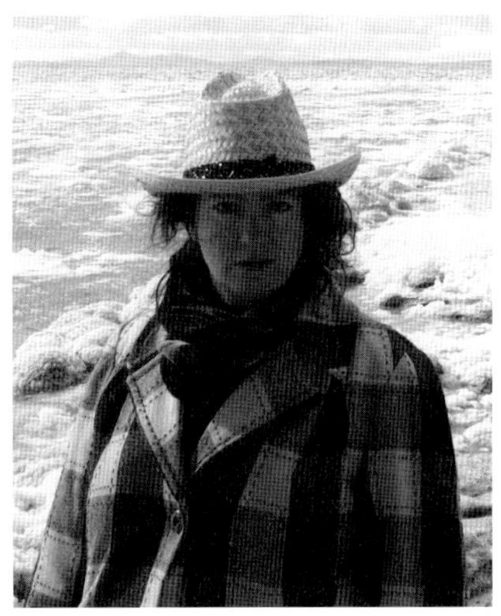

The work often starts from a cliché about a place or material and an attempt to move beyond it. I keep returning to the personal, the domestic, the local. It is challenging to look at things under your nose, the things we take for granted.

Anya Gallaccio, "Dust Bunnies and Coffee Stains: Anya Gallaccio in conversation with Clarrie Wallis", 2012

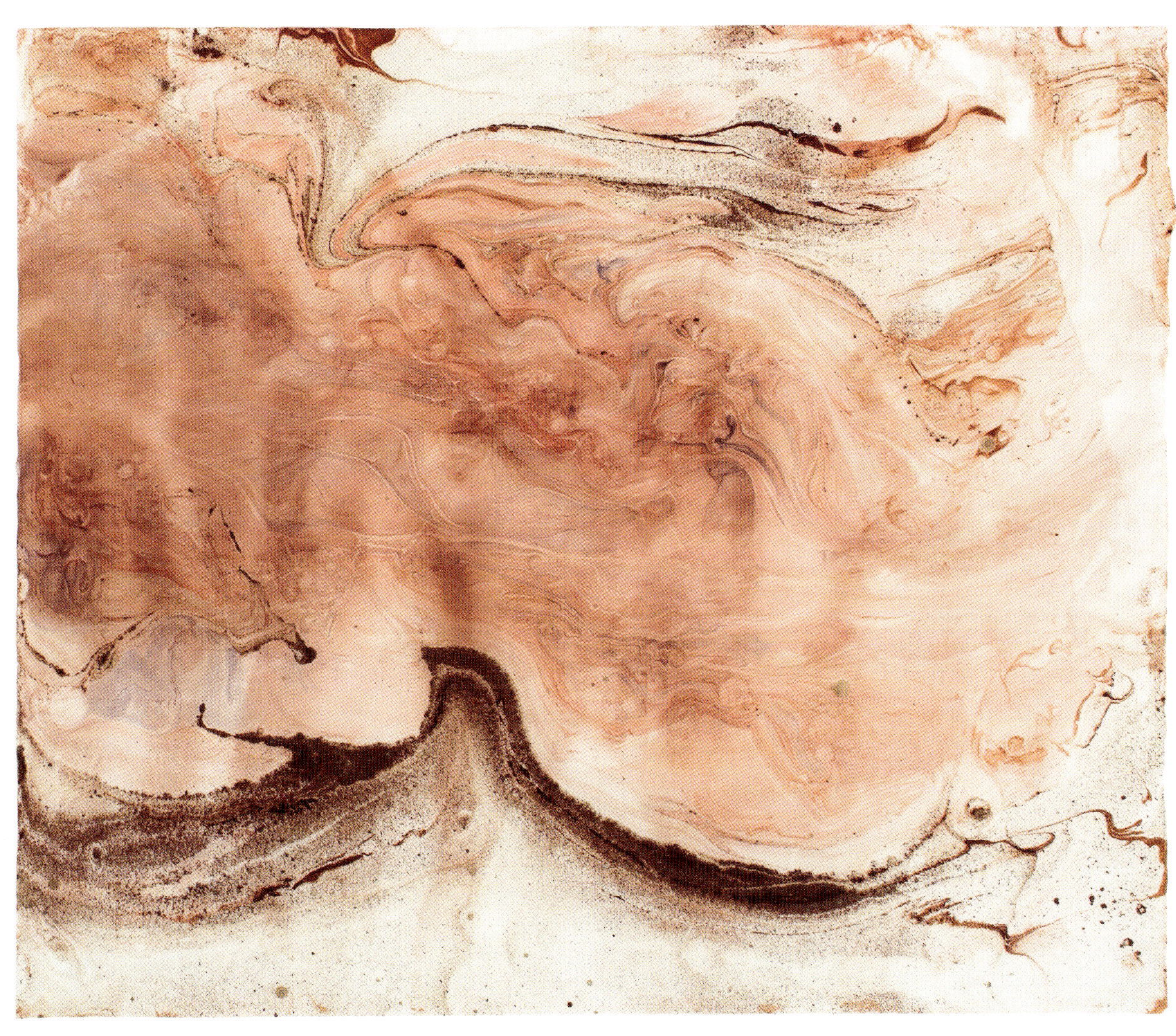

Untitled, Imagined Dirt Landscapes, 2016
Dirt and mixed pigment on paper
505 × 603 mm, framed

Henri Gaudier-Brzeska

Movement is the translation of life, and if art depicts life, movement should come into art, since we are only aware of it because it moves.
Henri Gaudier-Brzeska (1912), Jennifer Powell, ed., *Henri Gaudier-Brzeska*, 2015

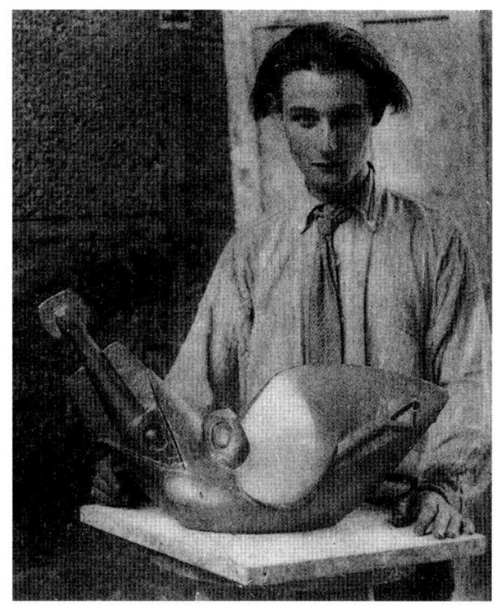

Born in Saint-Jean-de-Braye, France, 1891
Died in Neuville-Saint-Vaast, France, 1915
Lived and worked in Paris and London

By the age of twenty-three, Henri Gaudier-Brzeska had produced over two thousand drawings. At this young age, he also lost his life whilst serving with the French army in 1915. The drawings selected for *Actions* all communicate Gaudier-Brzeska's incessant search for new form. Gaudier-Brzeska usually worked quickly: his process of drawing reflected the pace of contemporary city life. The sweeping single lines from which *Sketch for "Bird Swallowing a Fish"* (c.1914) is composed, demonstrate the minimal number of marks that the artist needed to create a powerful image that is filled with movement. This drawing is likely to be a preparatory sketch for one of Gaudier-Brzeska's most iconic sculptures in the Kettle's Yard collection, made whilst he was in London (the city that he made his home from 1911 onwards). Carved out of plaster in 1914, *Bird Swallowing a Fish* combines organic and mechanized forms in a sculpture that bursts with the tension that characterizes much of Gaudier-Brzeska's work. It was produced whilst he was an active member of the Vorticist group; a collection of artists who both used, and moved beyond, Cubist and Futurist ideals to promote an abstraction that communicated the energy and the physical and technological changes of the modern world.

Gaudier-Brzeska was influenced by non-Western art and culture, which he often studied in the collection of the British Museum. This included a deep fascination with Chinese and Japanese calligraphy. The calligraphic ink drawing in *Actions*, *Vorticist Figure (Bird)* (c.1913/14) is executed with delicate but confident brush-strokes created through the fluid movement of the hand. This drawing does not relate directly to any of Gaudier-Brzeska's sculptures and his drawings were often independent experiments on the page. Gaudier-Brzeska's practice of drawing was part of his everyday life and he employed various techniques to capture images of the world around him. From a young age, he filled sketchbooks whenever he travelled. He drew from life in London's parks and zoos and he was obsessed with figures or animals in action – boxers, swordfighters, even animals fighting; dancers, women floating through the park with skirts blown by a gust of wind, birds landing on water. In the life drawing studio which he attended, Gaudier yearned for the models to move around – to walk, run and dance, and when they did not, he moved instead. In the wresting studio, which he visited in 1912, he watched as men turned in the air and attempted to capture the physicality of their bodies in motion. Gaudier-Brzeska moved incredibly rapidly between styles. He often drew or sculpted the same subject using representational and then abstract forms or vice versa. It is through the latter geometric abstraction, and particularly his Vorticist-inspired works, that Gaudier-Brzeska's influence on the changing images of twentieth-century art is most acutely felt. **JP**

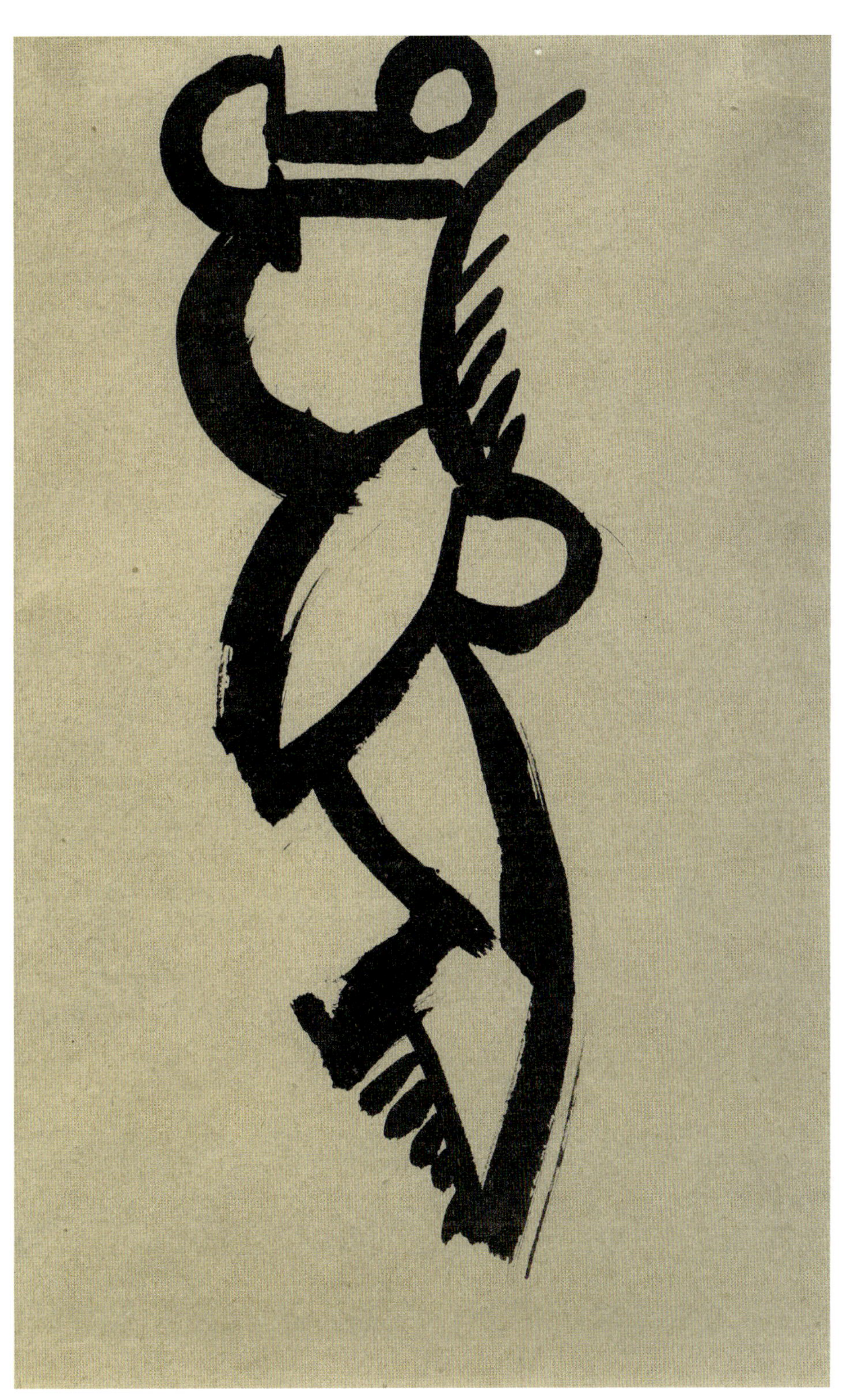

Vorticist Figure (Bird), c.1913/14
Ink on paperw
211 × 140 mm

Barbara Hepworth

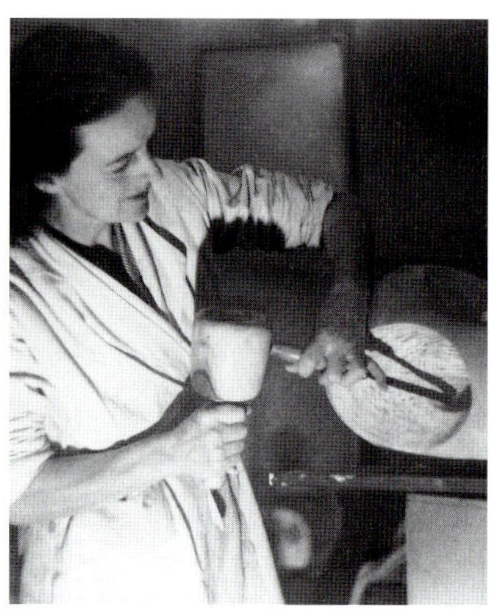

Born in Wakefield, England, 1903
Died in St Ives, Cornwall, 1975
Lived and worked in St Ives

Barbara Hepworth is best known as a visionary sculptor. Her works on paper are less often studied but remain equally vital and were a central aspect of her practice. *Two Figures, Yellow and Brown* (1947) combines oil paint and pencil drawing on hardboard. Two geometric forms, or 'figures' seemingly conjoin, rotate, and perhaps even dance as one. The vibrant yellow shape at the centre of the composition sings out against the thin painted ground that allows the hardboard to peek through. Hepworth's works are characterized by an increasing engagement with abstraction through a variety of materials, each of which is appreciated for its particular qualities and possibilities. She made art with an intelligent awareness of the conflict-bound period in which she lived and often saw in her abstract forms a means of escape, returning to the primeval or moving into the spiritual.

Two Figures, Yellow and Brown was donated to Kettle's Yard by Hepworth's friend, the composer Priaulx Rainier. Various titles have been attributed to it including *Group for Sculpture (Contrapuntal Forms)*. Hepworth used this title in the extensive catalogue of works that was established under her supervision in the early 1960s. This suggests that she, at the very least, related the work to her later carved Irish blue limestone sculpture that was commissioned for the 1951 Festival of Britain, *Contrapuntal Forms*. Priaulx Rainier helped Hepworth to realise this commission and received the drawing as a gift in the same year. The Festival of Britain was a government-backed re-assertion of the country's strength in arts and industry, staged to demonstrate that "the image of the world could be different" following the devastation of war. *Two Figures, Yellow and Brown* also relates to Hepworth's earlier series of drawings produced during the Second World War. She described these works as "drawings for sculpture" but insisted that this relationship was only a general one, best expressed through her exploration of form, rhythm and space in both her two and three-dimensional works.

Hepworth was born in Wakefield, Yorkshire, now the home of the Hepworth Wakefield gallery (opened 2011). Her first major retrospective exhibition was at the Whitechapel Art Gallery, London, in 1954 and her most recent was at Tate Britain in 2016. Hepworth described the experience of drawing with a pencil over painted hard surfaces as having a particular kind of 'bite'. She continued that "one is then lost in a new world of a thousand possibilities because the next line in association with the first will have a compulsion about it which can carry one forward into completely unknown territory." It is arguably Hepworth's commitment to this search for unknown territories in her art that positions her as a seminal British artist of the twentieth century. **JP**

We are fortunate to be living in a time when new forms are being created in architecture, sculpture, painting and music – new forms which, I feel, derive from the basic nature of life, but which come to terms with the particular difficulties presented by our civilization. These new forms in the cultural pattern of today are the core of our future life and it seems to me that they are in accord with past tradition because they spring from a profound response to life itself.
Barbara Hepworth, 1954

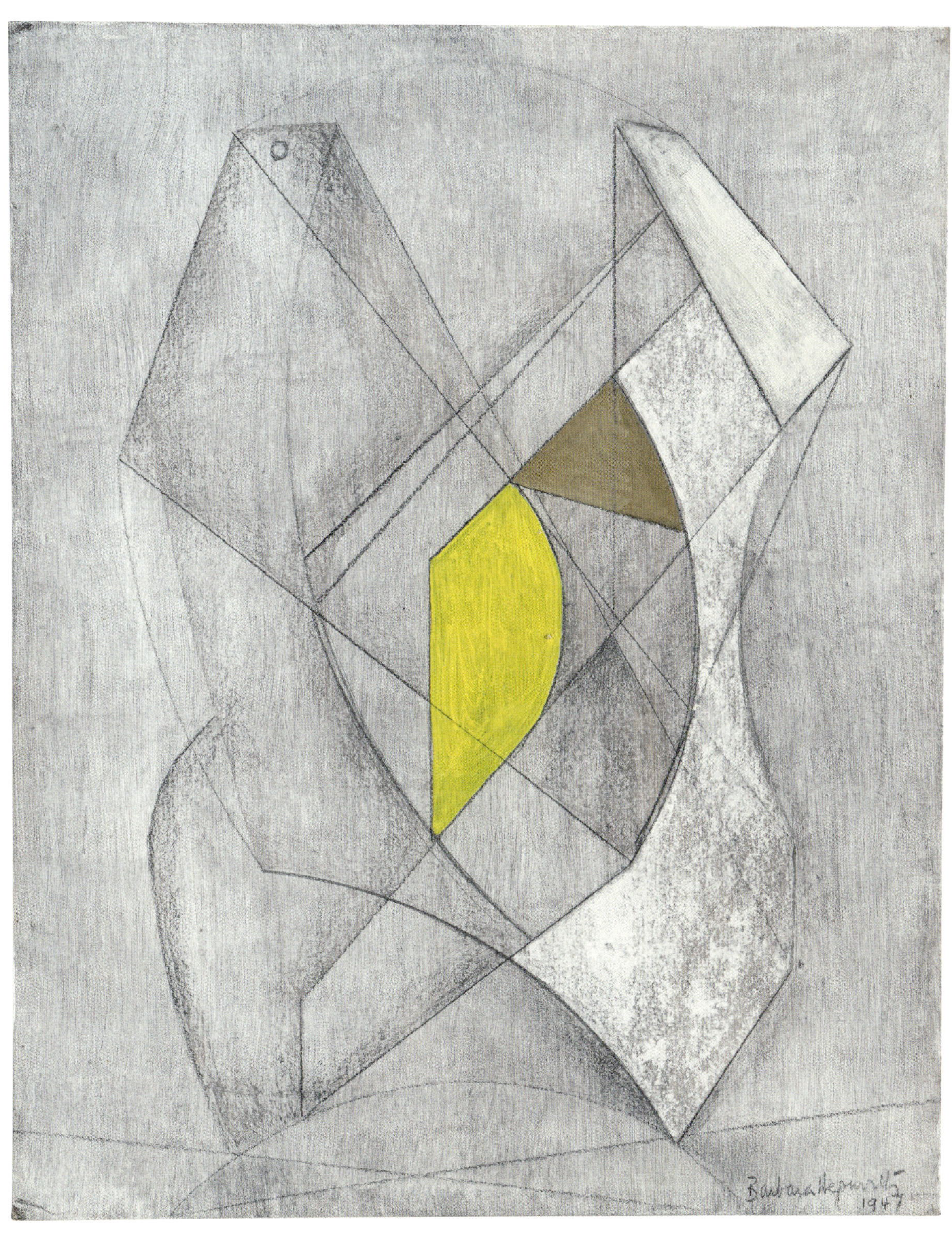

Two Figures, Yellow and Brown, 1947
Oil and graphite on hardboard
290 × 235 mm

Callum Innes

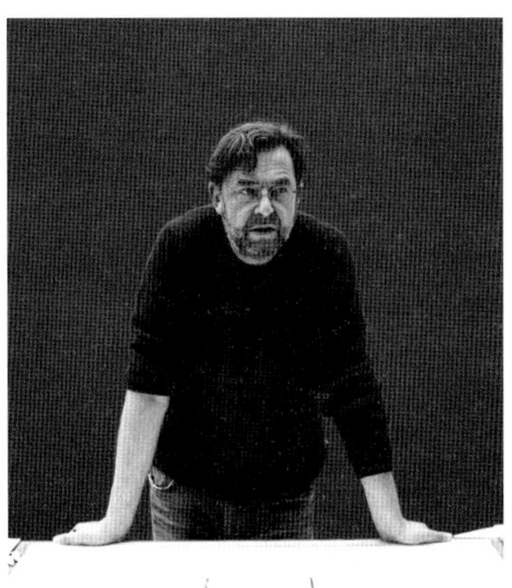

Born in Edinburgh, 1962
Lives and works in Edinburgh

For *Actions* Callum Innes has selected a group of five new watercolours produced in the summer of 2017. They are made following a procedure the artist established in the late 1990s with a group of works called *Exposed Watercolours*. One colour is brushed horizontally across the paper, followed by another colour, diluted with water, painted vertically over the top of the first. The body of the paper is left with a delicate pale trace, a memory of what once was. Only at the vertical edges do the original colours survive as imprecise glowing lines, laying open the artist's action.

It is possible to define Callum Innes' whole artistic practice within the idea of two actions: addition and subtraction. His paintings and watercolours over a thirty-year period have explored with infinite subtlety what happens when you add an area of colour to canvas or paper, and then change that colour through using turpentine or water, thinning and dissolving the original paint. This distinct process, and the viewer's awareness of the structure and precision of each painting, is critically offset by our experience of the embedded risk. Innes' controlled experiments are always unpredictable. Their achievement is in the balance they strike between the known and the unknown, between a sense of giving and of holding back, and their revelation of the richness and mystery of our relationship to form and colour.

At Kettle's Yard, Innes' watercolours will be hung in the new Research Space, a room for both the public and university researchers, a place for finding out more, for thinking, for new ideas. Innes' new watercolours, with their vibrant titles: *Red Violet / Turner Yellow* and *Transparent Orange Rose / Delft Blue* express a parallel endeavor, a repeated searching after something. Poised and luminous, they too offer space to pause, for uncertainty as well as discovery. **AN**

Watercolour suits Innes' method and approach. But we should, I think, make an even stronger claim: watercolour has a privileged position in his work, not only because he has consistently worked in the medium, but because it dramatises something about the liquidity of painting. By this I don't mean fluid gestures, but the action of dilution, the making clear of a liquid, and often limpid, state of translucency.

Briony Fer, "Colour Process Time", 2016

Transparent Orange Rose/Delft Blue, 2017
Watercolour on Canson Heritage 640gsm
560 × 760 mm

Mary Kelly

I think it is culturally overdetermined that the ideal will be (for want of a better term) masculine. And my project, in short, is to see what that means for women.

Mary Kelly, "Mary Kelly and Margaret Iversen in conversation", 1994

Born in Fort Dodge, USA, 1941
Lives and works in Los Angeles

Artist, educator and writer Mary Kelly's *Love Songs: Flashing Nipple Remix* (2005) consists of three light-boxes containing large black-and-white photographic transparencies. The re-enactment recorded in the three photographs is based on a snapshot of a street theatre protest that took place outside the Miss World Contest held at the Royal Albert Hall in London in 1971. Kelly was living and working in London at the time, having moved there in 1968 to undertake postgraduate study at Saint Martin's School of Art. Here she began her long-term critique of conceptualism, informed by the early women's movement. The re-enactment was carried out by five young women, dressed in black and wearing the same lights as the original protestors, who shook their bodies, generating dazzling, spiralling trails of light. Kelly has commented: "Doing it again, I was trying to ask – what's passed on from one generation to the next?" The re-enactment was part of Kelly's long-term project on the theme of collective memory, *Love Songs* (2005–07) which involved collaborating with younger women on the restaging of protest photographs from her archive.

While in London, Kelly worked collaboratively with the Berwick Street Film Collective on the documentary *Nightcleaners* (1970–75), which focused on women who work unsociable hours and the installation, *Women & Work: A Document on the Division of Labor in Industry* (1975). Kelly's iconic work on the mother/child relationship, *Post-Partum Document* (1973–79) painstakingly documented her infant son's development over a period of seven years, and contained elements such as *Analyzed Fecal Stains and Feeding Charts* (1974) which consisted of twenty-eight framed nappies and their contents, with a list below of the food items ("Two teaspoons cereal, one teaspoon carrot") consumed by her infant son. Kelly recalled that while she used a visual strategy similar to that of artists like Lawrence Weiner, Dan Graham and Victor Burgin, she brought in questions and debates from outside the art context, to engender a confrontation between feminism and conceptualism. Kelly's work has continued to address questions of sexuality, identity and historical memory in the form of large-scale narrative installations, such as her four-part work interrogating women's relation to the body, money, history and power called *Interim* (1984–89). Part 1 of *Interim* (*Corpus*) was developed while Kelly was the first female artist in residence at Kettle's Yard and New Hall College in Cambridge. Since the 1990s, Kelly's work has focused on the issue of war, as for example, employing the ephemeral medium of compressed lint (sourced from her tumble drier) to form text in intaglio for the installation *Mea Culpa* (1999). Since 1996, Kelly has been Professor of Art and Critical Theory Art in the School of Art and Architecture at the University of California, Los Angeles where she has established an Interdisciplinary Studio area for graduate students engaged in site-specific, collective and project-based practices. **SL**

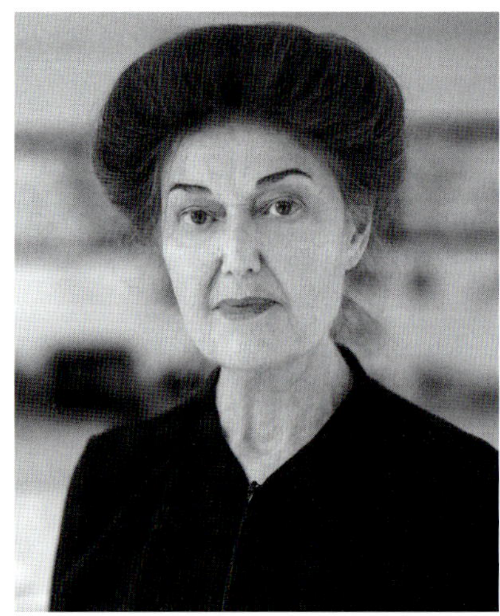

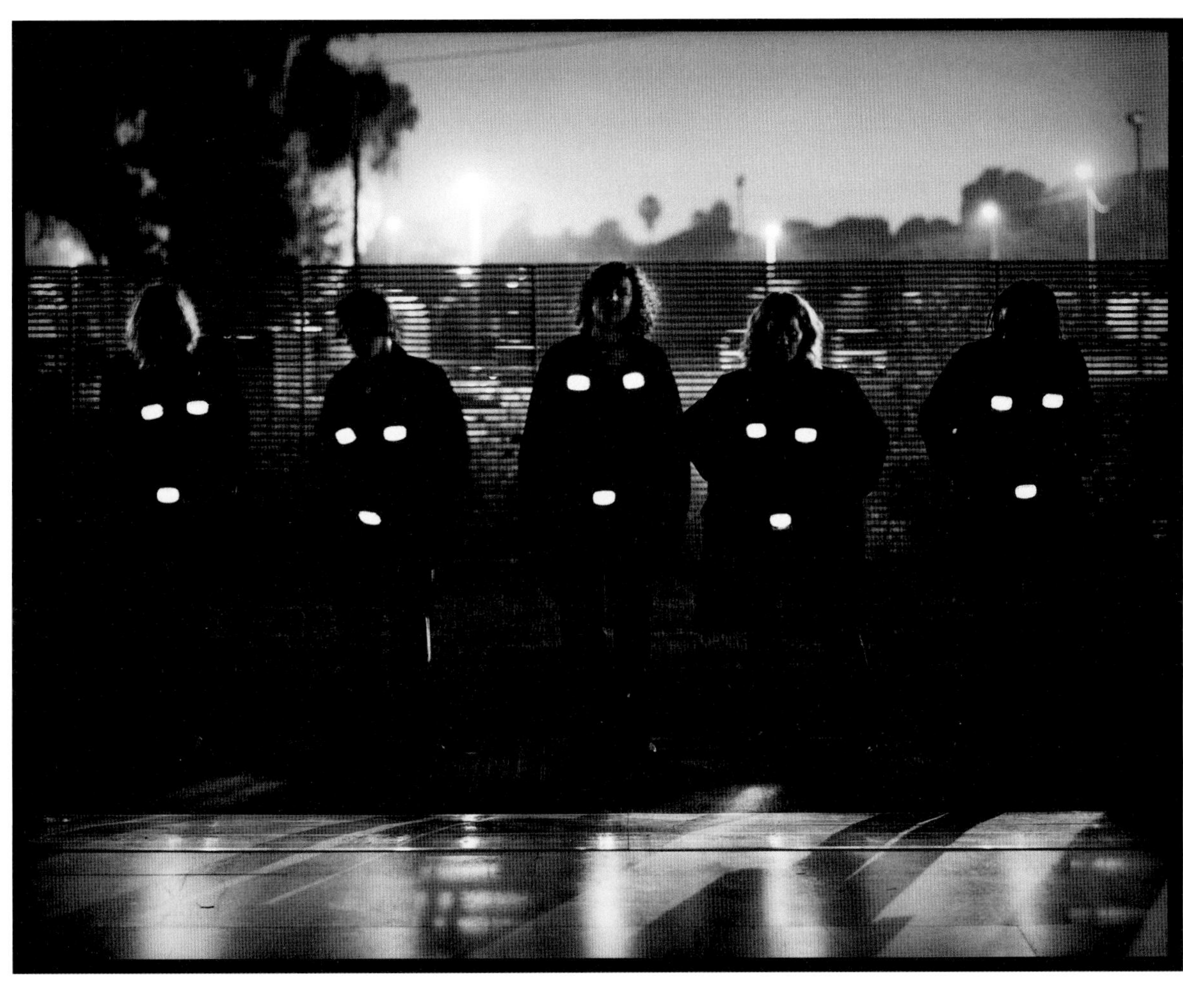

Love Songs: Flashing Nipple Remix, 2005
Transparencies (Black and White) mounted on light-boxes
965 × 1219 mm

Idris Khan

To take a picture is to have an interest in things as they are, in the status quo remaining unchanged (at least for as long as it takes to get a "good" picture), to be in complicity with whatever makes a subject interesting, worth photographing – including, when that is the interest, another person's pain.
Susan Sontag, *On Photography*, 1977

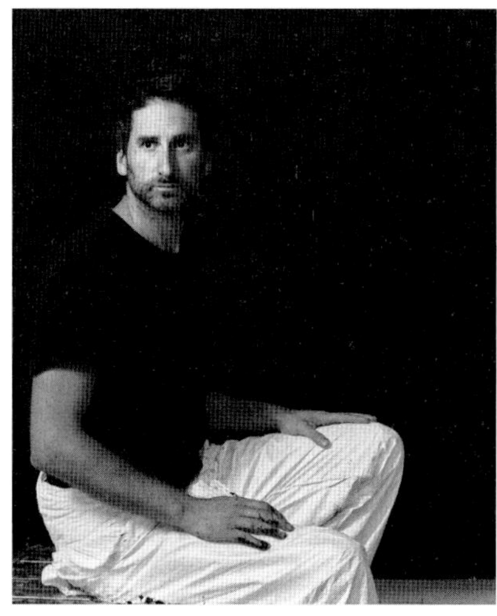

Born in Birmingham, 1978
Lives and works in London

Idris Khan is an artist known for his meditative, densely layered works that draw upon philosophical, literary, religious and political themes to make engrossing and emotionally affecting paintings, photographic prints and sculptural works. For *Actions*, Khan has created a new site-specific wall drawing which will extend over the large windows of the new Sackler Gallery at Kettle's Yard, using repetitively stamped marks. Superimposition of printed marks is a characteristic method used by the artist, who builds up layers of words, phrases and symbols on the surface of paintings, works on paper, sculptures and wall drawings, over a period of days or weeks to generate palimpsest-like images.

As a master's student at the Royal College of Art, Khan began using digital technology to overlay and combine sequential material such as every Bernd and Hilla Becher photograph of a gable-sided house and every stave of Chopin's *Nocturnes*. In 2004, when Khan graduated, he attracted praise for a single image he produced by scanning, condensing and digitally layering every page from the Qur'an. The work took two months to make, his father's copy of the Qur'an having to be correctly handled for every one of its 1,953 page-scans, and was the first time Khan had directly referenced his cultural heritage in his practice. In 2012, Khan was commissioned to make a wall drawing for the British Museum exhibition, *Hajj: Journey to the Heart of Islam*, which focused upon one of the five pillars of Islam central to Muslim belief: the pilgrimage to Mecca that every Muslim must make at least once in their lifetime if they are able. Khan's monumental floor installation, *Seven Times*, was also installed in the museum's Great Court, comprising 49 blue-black steel cubes. Each cube had the proportions of the Kaaba, the sacred black, gold and white structure located inside the Grand Mosque in Mecca that is considered the centre of the Muslim world and around which pilgrims are required to walk seven times. In 2017, Khan's solo exhibition *Absorbing Light* at Victoria Miro presented his most overtly political work to date, a meditation on Syria's notoriously brutal government-run Saydnaya prison, where Amnesty International estimate as many as 13,000 people were executed without trial between 2011 and 2015. The exhibition included the sculptural floor piece *Absorbing Light, 46* (2017), in which prisoners' verbal testimonies and Khan's responses to them were cast in numerals and letterforms, on the surfaces of forty-six bronze blocks, and three large, vertical monochrome paintings entitled *The Pain of Others (No. 1)*, *(No. 2)* and *(No. 3)*, (2017). **SL**

The Pain of Others (No.2) (detail), 2017
Ink and acrylic on diabond panel with aluminium subframe
2670 × 1880 × 60 mm

Issam Kourbaj

I smelt the ink of each of its pages. It was so new, so crisp. And I counted the number of its light-green and purple pages a few times. I touched its embossed lettering and its leathery shoulders slowly. It was my first ever, and I had only just received it. It was the recognition of my place in the universe. My passport was my icon of other worlds.
Issam Kourbaj, *Eye and Other Magic Moments*, 2008/9

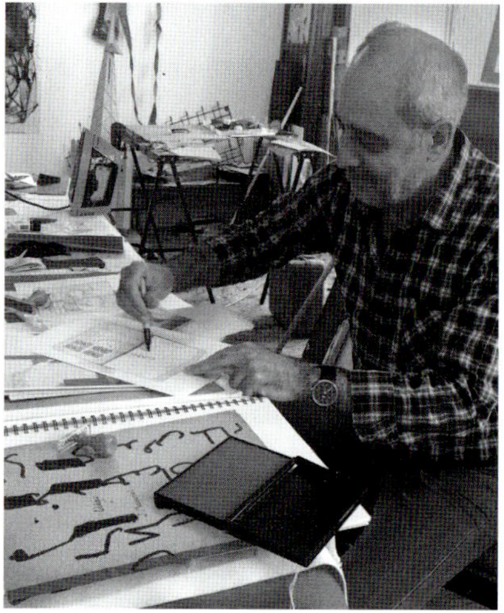

Born in Soweda, Syria, 1963
Lives and works in Cambridge

For *Actions* Issam Kourbaj has developed his ongoing idea, creating a work for every day that is 'lost' to the conflict in his homeland. *I will be here* (2018) takes the form of copied pages from his expired Syrian passports which have at some stage been surrendered to bureaucracy and stamped with the word *CANCELLED.* A page is pinned to the walls at Kettle's Yard each day of the exhibition and re-stamped by the artist as a form of protest against those who prohibit his movement, the very same authorities that are responsible for the continuing devastation wrought on his Syrian compatriots. Kourbaj recalls the excitement and hope brought to him as a young man by the arrival of his first passport and the prospect of foreign travel, having had a modest upbringing in a mountainous region in southern Syria. On leaving home in the 1980s he quickly began to experience difficulties moving between Syria and Russia, where he was studying, Eastern Europe and Britain, because of his nationality. Though now living happily with his family in Britain, Kourbaj has not escaped the feeling of being an outsider and yearns to see his homeland. He is not optimistic about having the opportunity to return. Through his ongoing projects he not only questions the atrocities that prevent him from doing so, but the wider notion of identity and what 'home' means for him, us and the many others affected by conflict and political upheaval across the world.

Since the beginning of the conflict in Syria, Kourbaj has been working tirelessly to make work that articulates the unimaginable destruction and loss inflicted on ordinary people and his cultural heritage. His works are both fleeting and sobering; objects laid out inside all too recognisable white refugee tents, Arabic script written by hand on the covers of old books, matches lit and extinguished: these are humble materials used with care to create moments of great poignancy. Kourbaj's project *Another Day Lost* (2015) was recently presented at the Penn Museum, Philadelphia and the British Museum in London. His installation *Dark Water, Burning World* (2017) was installed at the Victoria and Albert Museum as part of Refugee Week in 2017. **GH**

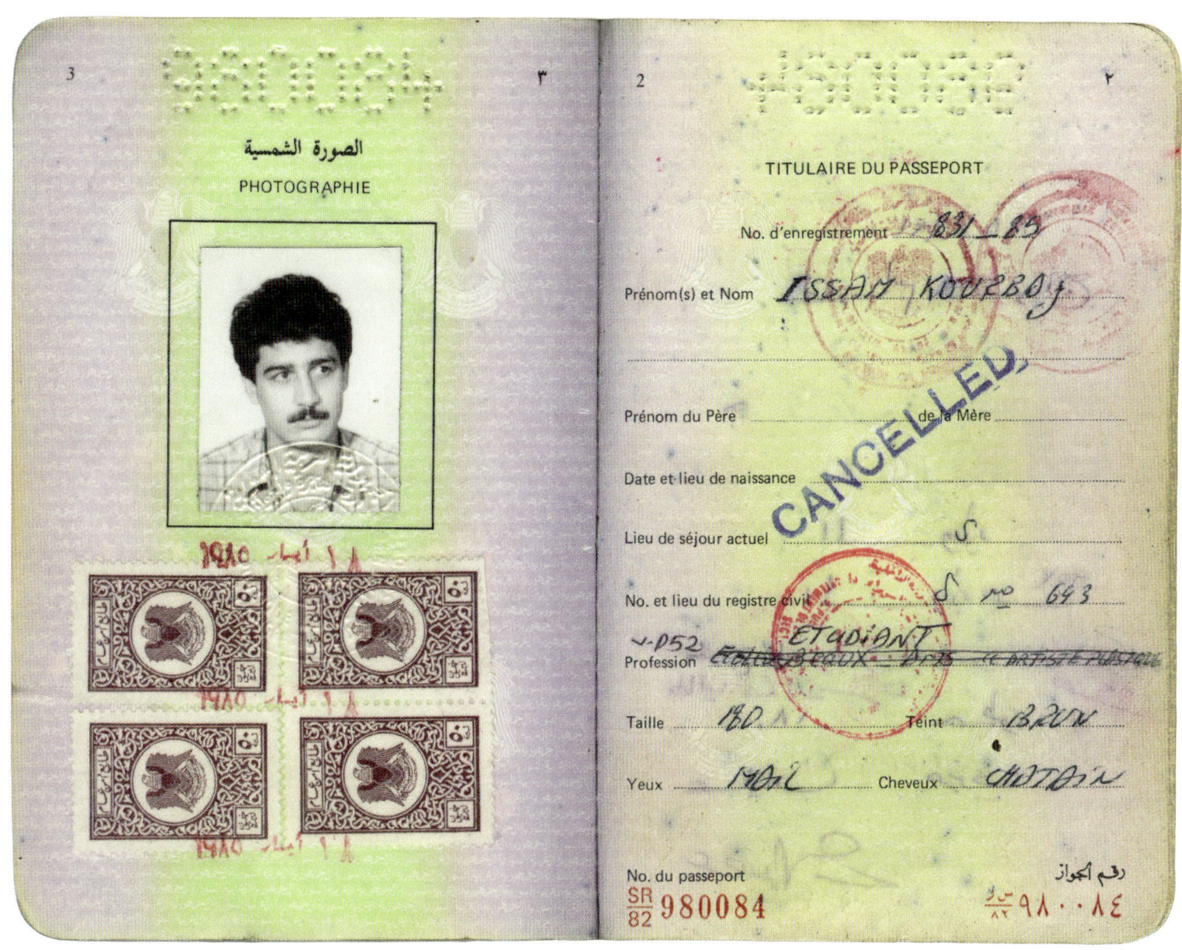

I will be here (detail), 2018
سوف أكون هنا، ٢٠١٨
Two Syrian passports belonging to the artist,
rubber stamps and photocopies on paper
Dimensions variable

Linder

Born in Liverpool, 1954
Lives and works in Derbyshire, England

For *Actions*, Linder has created two new photomontages which combine publicity photos of 1950s and 1960s French film stars with cut-outs from a contemporary auction catalogue of modernist furniture. Linder explains that as she made the works, she thought of Helen Ede, who together with her husband, Jim Ede, founded Kettle's Yard. She says, "There were only female figures in the black-and-white publicity photos and as I worked with them, I thought of Helen Ede's self-effacement." Linder was also stirred by the closing sentence of Herbert Read's 1944 letter to Naum Gabo, in which he proposes, "You must not expect a direct reaction from a work of art in modern society; but dropped like a foreign substance into that agitated sea, it might, without losing either its identity or its purity, effect a transformation both rich and strange."

Linder studied graphic design at Manchester Polytechnic, where she began experimenting with photomontage. After meeting local musicians Pete Shelley and Howard Devoto at a Sex Pistols gig in 1976, she concentrated on working solely on collage, using magazines, a sheet of glass, a scalpel, scissors and inexpensive glue. Her work critiqued the sexual politics of the 1970s, in particular the stereotypical gender roles depicted in men's magazines like *Playboy* and in popular women's magazines such as *Family Circle*. One of her best-known compositions – a naked woman with an iron for a head and her nipples replaced with grinning lipsticked mouths – appeared on the sleeve of the first single by Shelley and Devoto's band, Buzzcocks, *Orgasm Addict* (1977). In 1978, Linder formed the band Ludus (1978–83) and she also collaborated with writer Jon Savage on the fanzine *The Secret Public*, to articulate an alternative to the male, heterosexual punk narrative.

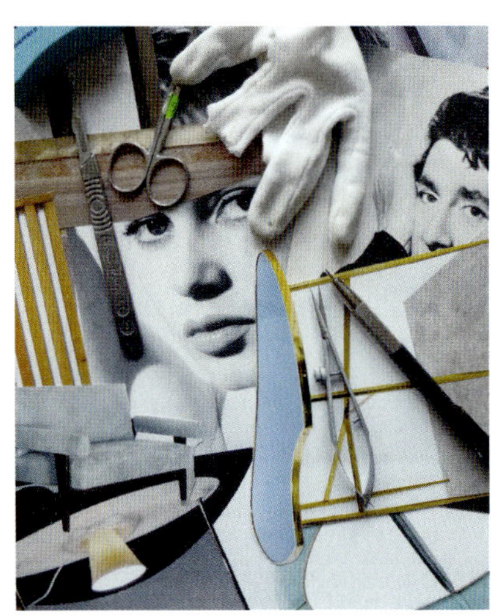

In recent years, Linder's photomontage and performance works have become more closely intertwined. In 2013, Linder began a year-long artist's residency at Tate St Ives, researching Barbara Hepworth's love of dance and her engagement with landscape. Her solo exhibition at Hepworth Wakefield the same year, included collage both as two-dimensional prints and as three-dimensional light-box sculptures, and culminated in a new performance piece *The Ultimate Form*, realised in collaboration with Northern Ballet and choreographer Kenneth Tindall. In 2016, Linder developed her research on Hepworth further, making a work inspired by a photograph of the sculptor dressed as Juno, the goddess of marriage, at the 1956 S. Ives Art Ball, two years after her divorce from Ben Nicholson. Linder designed a coiled, circular psychedelic carpet, with thirteen eyes embroidered across it, called *Diagram of Love: Marriage of Eyes* and worked with seven dancers from the Northern Ballet to choreograph a dance piece employing the carpet as a sinuous flowing form. **SL**

I think the act of collage, of creating one's own collage, is becoming more essential, almost as a survival tool. Unless one is very careful, one gets bombarded by ungainly, repetitive imagery. The act of withdrawing from the world and trying to create an alternative collage becomes more and more important.
Linder, quoted in Emily King, *Linder*, 2015

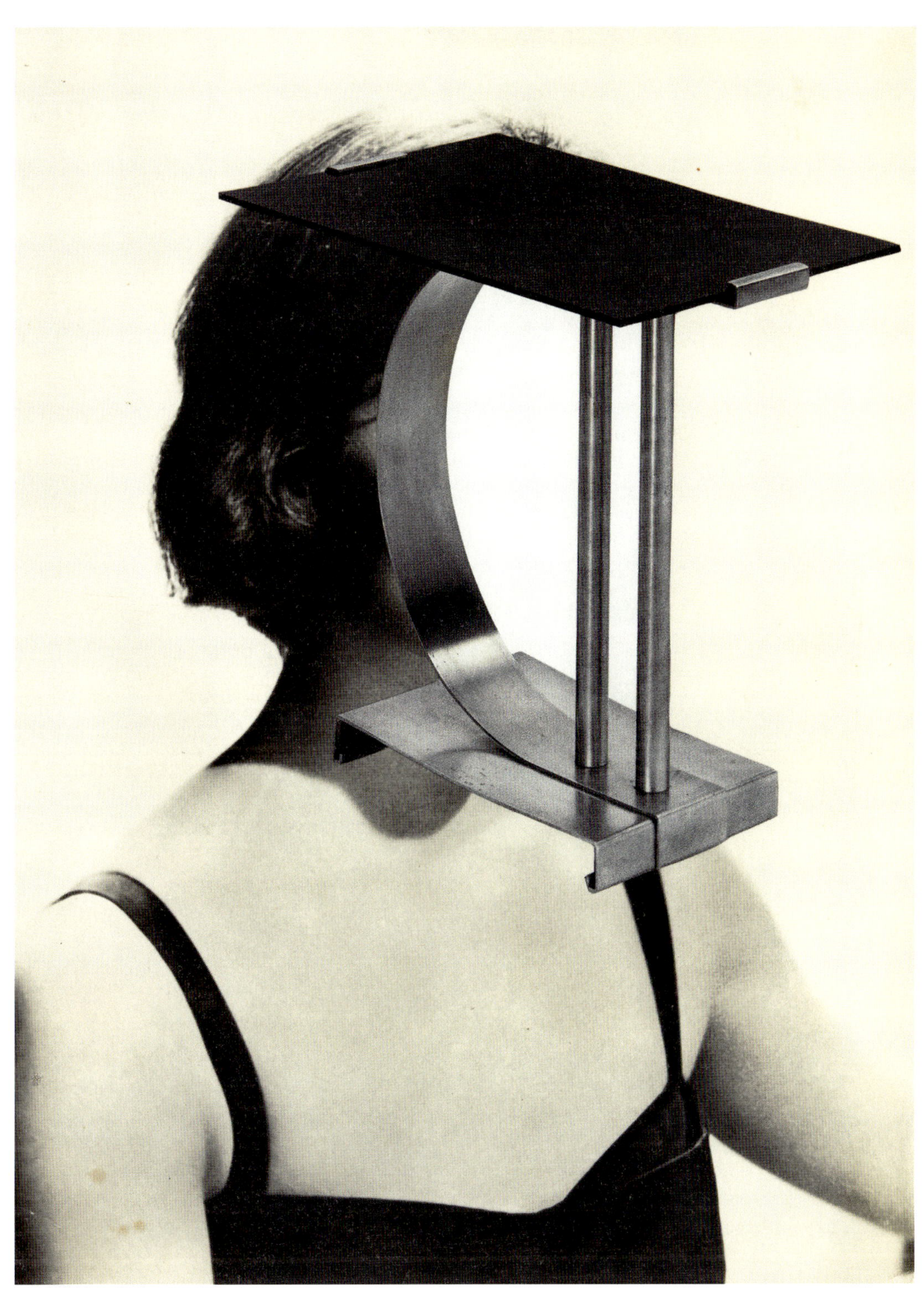

Mayniel Relief, 2017
Photomontage
227 × 168 mm

Richard Long

Born in Bristol, 1945
Lives and works in Bristol

In 1967, Richard Long, then a second-year student at Saint Martin's School of Art, took a train out of London to the first countryside he reached. He stopped at the first suitable field he found, where he walked backwards and forwards until the flattened turf became visible as a line. Long photographed the result of his action, a work he called *A Line Made by Walking* (1967). This physical trace in the field marked the beginning of a career combining photography, sculpture and text works, but stemming from the experience of solitary walking, looking and making marks in the landscape. Much of Long's work is created as a result of walks he has taken in remote parts of the world, such as the 1,030-mile walk he carried out in 1998, from the southernmost point of mainland Britain to the northernmost. He always uses naturally occurring materials to create his works, as in gallery-based works *Norfolk Flint Circle (1990)* and *Red Slate Circle* (1998), created with slate from the border between Vermont and New York State. He explains that he sees his interventions in the landscape as registering his passage, either in a way which might last, but which could just as easily be impermanent. He says, "I'm not interested in making monuments, but the other point of view is to leave absolutely no mark - take only photographs and leave only footprints. There's quite interesting territory between those two positions - like moving stones around, making works which disappear, or making water marks – many ways of being an artist in a landscape."

Long was born in Bristol and has lived in the area all his life. As a boy, he played on the Downs, in the limestone caves of the gorge, and on the towpaths on the banks of the River Avon, where he was fascinated by the river's marked differential between high and low tide. River Avon tidal mud is one of Long's favourite materials, which he values for its geological significance ("a mixture of time, water and stone") and describes as "unbelievably strong and viscous. It has all the natural binding qualities, like cave paintings." Long has often used mud from the River Avon to realise wall works in gallery settings, although he has also used mud from other places including the Hudson River, the Rhone Valley, and Braga mud from northern Portugal and Cornish white china clay. Long used this last material to create *Waterfall Line* (2000), a site-specific wall work commissioned for the opening of Tate Modern, composed on a black-painted wall upon which the artist worked with his gloved hand with the watery clay. **SL**

A walk marks time with an accumulation of footsteps. It defines the form of the land. Walking the roads and paths is to trace a portrait of the country. I have become interested in using a walk to express original ideas about the land, art and walking itself.
Richard Long, "Words after Fact", 1982

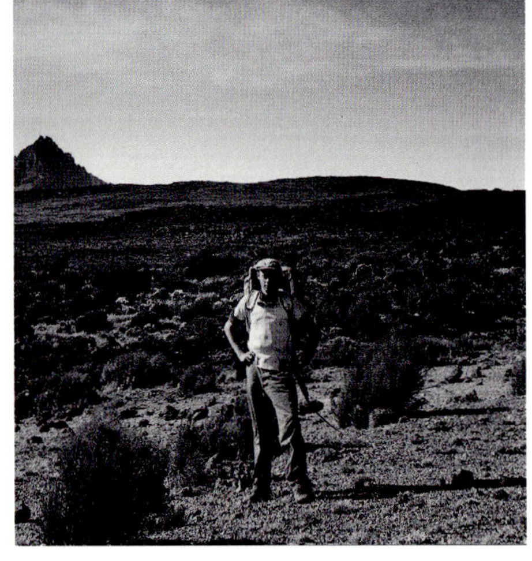

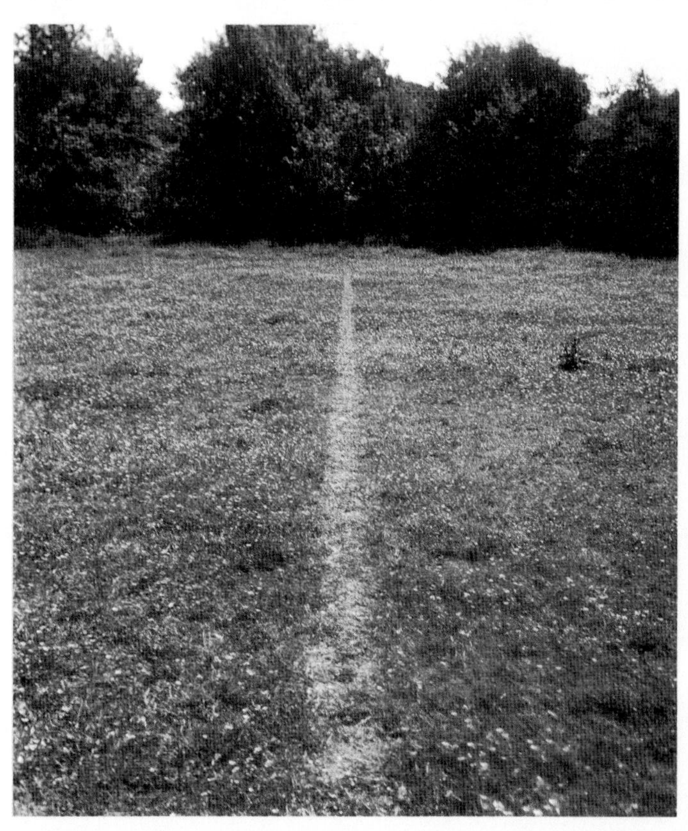

A Line Made by Walking, 1967
Gelatin silver print on paper
375 × 324 mm

Melanie Manchot

The Ladies *continues an on-going enquiry into group portraiture as a mode of questioning the relationship between individual and collective forms of subjectivity. Performativity and participation are core methodologies across both photographic and moving image works and here the interaction with a group of women grew into a form of collaborative exchange. The works enact relationships between highly authored architectures and a group of Cambridge residents whose presence in these spaces raises questions of belonging and agency. The images are loosely based on works from the history of feminist performance as well as gestures and motifs from painting and archive photographs.*
Melanie Manchot, 2017

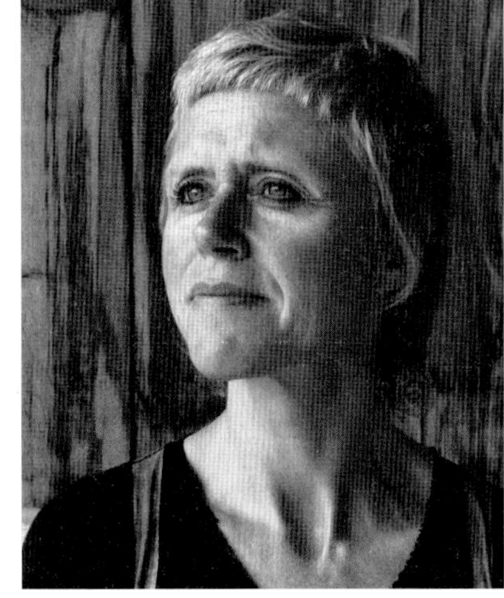

Born in Witten, Germany, 1966
Lives and works in London

Melanie Manchot's new body of work for *Actions* has involved the artist photographing a group of Bangladeshi women who live in Cambridge, in a number of iconic settings including the Cambridge Union Debating Chamber, the seventeenth-century Wren Library and the neo-Gothic Dining Hall at King's College. These beautiful, painterly images show the women, dressed in vibrant, embellished traditional dress, arranged in groups, seated, standing or perusing volumes of books. The women's obvious camaraderie overwhelms the incongruity of the settings, bestowing each scene with a quality of grace and comfort familiar from Vermeer paintings of women in interiors. These sensitive and vivid tableaux result from Melanie Manchot's skill in inspiring trust in her subjects, whether strangers or her closest intimates.

Manchot first received considerable critical acclaim for her series of fourteen C-prints, Liminal Portraits (1999–2000), a group of large-scale colour portraits of the artist 's mother, who was then 65, in which she appears partially unclothed. Manchot explained, "It was about the representation of women and the notion of beauty – particularly when women are beyond a certain age. In many ways, they are incredibly beautiful, but they reach a point of invisibility. Their bodies may be complicated, a little bit unruly, beyond what we readily accept." In 2004, Manchot began working with group portraiture in a body of work called Groups+Locations (Moscow) (2004), in which groups of Muscovites of different ages were posed in famed locations including the Metro and outside the Pushkin Museum and the Cathedral, for a series of photographs that explore notions of the collective and community.

Since then, Manchot has often used her practice as a means to show how bodies can reanimate the urban environment, as for example in her film *Kiss* (2009) of a young couple embracing on the top deck of a London bus, or her film *Tracer* (2013), in which she recorded the free-running exploits of a group of parkourists at locations along the route of the Great North Run. Manchot has also continued to explore the passing of time as revealed through bodily changes, perhaps most notably by turning her camera on her daughter, Billie. In 2008, Manchot began filming her daughter, then aged eleven, with a Super-8 camera for a minute every month – a process that was repeated every month for the next seven years, culminating in the installation *11/18* (2016), which recorded her daughter's transition from playful child to poised young woman. **SL**

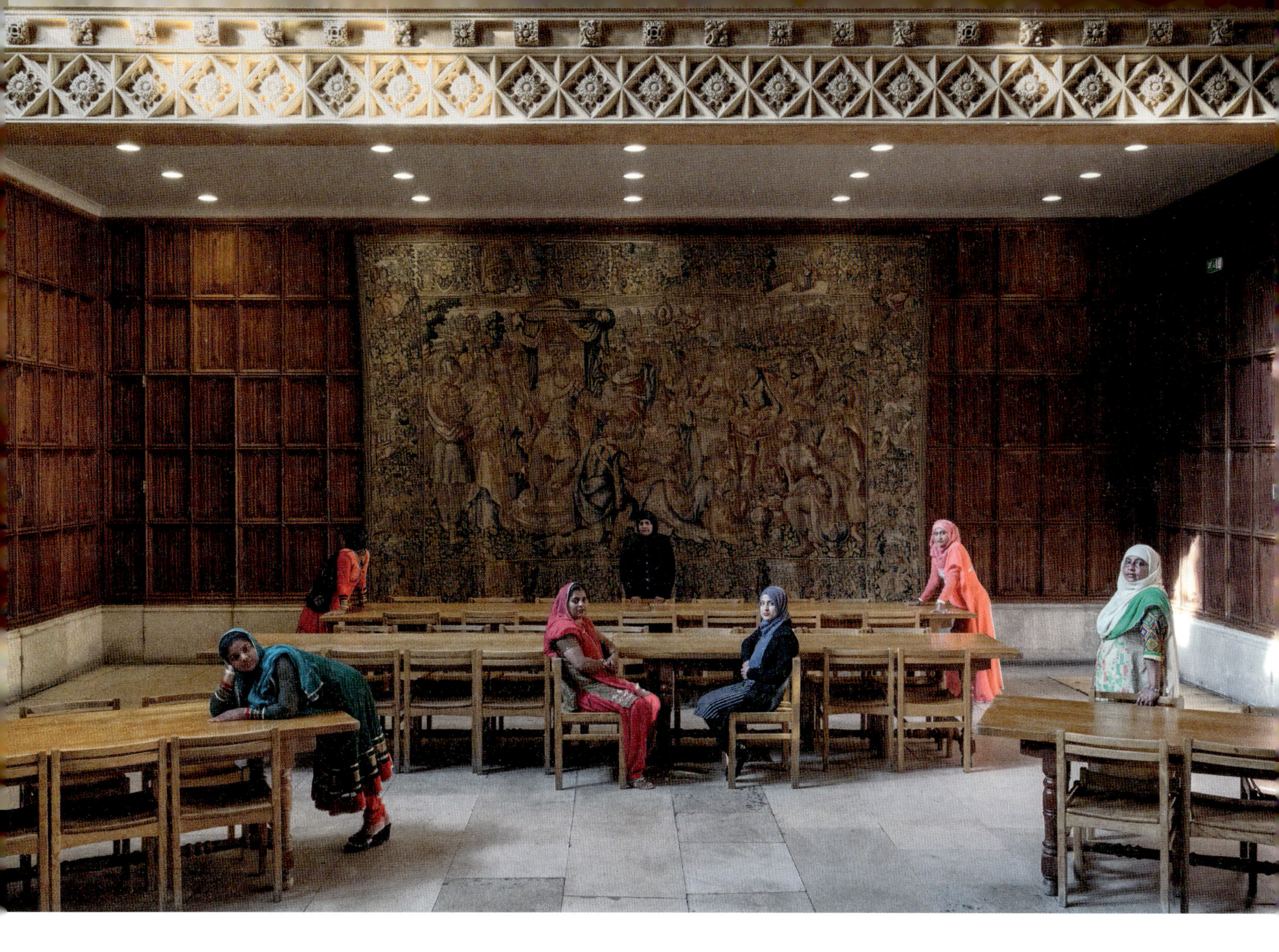

The Ladies (King's Dining Hall), 2017
Digital C-print
1200 × 800 mm.

Julie Mehretu

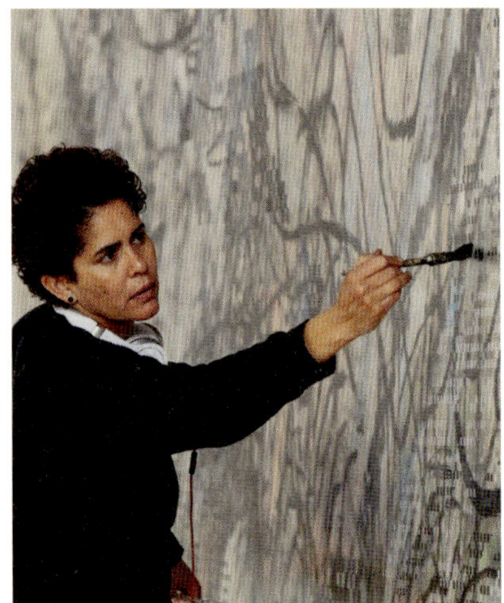

Born in Addis Ababa, Ethiopia, 1970
Lives and works in New York

In recent works by Julie Mehretu, the surface of each painting is an animated mass of grey marks, lines, smudges and stains. There is no still centre: everything is moving, swirling, falling. It is as if we are engulfed in the immediate aftermath of an explosion, in the seconds before the detritus and dust settle to reveal a changed landscape. Mehretu's rich and dynamic use of paint holds us there, in a suspended moment of shock and possibility.

The year 2012 marked a decisive shift in Mehretu's work. The new *Grey Paintings* were no longer grounded in architectural renderings, but generated and abstracted from news photographs of particular global events and upheaval: the humanitarian crisis in Syria, turmoil in the Middle East and, in the USA, race riots following the extrajudicial killings of African-American men. The artist Glenn Ligon has described Mehretu's process in relation to her work *Conjured Parts (epigraph), Aleppo* (2016), in which a photograph of a Free Syrian Army soldier surveying the ruins of a Damascus neighbourhood becomes Mehretu's departure point for the painting. After blurring and manipulating the image using Photoshop, it was then projected and airbrushed onto the canvas. In the finished painting, the image, which underpins the composition, is the faintest presence, obliterated by the artist's urgent, gestural brush marks.

Mehretu acknowledges a continuing dialogue with twentieth-century abstraction, especially the large-scale works of American artists. Her new paintings, with their specific address to current world events, reanimate the potential of abstraction to offer a charged space for ideas and feelings. They are concurrently assured and questioning. How do we interpret and comprehend the images the media give us? What is our responsibility as citizens, as artists to speak out? How can art offer other images that are both authentic and generative, while reflecting the complexity of our embattled and disputed times? If we understand Mehretu's paintings as process, in a state of constant becoming, every mark is a live action, and each action the creation of new space; offering light out of darkness. **AN**

That we can follow the evolution of Mehretu's painting over time and for it to speak to us in its semantic depth as we attempt to negotiate the complex dimensions of our present is proof of the force of her art. For it is not simply a matter of composition and gesture, contour and image, substrate and surface, brought together to produce the powerful aesthetic effect of her work. There is the emancipation of the act of making and the mindful intelligence of physical abandon that reflects a vital grounding in the world in which we recognise ourselves, and in which we participate.
Suzanne Cotter, "The Alien Discontinuum: On painting and participating in the work of Julie Mehretu", 2017

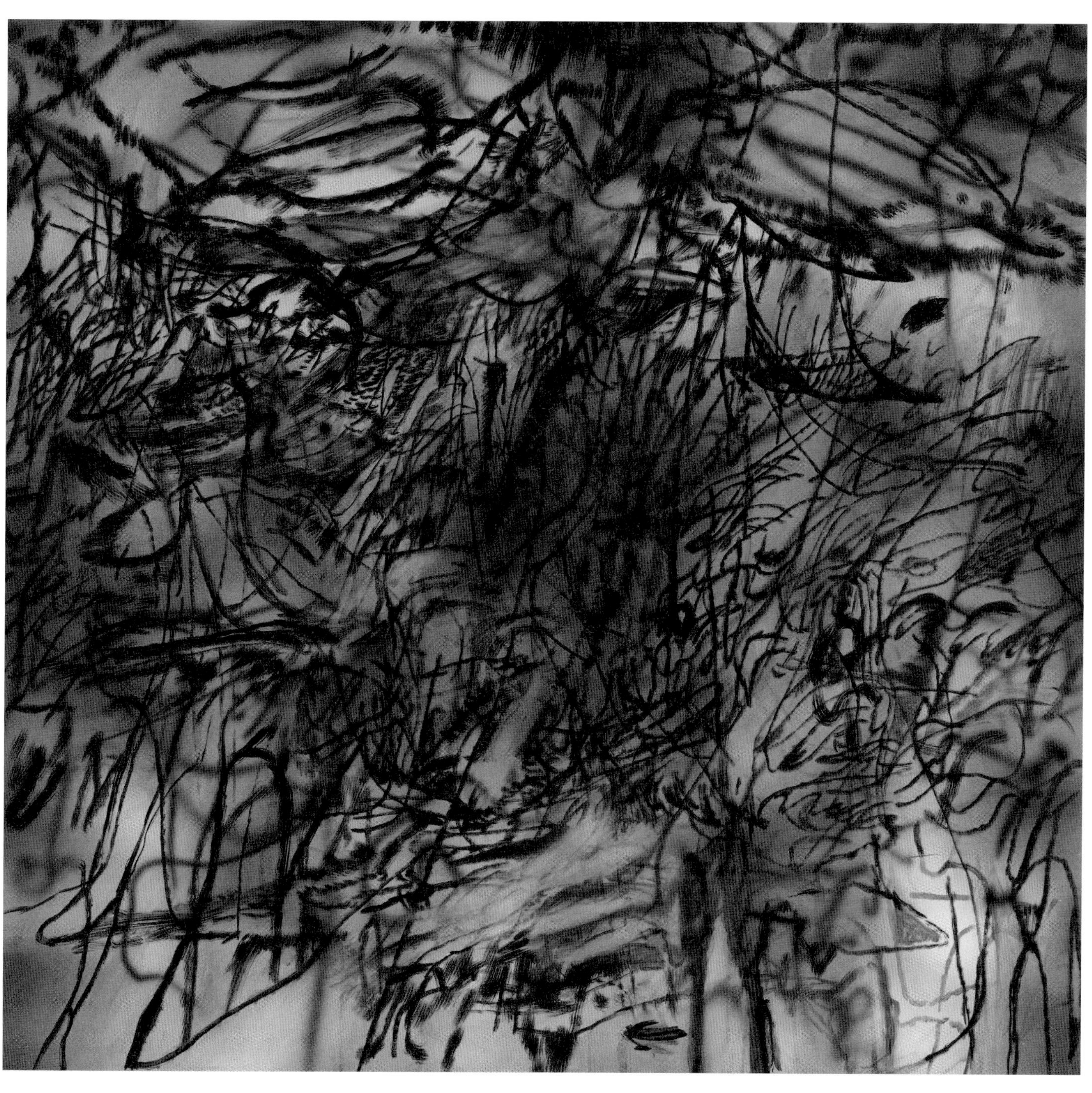

Ghosthymn, 2017
Ink and acrylic on canvas
1710 × 1810 mm

Gustav Metzger

Born in Nuremberg, Germany, 1926
Died in London, 2017
Lived and worked in London

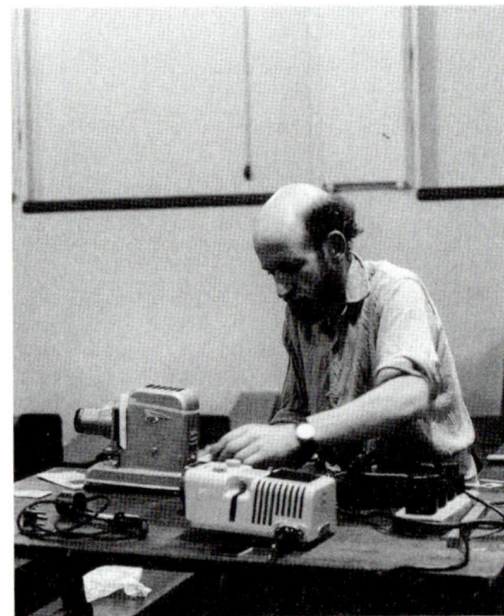

Gustav Metzger outlined his notion of *Auto-Destructive Art* in his first manifesto published in 1959 and presented it at a number of Lecture/Demonstrations, where physical experiments using a range of materials and processes would be carried out in front of a live audience. Familiar materials would be forced to undergo some sort of transformation or revert into a state of flux. Two of these seminal lectures took place at the University of Cambridge in 1960 and 1965. *The Chemical Revolution in Art* in 1965 included an experiment whereby drops of ink were injected into a solution of glycerin and water, which was magnified and projected, with the heat of the projector shifting the behavior of the materials and the visual effect created by the projection. This process and others would later inform Metzger's celebrated work *Liquid Crystal Environment* (1965, remade 2005), which was shown at Kettle's Yard in 2014 in *LIFT OFF!*, when Metzger returned to Cambridge in the final stages of his life to revisit other early experimental works from the 1960s using heat, air and water, and to make new photographic works using fibre-optic light.

Metzger was a radical artist and political activist who was a member of the anti-war group *Committee of 100* and developed the concept of *Auto-Destructive Art:* an active art that could simultaneously destroy and create itself. Arriving in Britain in 1939 after fleeing Jewish persecution in Germany and losing his parents to the concentration camps, Metzger quickly became engaged in the visual arts, enrolling at the Cambridge School of Art in 1945 before joining life-drawing evening classes in London, led by the artist David Bomberg who became key to inspiring Metzger's ambitions to develop as an artist. He later moved to King's Lynn in Norfolk in the 1950s where he painted and developed his *Acid Nylon Paintings.* Perhaps as a result of his troubled upbringing, Metzger strongly believed that the role of the artist carried with it a moral responsibility "to help the world", and as such his original and devoted interweaving of issues in art, politics, ecology and society would contribute towards how artists today consider their practice in the wider context of the world. **GH**

It was my duty to help the world, and so by defining, by localizing one destructive activity, one problem of violence and danger within art, within world art, I would be doing what I am supposed to do as a moral obligation. My moral obligation is to light, light up the world, light up issues facing the world. I think this is something which goes back to me, in World War II, reading these books, and wondering whether I shouldn't commit my whole life to revolution, to a fundamentally dangerous way of living.

Gustav Metzger, "Gustav Metgzer in conversation with Clive Philpott", 2009.

Auto-Destructive Art, Machine-Art, Auto-Creative Art, 1961
Offset print on paper
28.2 × 21.7 cm

AUTO-DESTRUCTIVE ART

Demonstration by G. Metzger

SOUTH BANK LONDON 3 JULY 1961 11.45 a.m.—12.15 p.m.

Acid action painting. Height 7 ft. Length 12½ ft. Depth 6 ft. Materials: nylon, hydrochloric acid, metal. Technique. 3 nylon canvases coloured white black red are arranged behind each other, in this order. Acid is painted, flung and sprayed on to the nylon which corrodes at point of contact within 15 seconds.

Construction with glass. Height 13 ft. Width 9½ ft. Materials. Glass, metal, adhesive tape. Technique. The glass sheets suspended by adhesive tape fall on to the concrete ground in a pre-arranged sequence.

AUTO-DESTRUCTIVE ART

Auto-destructive art is primarily a form of public art for industrial societies.

Self-destructive painting, sculpture and construction is a total unity of idea, site, form, colour, method and timing of the disintegrative process.

Auto-destructive art can be created with natural forces, traditional art techniques and technological techniques.

The amplified sound of the auto-destructive process can be an element of the total conception.

The artist may collaborate with scientists, engineers.

Self-destructive art can be machine produced and factory assembled.

Auto-destructive paintings, sculptures and constructions have a life time varying from a few moments to twenty years. When the disintegrative process is complete the work is to be removed from the site and scrapped.

London, 4th November, 1959 *G. METZGER*

MANIFESTO AUTO-DESTRUCTIVE ART

Man in Regent Street is auto-destructive.
Rockets, nuclear weapons, are auto-destructive.
Auto-destructive art.
The drop drop dropping of HH bombs.
Not interested in ruins, (the picturesque)
Auto-destructive art re-enacts the obsession with destruction, the pummelling to which individuals and masses are subjected.
Auto-destructive art demonstrates man's power to accelerate disintegrative processes of nature and to order them.
Auto-destructive art mirrors the compulsive perfectionism of arms manufacture—polishing to destruction point.
Auto-destructive art is the transformation of technology into public art. The immense productive capacity, the chaos of capitalism and of Soviet communism, the co-existence of surplus and starvation; the increasing stock-piling of nuclear weapons—more than enough to destroy technological societies; the disintegrative effect of machinery and of life in vast built-up areas on the person,...

Auto-destructive art is art which contains within itself an agent which automatically leads to its destruction within a period of time not to exceed twenty years.
Other forms of auto-destructive art involve manual manipulation. There are forms of auto-destructive art where the artist has a tight control over the nature and timing of the disintegrative process, and there are other forms where the artist's control is slight.
Materials and techniques used in creating auto-destructive art include: Acid, Adhesives, Ballistics, Canvas, Clay, Combustion, Compression, Concrete, Corrosion, Cybernetics, Drop, Elasticity, Electricity, Electrolysis, Electronics, Explosives, Feed-back, Glass, Heat, Human Energy, Ice, Jet, Light, Load, Mass-production, Metal, Motion Picture, Natural Forces, Nuclear energy, Paint, Paper, Photography, Plaster, Plastics, Pressure, Radiation, Sand, Solar energy, Sound, Steam, Stress, Terra-cotta, Vibration, Water, Welding, Wire, Wood.

London, 10 *March,* 1960 *G. METZGER*

AUTO-DESTRUCTIVE ART MACHINE ART AUTO CREATIVE ART

Each visible fact absolutely expresses its reality.

Certain machine produced forms are the most perfect forms of our period.

In the evenings some of the finest works of art produced now are dumped on the streets of Soho.

Auto creative art is art of change, growth movement.

Auto-destructive art and auto creative art aim at the integration of art with the advances of science and technology. The immidiate objective is the creation, with the aid of computers, of works of art whose movements are programmed and include "self-regulation". The spectator, by means of electronic devices can have a direct bearing on the action of these works.

Auto-destructive art is an attack on capitalist values and the drive to nuclear annihilation.

23 *June* 1961 *G. METZGER*

B.C.M. ZZZO London W.C.1.

Printed by St. Martins' Printers (TU) 86d, Lillie Road, London, S.W.6.

Oscar Murillo

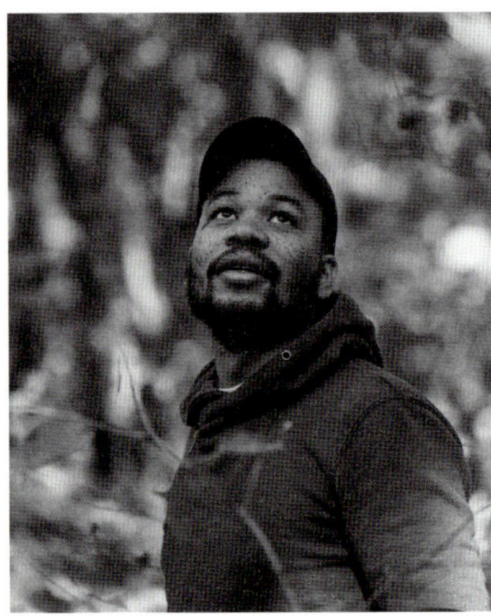

Attempts to understand artistic practice through action and labour are present throughout his process, including his laborious approach to painting, of which he says, "paintings are by-products of being in the studio and making work". Marking, dyeing, cutting, and stitching canvas comprise the physical activity needed to reflect on the notion of work, its place and displacement in the world.
Emma Enderby, "Meaning Belongs to People, Oscar Murillo", 2017

Born La Paila, Colombia, 1986
Lives and works in various locations

An energised synthesis of material, imagery and ideas *Tamawuj* was made over the summer and autumn of 2017 and is being exhibited for the first time in *Actions*. The title of the work comes from the title of the Sharjah Biennial 13 (2016), in which Murillo participated. According to the Biennial information, *Tamawuj*, a noun in Arabic, is defined as "a rising and falling in waves, but also a flowing, swelling, surging, fluctuation or a wavy undulating appearance, outline or form." Murillo's careful choice of title reflects his approach to making art, in which all his activities aim to accumulate and create meaning within a dynamic, continuous cycle.

Tamawuj will have started its life as a number of canvas sections on the floor of Murillo's London studio, gathering not only paint using a range of techniques, but also dust, dirt and footmarks. The screen-printed images (added when the canvas sections travelled to New York) of a heroic looking Polish woman and a Geisha girl are appropriated from a bank note and tea packaging. Murillo is interested in the claims that such images appear to make, their status as 'floating' signs in which difference and identity is subsumed within globalised economic systems.

Worked on again, back in London, the paintings come together in their final form as stitched collages. Their journey mirrors the artist's own itinerant life. An immigrant, with his family, coming from Colombia to the UK as a child, it is as if crossing borders is almost a physical necessity, a means of repeatedly asserting and questioning his own relative freedom. While on planes Murillo continues to make work, drawing in a series of books which document, through photographs and text, the lives of his family and friends in Colombia and the UK since the 1970s. In another open-ended project *Frequencies* (2013–), Murillo has organised for small canvases to be attached for a period of months to school desks in over thirty countries. Children have responded with drawings, poems and doodles, sometimes revealing their hopes and fears, while the canvases show the marks, stains, and wear of everyday use. As much a part of his practice as his paintings, videos and events, Murillo often includes the display of a group of these canvases within his installations, as in his 2017 exhibition at the Haus der Kunst in Munich.

Emma Enderby has described Murillo's work as one of "active displacement and hybridisation, constantly collapsing distinctions". In *Tamawuj*, with its red, spray-painted 'pan-national' and three looping arcs, there is a tremendous energy and life. Are Murillo's words, with their suggestion of unity beyond political borders, a declaration or a proposition? Here, as in all his work, Murillo, addresses himself to us, testing the boundaries of what art can be and what it can do. **AN**

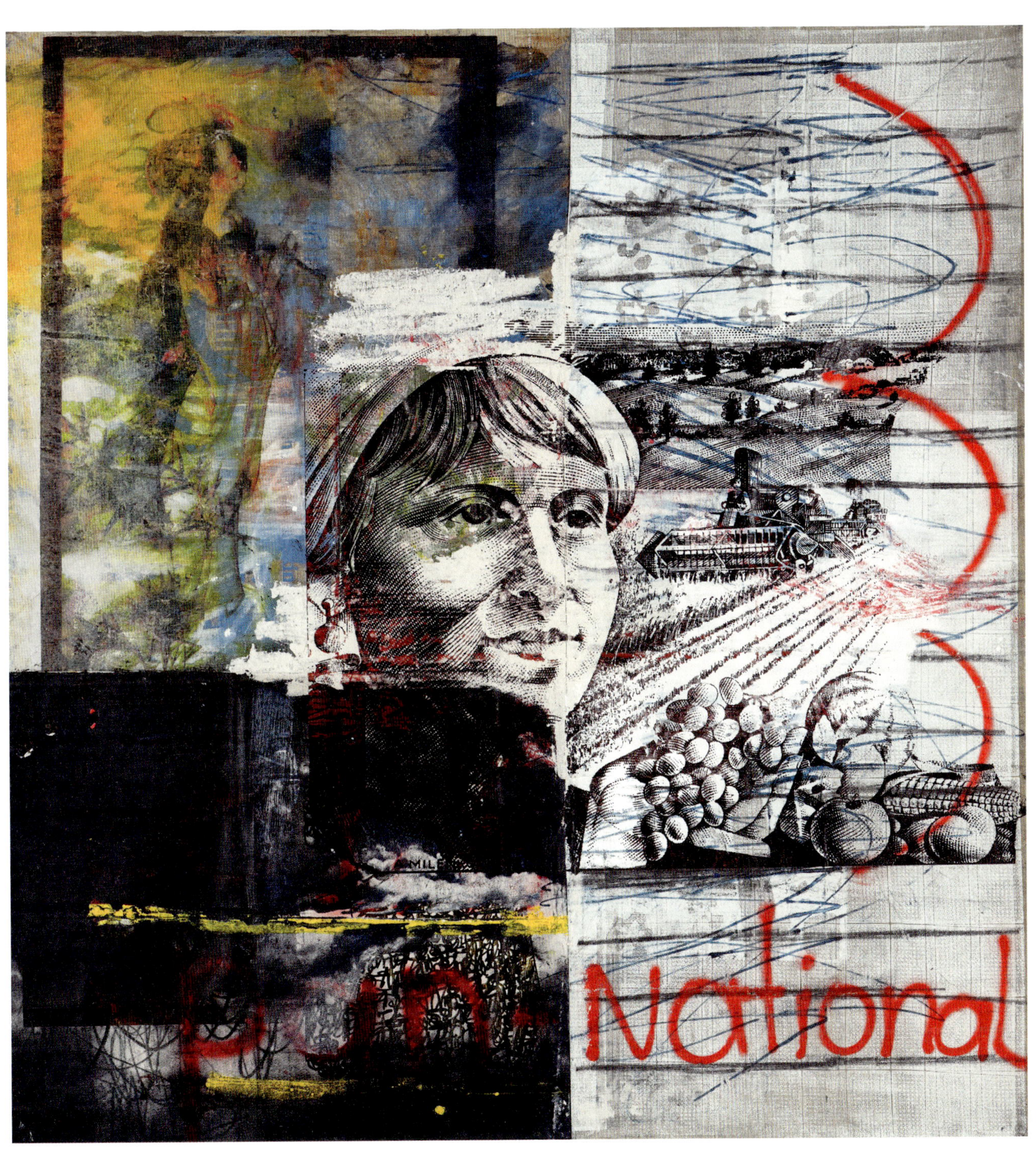

Tamawuj, 2017
Oil, oil stick and graphite on canvas and linen
2290 × 2390 mm

Ben Nicholson

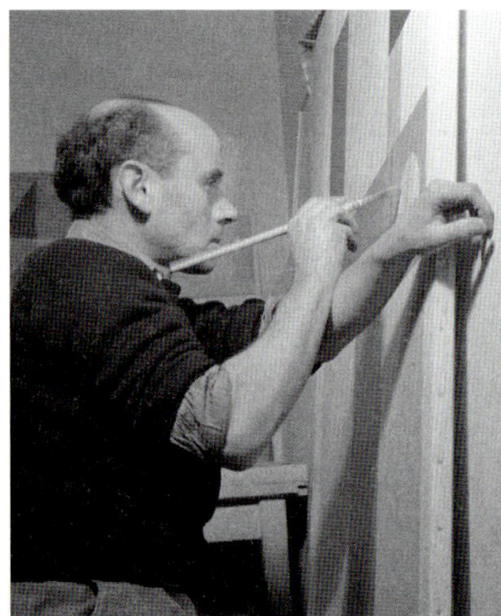

Born in Buckinghamshire, England, 1894
Died in London, 1982
Lived and worked in London and St Ives

Ben Nicholson's *1936 (white relief), second version, 1957* (1957) has an arresting quietness and simplicity that can still make us halt when we encounter it. This work is a later version of a 1936 relief. It is composed of a single square and circle, which protrude from, or regress into, the rectangular wooden baseboard. It is one of a series of geometric reliefs that Nicholson began to carve between 1933 and 1937: his first purely white relief was made in 1934. The noticeable shadows that are enhanced by the monochrome nature of this wall-based work further enrich its sculptural qualities. Traces of the artist's hand also interrupt its mathematical precision and Nicholson sometimes deliberately heightened these tensions by combining hand-drawn shapes with those executed with a compass or ruler.

Nicholson's works of the 1920s and early 1930s focused largely on landscape and still life subjects. He had previously experimented with geometric abstraction and colour in a small number of paintings of the mid-1920s. The white reliefs, however, marked an ambitious shift in his aesthetic. Speaking about his reliefs in 1941, Nicholson insisted that his overriding concern was for their potential to open up and create space. However, many contemporary sources and relationships converged around the time of their first production in 1934. A meeting with the artist Piet Mondrian in his Paris-based studio the year before directly inspired Nicholson's first relief work. Nicholson recalled the silence and light that filled Mondrian's studio. The geometric, white and light-filled spaces of contemporary architecture also connected with Nicholson's practice. Indeed, he was a co-founder of the short-lived group Unit One (in 1933), which promoted dialogues between international architecture, painting and sculpture. Nicholson was also working increasingly with the sculptor Barbara Hepworth, having begun a relationship with her in 1932. It was whilst sharing her studio in 1936 that he made one of only two white relief sculptures. In 1937 Nicholson co-edited *Circle*, with Kettle's Yard architect Leslie Martin and artist Naum Gabo. Four of Nicholson's white reliefs were reproduced in this journal, which advocated a new art that reflected the universal concerns of the modern world and promoted abstract experiment.

The painter and close friend of the artist, Paul Nash, suggested that Nicholson's white reliefs were "something like a new world". *1936 (white relief), second version, 1957* (1957), contains only three main shapes. It reflects Nicholson's confidence that abstract form arranged in space could offer limitless possibilities, which unconfined by references to time or place, could inspire intense aesthetic emotion. Nicholson acknowledged the spiritual dimensions of his interests, proposing that both painting and religious experience shared this common search for the infinite. **JP**

A painter doesn't live in a vacuum but contributes to and reflects the spirit of his time. This is evident today in abstract art where his interest is in the universal and in freedom from local restrictions. Abstract art doesn't arise 'out of the blue' and has a vitality only when it grows out of the painter's personal experience of living; it must start from something and this is what it starts from.

Ben Nicholson, "More or Less About Abstract Art", 1961

1936 (white relief), 1936, second version 1957, 1957
Oil on carved board
644 × 876 mm

Harold Offeh

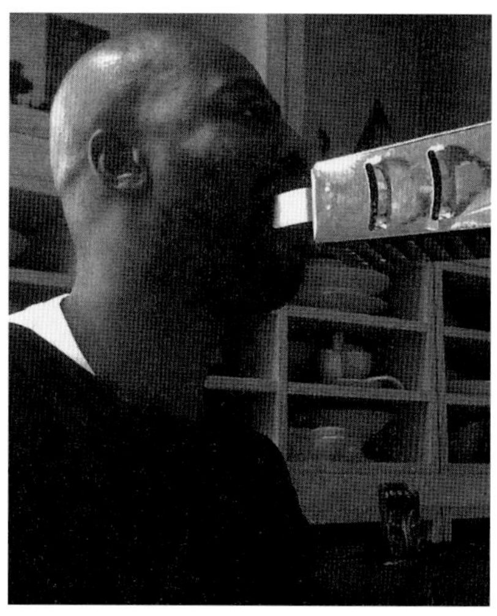

Born in Accra, Ghana, 1977
Lives and works in Cambridge

Harold Offeh's new performance for *Actions* was inspired by an inventory of 'non-art' objects in the Kettle's Yard House written by Jim Ede in 1974. The Inventory documents the personal histories associated with a range of objects, including plates, bowls, glasses, furniture and shells in the Kettle's Yard House, collected by Ede throughout his life. Ede's travels, acquaintances, aesthetic tastes and ceaseless power to perceive value in objects, where others perhaps couldn't, are revealed through this unique document. Offeh explains, "The notes are less concerned with economic value and more with the personal history and social value and function of each of the objects. They are an archive of the archive. As a list of 107 objects collected over a lifetime, the document becomes a great narrative portrait of Jim Ede." In a succession of live actions Offeh invites an audience to view a group of objects, displayed through physical interactions with his body and a screen. The work follows Offeh's year-long engagement with Kettle's Yard as the Open House Artist in Residence in 2017, during which time he worked with local community groups to unlock the wealth of creativity and history in north Cambridge.

Offeh uses performance and durational works as a means to examine cultural archives, collective memory and issues of identity, often using his body as a tool to expose and activate historical images. In his ongoing project *Covers,* he attempts to embody a number of famous images from popular culture, including Grace Jones' impossibly sculptural pose struck for the cover of her album *Island Life (Graceful (Arabesque 1)* (2008). Offeh puts his body to work, setting it a simple task that pushes its physical boundaries until failure is inevitable. Many of these works are funny and Offeh regularly uses humour as a means of communication, but his act is serious in confronting us with questions about contemporary culture. He is interested in the potential of reenactment as a method of understanding the past through direct experience, seeking inspiration in everything from eccentric costumed battle re-enactments to homemade YouTube parodies. There is a generosity in Offeh's practice; he believes that everybody has a valuable contribution to make to culture. **GH**

24. 2 shells. These were found near each other on a beach near Ceuta. Had it not been for Dali's teaching, I doubt if I would have bothered to pick them up – they would merely have been broken shells whereas now they are most treasured.

30. Candlesticks – these were purchased over 100 miles apart for 1/- each in Mazagan and Taroudant (French Morocco).

31. Shells – several of these shells belonged to Gaudier-Brzeska, some to Ian Fairweather and the glass "dish" to Mrs Dempster of Morocco.

48. Goblet – was given to me by Ben Nicholson.

55. Two fossils from Pescadero south of San Francisco. If you waited long enough they fell out of the cliff face into your hands.

76. Cups and saucers purchased after an air raid on Hull 1944 and in constant use by us until we left Kettle's Yard.

Jim Ede, "Notes on the Inventory", 1 November 1974

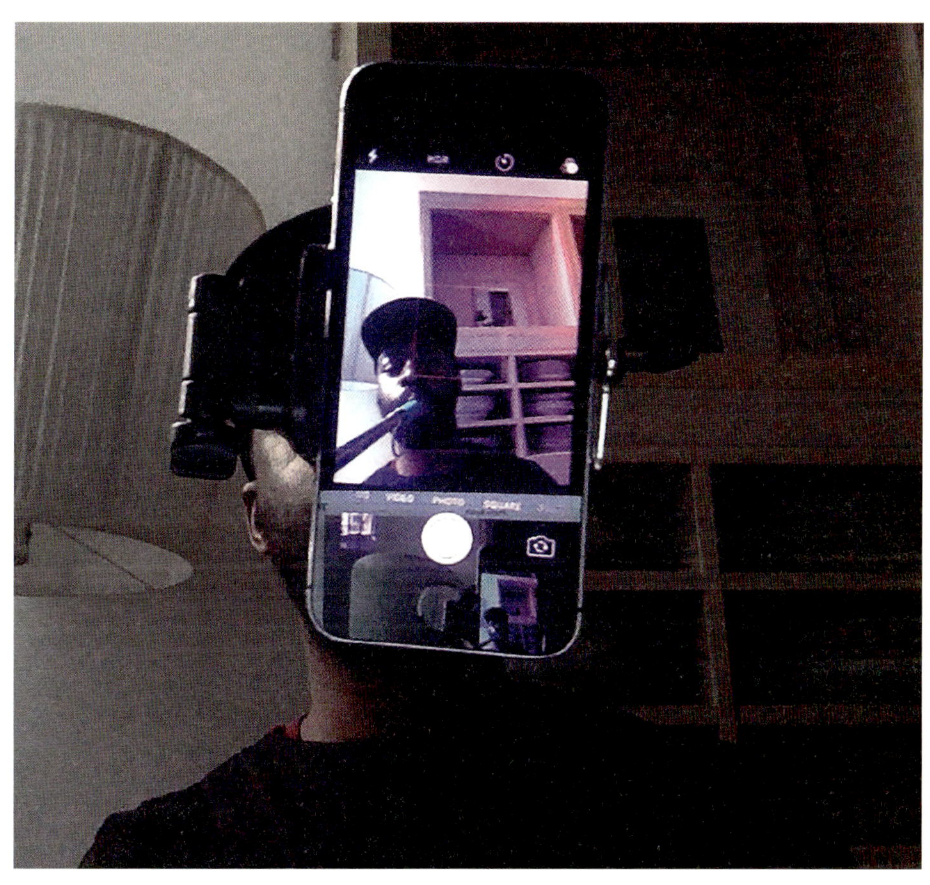

Object Action 1 (Selfie), 2017
Digital photograph

Cornelia Parker

I prefer things when they're fractured for some reason. I've always responded to fragmented things: if something's squashed in the road, I'm drawn to it. A squashed object is much more interesting than an intact one and I think brokenness is very much a part of society. Civilisations fall, for instance, or a very recognisable object can become mysterious and more open to interpretation when it's in pieces. To me, that's more interesting than what is whole.
Cornelia Parker, "In Conversation with Cornelia Parker", 2013

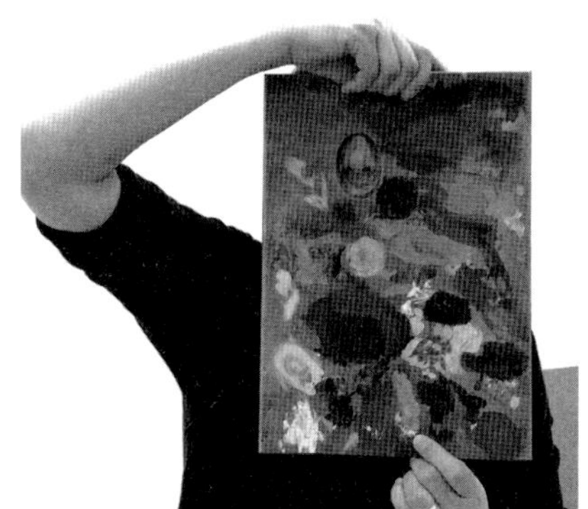

Born in 1956, Cheshire, England
Lives and works in London

For *Actions*, Cornelia Parker has created a veil of marks upon the two window panes in Helen Ede's bedroom in the Kettle's Yard House, using chalk from the white cliffs of Dover, in an intervention that beckons forth notions of home, identity – and the presence of the room's former occupant. Between 1957 and 1973, when the Edes lived in the House, Helen, whose two daughters were grown up, would often withdraw to her light-filled room for peace and recuperation from her intertwined roles as wife and host. Helen's room lay outside of Jim Ede's carefully considered arrangement of the rest of the House: simply decorated, it has an ambience of solitude and contemplation similar to that conjured in Virginia Woolf's essay "A Room of One's Own" (1929).

Parker's work for Helen Ede's bedroom is one of a series of recent projects in which the artist has examined ideas of transition, transference and the psyche. After being inspired by a collection of small tokens left by mothers with their abandoned babies, Parker selected over sixty artists to participate in the exhibition *Found* (2016) at the London Foundling Museum. She commented, "In order for something to be 'found', it has to at some point in its history been 'lost'." Also in 2016, Parker created *Transitional Object (PsychoBarn)* for the roof garden of The Metropolitan Museum of Art in New York. The artist dismantled a barn and reconfigured it as a replica of the Bates motel from Hitchcock's thriller *Psycho* (1960), where the deranged Norman Bates lived alone, imitating his dead mother. The title of Parker's work, *Transitional Object*, referred both to the artist's characteristic methods of construction, but also to psychologist D.W. Winnicott's term for the comforting toys which help young children to settle when separated from their parents.

Parker once said, memorably, "I resurrect things that have been killed off." Usually the artist carries out her resurrections through a transformation, as in her most famous work, *Cold Dark Matter: An Exploded View* (1991) an installation that consisted of the restored three-dimensional volume and contents of a garden shed exploded by the British Army at the request of the artist. The surviving fragments were painstakingly reassembled to create a frozen explosion, suspended from the ceiling, casting jagged shadows. Recently, Parker has continued arranging fragments into lyrical assemblage through her work as 2017 General Election Artist: over the last year she has maintained an Instagram account, @electionartist2017, a kaleidoscopic array of wry and thoughtful snapshots of politicians, campaigners, crowds at rallies, shop windows, market stalls, commuters on escalators, rough sleepers, graffiti and rubbish. **SL**

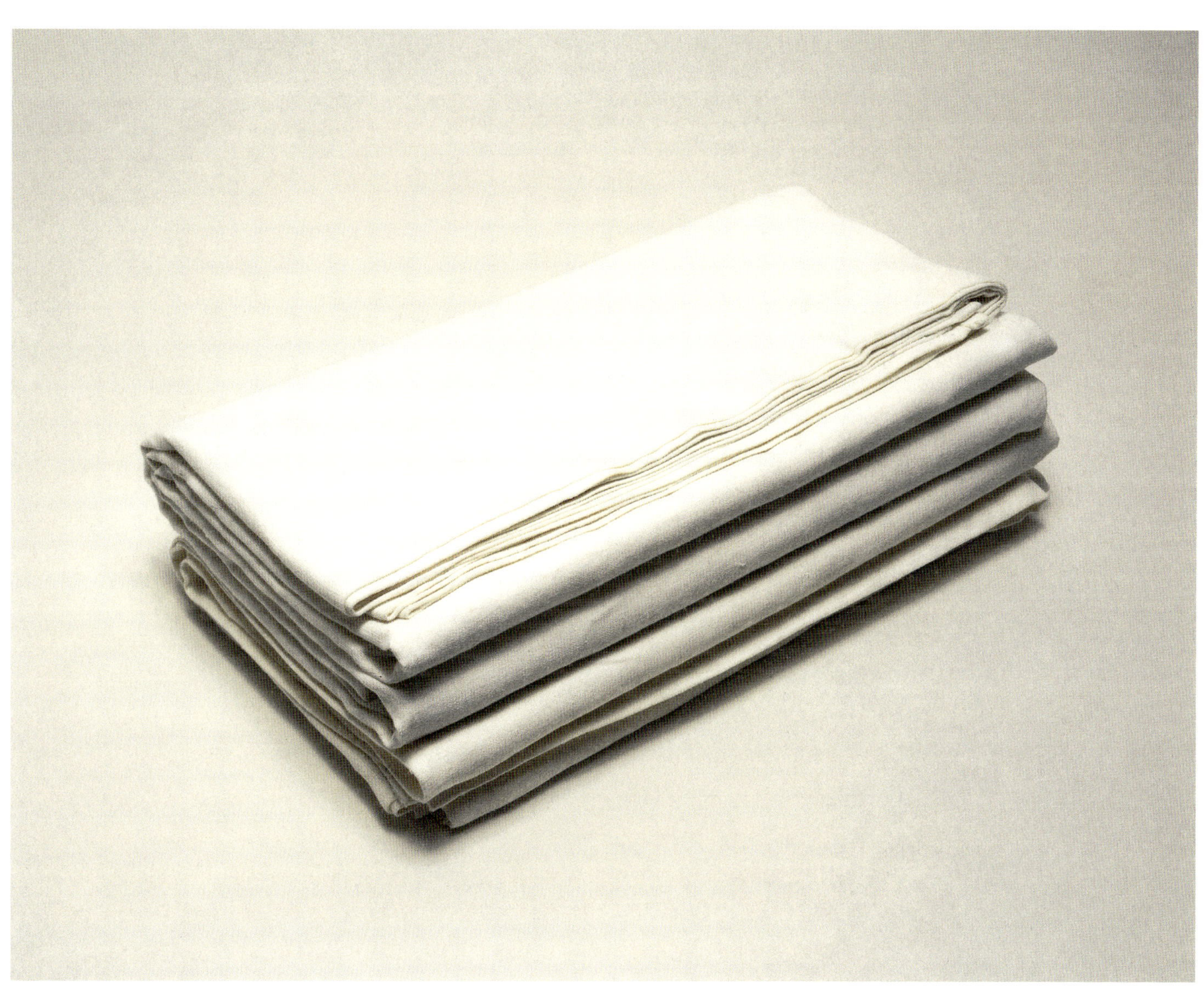

Inhaled Cliffs, 1996
Sheets starched with chalk from the White Cliffs of Dover
410 × 255 × 110 mm (folded)

Vicken Parsons

Born in Hertfordshire, England, 1957
Lives and works in London and Norfolk

For *Actions* Vicken Parsons is exhibiting a small group of new paintings made in 2017. The work illustrated here, like all Parsons' paintings, is small, unframed and untitled: oil paint on a thick wooden board. Grey and white paint marks convey the bare idea of a room. A block of white suggests light flooding in, only cut off by the lower edge of the painting. To the left are paler reflections. In the foreground, thin darker lines appear to delineate openings, an unfinished working out, a palimpsest; the traces of a place, a time, a memory. The black lines appear more intent, fixing or holding the idea of a space we can visually enter and comprehend, while the grey lines, expressive dashes, feel intuitive; as if the movements of a person have become visible, after the body has left.

Parsons' paintings have been described as visual poems. They offer the viewer many possible associations, yet her images are also imbued with a sense of precision and purpose. The colours and forms in her works both hold us in the present and draw us into the life of the mind. She has said of her works: "I'm constructing a space for your head to be in, in a way."

In 2013, Parsons made an installation of "painted objects" in St Peter's Church, next to Kettle's Yard. These groups of small painted metal blocks could, at first glance, be models for a modern city. As in the paintings, the colours and brush marks seem provisional, by turns confident and free, tentative and uncertain. A year later, paintings by Parsons were hung in the Kettle's Yard House, in spaces created due to a number of works being away on loan. Here, in the curated, light-filled rooms, the paintings quietly disturbed the familiar visual landscape with a burst of blue or a stripe of luminous yellow/green. Jim Ede, the creator of Kettle's Yard, would have admired their intelligence and ambition, their ability to open up worlds of possibility and feeling.

In Parsons' exhibition *Iris* at Alan Cristea Gallery in London in 2016/17, many of the paintings, for the first time, included a further layer of vertical and horizontal lines, as if rendering parts of a structure, a grid, somehow lying beneath and above the image. This new series of works offers a deep sense of engagement with the act of making a painting, while offering us not pictures but experiences. **AN**

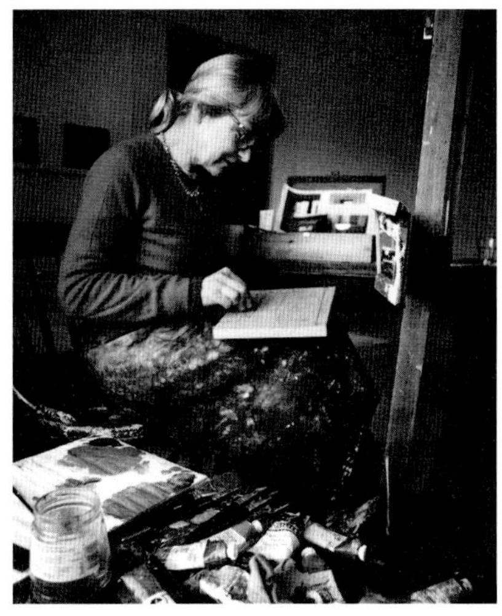

Though always conscious of looking at a fabricated object, the viewer of each work enters two spaces. One is a mysterious environment, different in each picture and experienced as three dimensional, that Parsons has brought into existence. The other is a demarcated flat domain – a tablet – into which field the viewer is drawn, and which acts as a kind of seismograph of Parsons' thought. In this creation these two worlds are co-dependent, both physically and psychologically. Each refers the viewer to the other, not alternately but simultaneously.

Richard Morphet, "Charged Spaces", *Vicken Parsons: Iris*, 2016

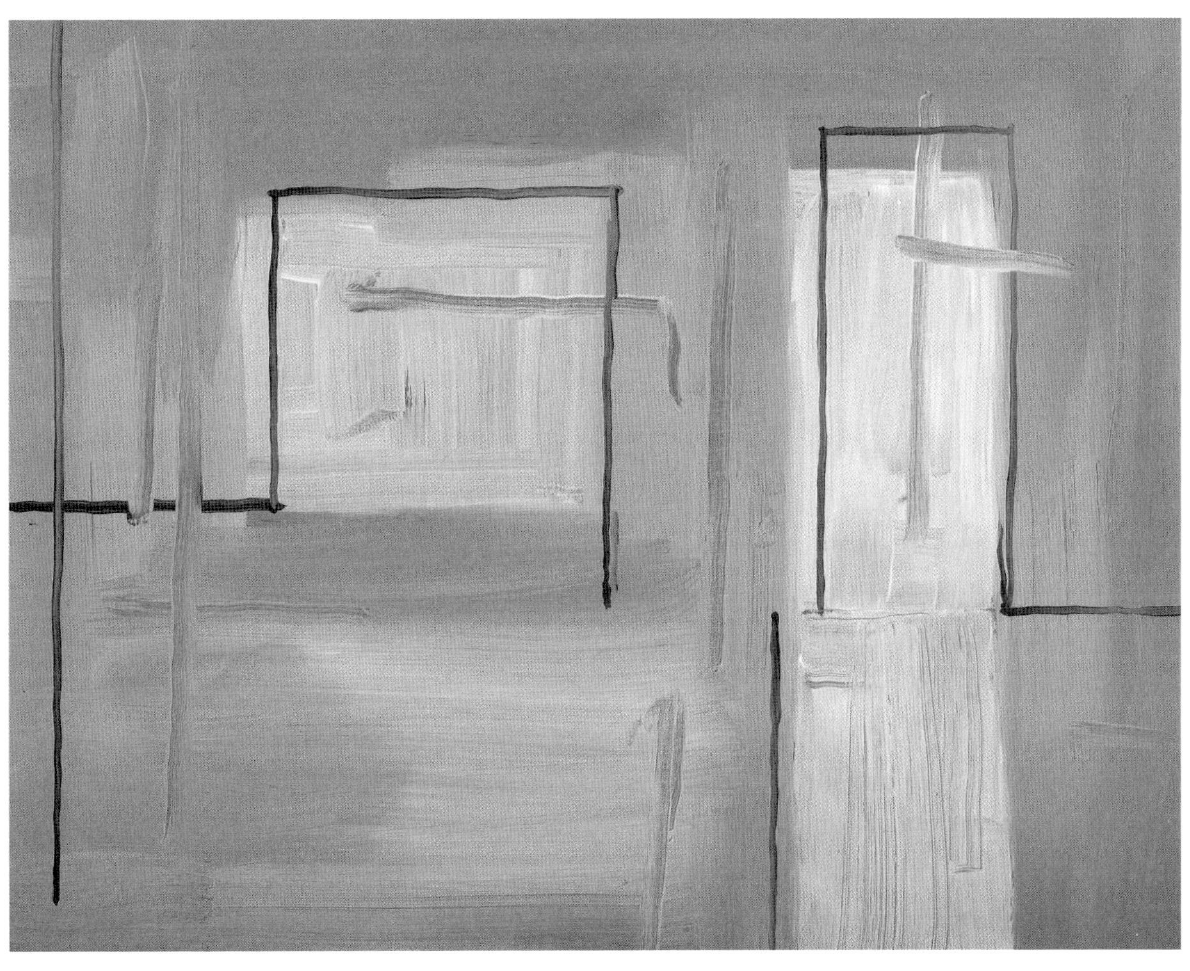

Untitled, 2017
Oil on wood
220 × 290 mm

Katie Paterson

Born in Glasgow, 1981
Lives and works in Berlin

For *Actions*, Katie Paterson presents her photographic documentation of a work which reflected on ideas of vast and extra-minute scale, *Inside this desert lies the tiniest grain of sand* (2010), shown within the transporting space of the gallery lift at Kettle's Yard. To produce this work, Paterson, who often works collaboratively with leading scientists and researchers, asked experts in nanotechnology to carve from a grain of sand collected from the Sahara Desert an almost infinitely smaller fragment – just 0.00005 millimetres across – which she then affixed to a normal-sized grain of sand, and deposited back in the immense dunes of the Desert, this final action captured in the photographic image. This piece reflects Paterson's characteristically poetic and imaginative approach, in which she translates expanded ideas of reality into something which can be held in the palm of the hand. Paterson first presented *Inside this desert lies the tiniest grain of sand* at Kettle's Yard in 2013, during a solo exhibition which also included the first display of her *Fossil Necklace* (2013), constructed with over 170 beads carved from fossils which chart the evolution of life on earth, from a dinosaur tooth to a squid's backbone, that in their sequential stringing together, chart the evolution of life on earth.

Paterson graduated from master's studies at the Slade in 2007 with an exhibition *Vatnajökull (the sound of)*, that signalled her working method of realising awe-inspiring yet approachable visions of the natural world via technology. Visitors to the gallery encountered a mobile phone number in the form of a neon sign – on dialling the number, they were connected to a microphone submerged in a lagoon in Iceland, transmitting the sound of a melting glacier. In 2013, Paterson used a process of casting, melting and recasting to transform an ancient meteorite, into a new version of itself, which visitors could touch, called *Campo del Cielo, Field of Sky*. The following year, 2014, Paterson became the first artist to send an artwork to the International Space Station when the smallest of her *Campo del Cielo* meteorites was launched into space and docked with the ISS. More recently, Paterson's practice of bringing the cosmos indoors has resulted in *Totality* (2016), commissioned by Arts Council Collection and Somerset House, which is a mirror ball composed of over ten thousand images of solar eclipses, nearly every one that has been documented by humankind either by illustration or photography. **SL**

Katie Paterson works with scales that make the Grand Canyon look like a crack in the pavement: the depths of geological and cosmological time, the breadth of the visible universe, the numbers of dead stars like grains of sand on an unmeasurable beach. What's happening here is a sort of domestication of the cosmic sublime: an illumination and illustration of that sense of scale, which neither makes it monstrous nor claims to have tamed it. It's less a bringing-to-heel than a bringing-indoors – folding all those impossible distances and sizes into everyday objects in the comparative intimacy of domestic space.
Paul Graham Raven, *New Scientist*, 2016

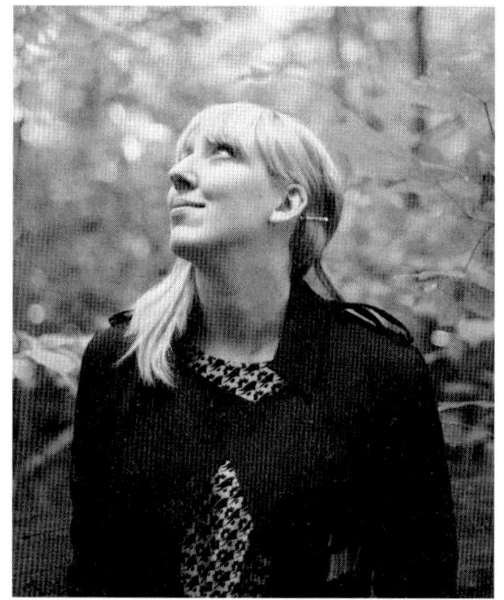

Inside this desert lies the tiniest grain of sand, 2010
Black-and-white silver gelatin photograph
500 × 401 mm

Zoran Popović

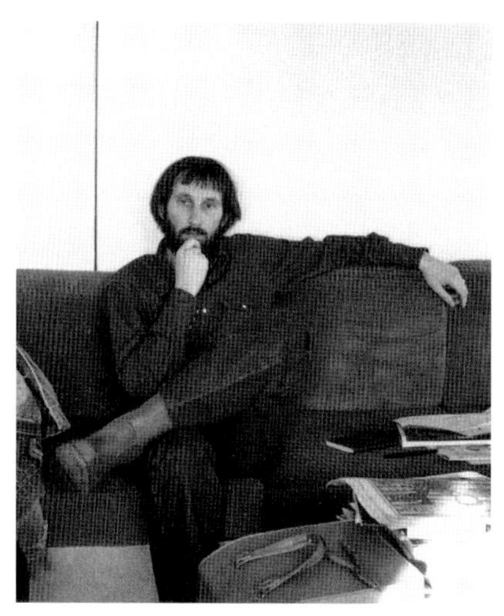

Art must be negative, critical, both towards the external world and in relation to its own language, its own (artistic) practice. It is pointless and hypocritical to be engaged, to speak and act in the name of some humanity, of mankind, political and economic freedoms, and to remain passive on the other hand in relation to the system of "universal" artistic values, the system that is the basic prerequisite of the existence of artistic bureaucracy, and therefore of the outrageous robbery perpetrated by star artists.
Zoran Popović, "For Self-Management Art", *Oktobar 75*, 1975

Born in Belgrade, Yugoslavia, 1944
Lives and works in Belgrade

Struggle in New York (1976) is a film that examines the role of art in modern society and politics through the eyes of young artists working in 1970s New York. Placing himself in this centre of Western capitalism, Popović follows a number of influential artists as they grapple with urgent issues ranging from gender inequality and oppression to the lack of diversity within institutional power structures. In this fascinating artwork, we find ourselves in the midst of a cacophonous musical performance by members of *Art and Language*, on a picket line outside the Whitney Museum of American Art, and in an interview with conceptual artist Ian Burn.

Perhaps due to his upbringing in socialist Yugoslavia, Popović is deeply critical of art that doesn't interrogate its surroundings, believing that "a politicisation of art is necessary". This belief flows through his work. In *Struggle in New York*, between sweeping shots of New York's financial district and the decayed streets of the Bronx, a group challenges the opening of the new art centre P.S.1, questioning the morality of its funding structure and ties to large corporations, and accusing it of using artists to serve the cultural elite rather than the deprived communities around it. In another scene, a group of young female artists campaign for equal rights and to break free of the influence of men and their intrinsic power in the arts. Although over forty years have passed since *Struggle in New York* was filmed, its demands feel no less urgent now than they did then.

Popović was one of a number of artists, including Marina Abramović, who were associated with the Student Cultural Centre (SKC) in Belgrade, where *Struggle in New York* was first shown in April 1977. The SKC was set up in 1968 by the Yugoslav state as a creative outlet for the burgeoning wave of rebellious young artists and students who challenged the political situation at that time. Popović first travelled to New York in 1974 to spend a year working in the studio of Joseph Kosuth, where he met other key avant-garde artists and contributors to the artist-led leftist publication *The Fox*, to which he also contributed. This time was key for Popović in solidifying his ideas around the value and form of art in society. On returning to Belgrade in 1975 he released a journal with other politically engaged Yugoslav artists and curators through the SDC, *Oktobar 75*, which included his essay "For Self-Management Art", where he discussed these ideas and called on other artists to question their values and review their position in relation to society and the art establishment. **GH**

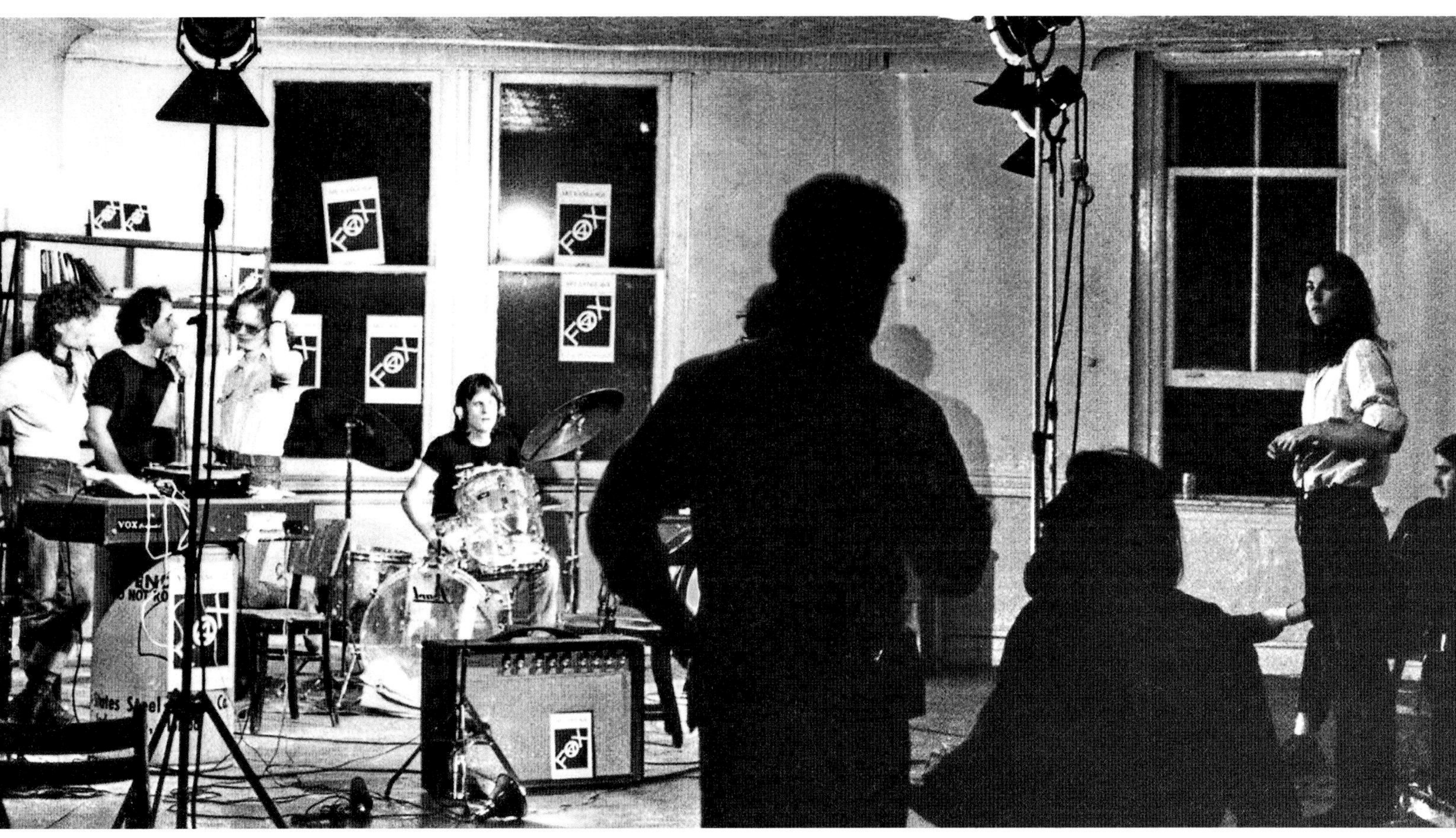

On the set of "*… And Now for Something Completely Different…*" a part of *Struggle in New York* filmed in 1976 by Zoran Popović. From left, Christine Kozlov, Mel Ramsden, Paula Ramsden, Jesse Chamberlain, Howard Schamest, Zoran Popović, Kathryn Bigelow, Larry Scharf.

Struggle in New York, 1976
16mm film transferred to DVD, 56 minutes 30 seconds, black and white

Khadija Saye

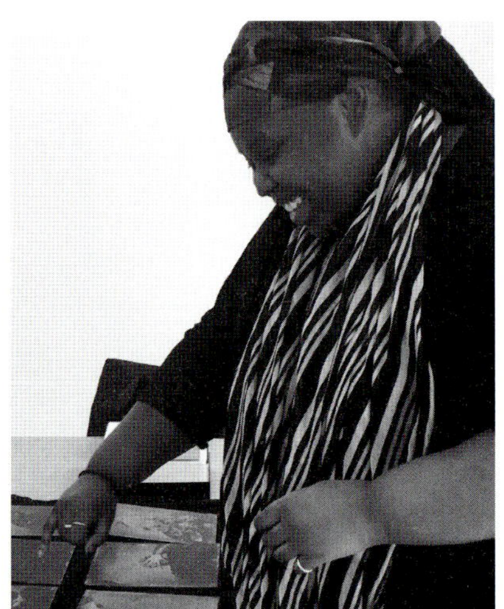

Born in London, 1992
Died in London, 2017
Lived and worked in London

The four photographic works by Khadija Saye in *Actions* are part of the series *Dwelling: in this space we breathe*, 2017. Poetic and powerful, they document the artist's use of traditional Gambian spiritual rituals as a means of healing. Saye's images are contemporary tintypes, an early form of photography popular in the 1860s and 1870s. For Saye the elaborate process of making each work, involving the wet-plate collodion method, was significant. It was another ritual to consciously undertake, also with uncertain outcomes and spiritual meaning, very different from the speed and disposability of image making in the digital era. From each session, Saye created a small number of unique plates, revealing the accidents and rich tonal range of the tintype process, with unfocused depths and mesmerizing detail. The tintypes in *Actions* are four of the six works selected to be exhibited as part of the Diaspora Pavilion at the 2017 Venice Biennale. Saye was the youngest artist to be included in this landmark exhibition.

In each of her images, the artist is seen physically relating to a ritual object or objects, from a bunch of cowrie shells apparently coming from her mouth to a cow horn applied to her back. When not viewed within their cultural and religious context, the actions can appear absurd. Saye hints at this in *Peitaw,* for example, where she appears to be using one arm to keep her 'prop' in place. The vintage appearance of each image reinforces the sense of the performative, of knowingly acting out each ritual.

Saye wrote of how her own life and spiritual needs were embedded within the new work: "Using myself as the subject, I felt it necessary to physically explore how trauma is embodied in the black experience." By using the tintype process and through her carefully set up poses and choice of clothing, Saye invokes the history of photography as a medium for the subjugation of black women as well as its positive potential today, when controlled by those being represented. However, Saye wanted her photographs to ultimately transcend any specific religion, place or person. It is the presence and inner strength of the artist as both subject and witness, represented in light and shadow, which ultimately shines most brightly through these remarkable photographs. **AN**

The journey of making wet plate collodion tintypes is unique in the sense that no image can be replicated and the final outcome is out of the creator's control. Within this process, you surrender yourself to the unknown, similar to what is required by all spiritual higher powers: surrendering and sacrifice. Each tintype has its own unique story to tell, a metaphor for our individual human spiritual journey. The process of submerging the collodion covered plate into a tank of silver nitrate, ignites memories of baptisms, the idea of purity and how we cleanse in order to be spiritually sound. The application of the collodion transcends the photographic process, it is a reflection, physical manifestation of my relationship to the deep-rooted tradition of African spirituality.

Khadija Saye, unpublished text, 2017

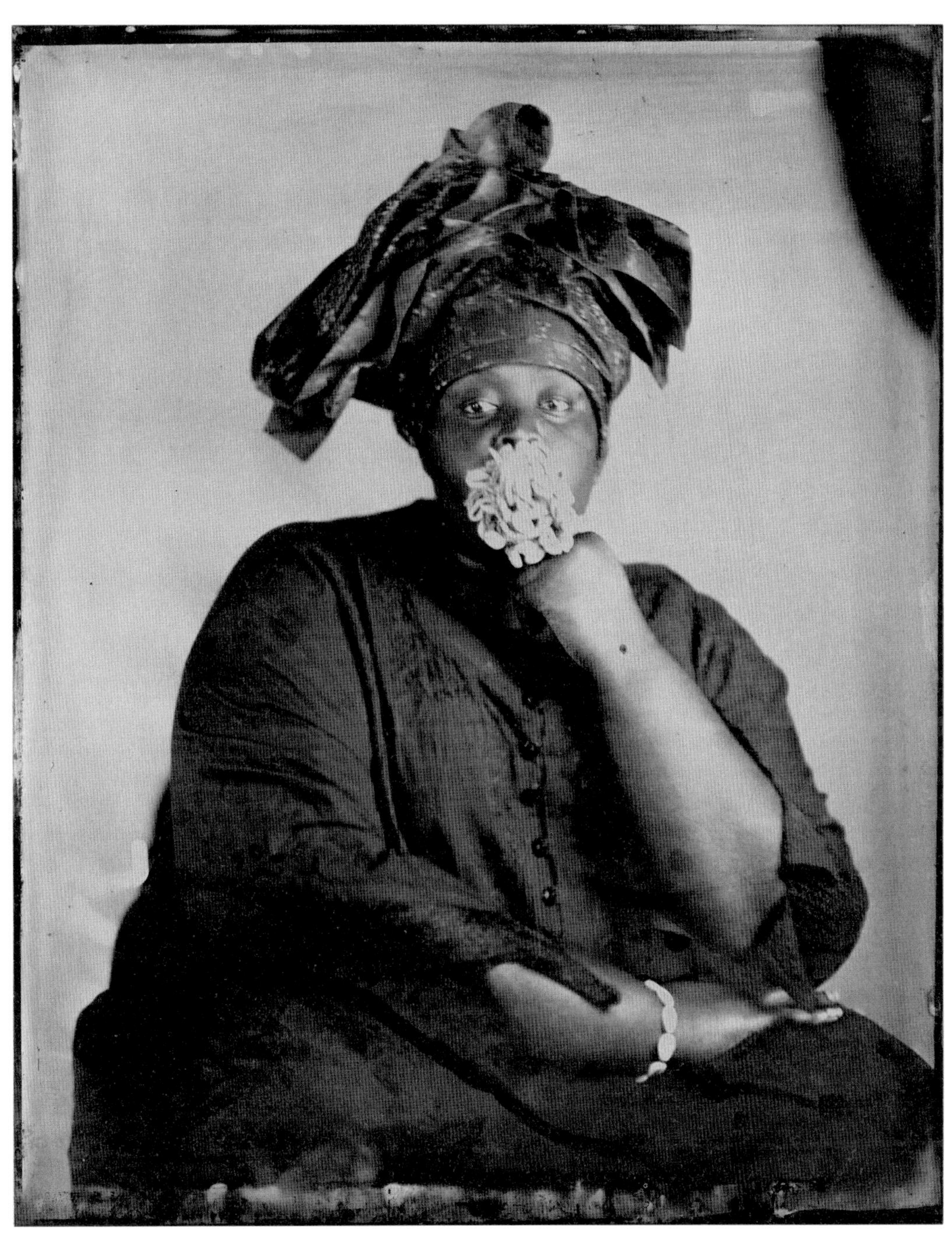

Peitaw, 2017
From the series: *Dwelling: in this space we breathe*
Photograph, wet plate collodion tintype on metal
250 × 200 mm

Emma Smith

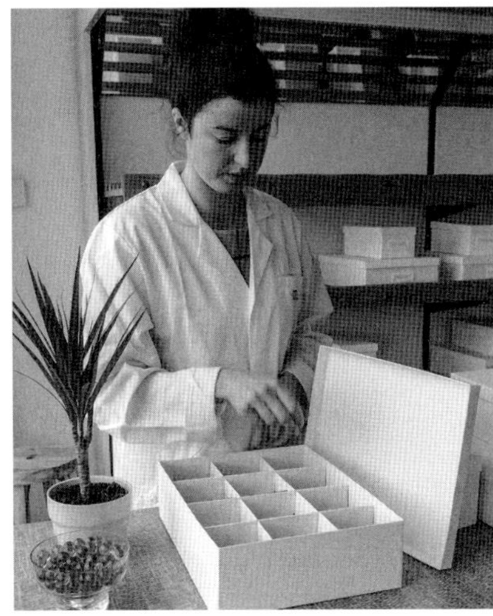

Born in London, 1981
Lives in Cambridge; works in various locations

For *Actions* Emma Smith has collaborated with a software developer to create an interactive online artwork where visitors are prescribed and gifted restorative performance instructions. This new work builds on a project commissioned in 2015 by Kettle's Yard through its Open House residency programme, *Variations on a Weekend Theme,* where Smith created a pop-up art apothecary, converting a disused bakery in North Cambridge. The project was inspired by Jim Ede's generosity in opening his home and collection to visitors and students in Cambridge, as well as his previous modernist 1930s home in Tangier, where he invited servicemen to take time away from their duties over the water in Gibraltar, believing art to be restorative and inextricably linked to life. Smith worked with residents in Cambridge to gather domestic knowledge and practices for dealing with our frenetic lives; modest, everyday actions that instill a sense of wellbeing such as flower arranging. Then, utilizing complex charts inspired by the domestic casebooks of sixteenth-century medical astrologers Forman and Napier, through research facilitated by the Department of History and Philosophy of Science at the University of Cambridge, Smith invited members of the public to embark on one-to-one consultations to prescribe their perfect restorative action. The walls were adorned with artworks from the Kettle's Yard House. Her new work re-envisions these charts in digital form to create an online version of the apothecary.

This work is typical of Smith's research-driven, socially engaged projects that bring people together in order to interrogate how we function and communicate as humans, with each other and our surroundings. Her work emerges through experimentation and exploration, developed through collaboration. She creates large-scale performance events, which anticipate their own dissemination and re-performance through installation, props, scripts and scores. **GH**

Her truly remarkable engagement with and curiosity about diverse fields of knowledge – ranging from mathematics to human sciences, to music, history and sociology is processed through an elaborated Ars Combinatoria. The processes by which she unites and crosses disciplinary ambits, continually shifting the methods and ways of doing and of analysing things, is one of the most remarkable features of her practice. This is due not only to the combinatory nature of the work but also her frequent use of very elaborated ludic tactics to introduce intelligent, erudite but also playful and funny riddles when working with people. This quizzical merging of various sources and kinds of knowledge is largely expressed through the activation and organisation of events that gather players and audiences together, becoming equal participants of performative moments that arise in a rather spontaneous manner.
Filipa Ramos, *Dwelling on Dwelling*, 2015

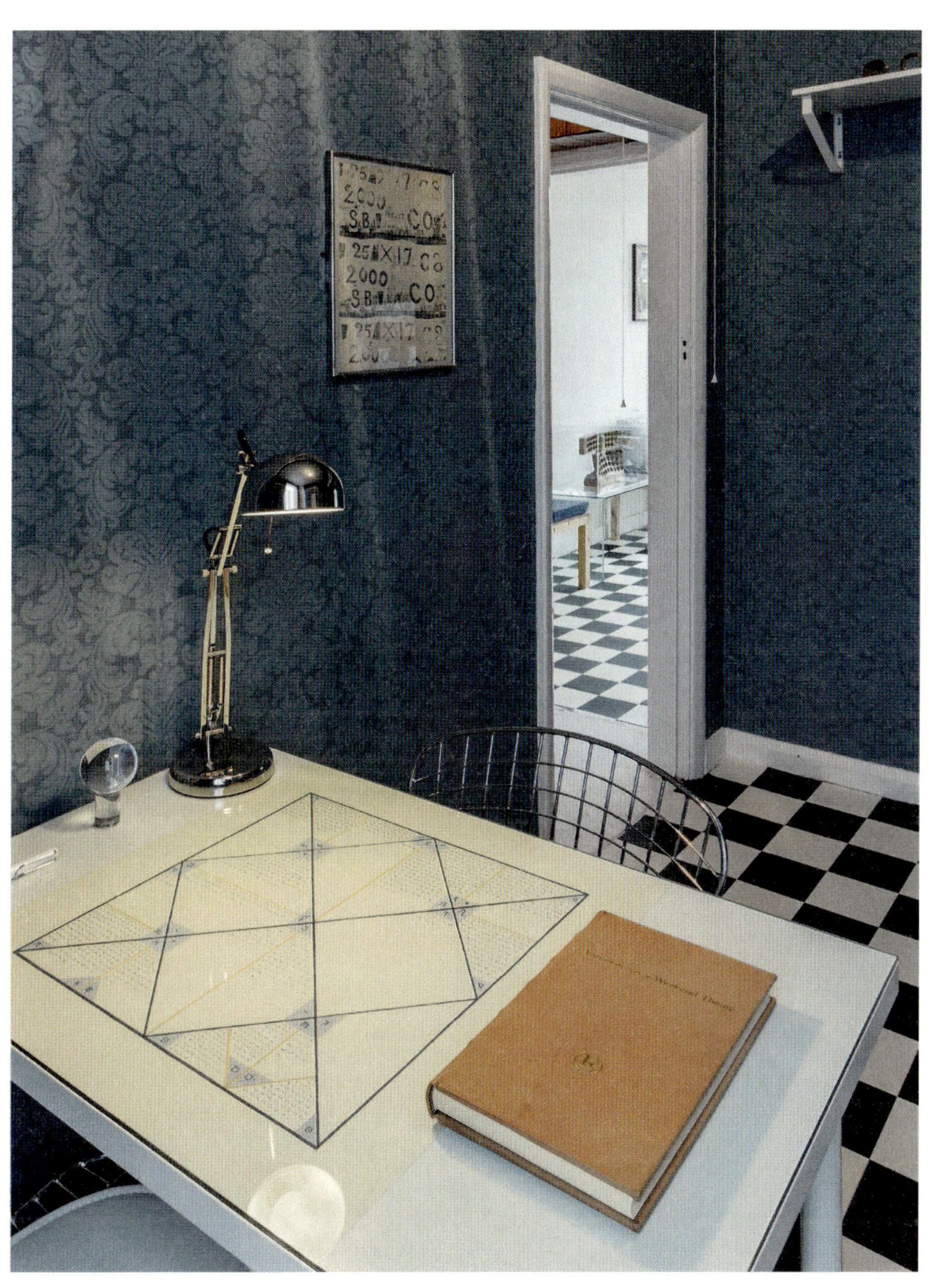

Variations on a Weekend Theme, 2015
Installation view

Caroline Walker

Born in Dunfermline, Scotland, 1982
Lives and works in London

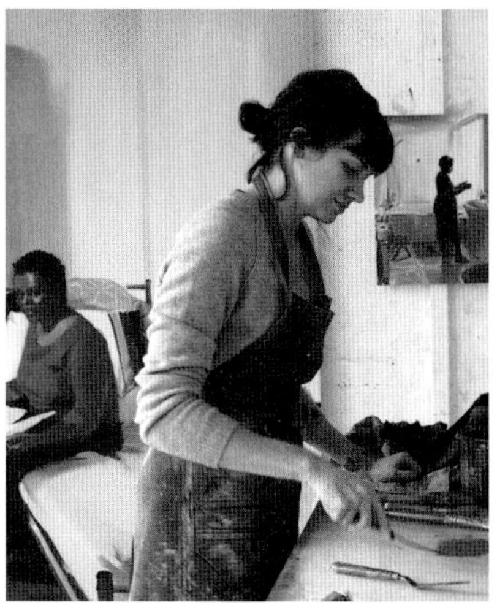

Caroline Walker's new series of paintings, titled *Home*, offers the viewer a less familiar portrayal of the refugee crisis. In collaboration with Kettle's Yard and the charity Women for Refugee Women, Walker met and photographed five women living in temporary accommodation, before making paintings of each in her studio. Walker's sensuous handling of paint brings to life the often banal detail of each room. The warmth with which Walker depicts the women contrasts with and foregrounds the potential isolation and latent anxiety of their situations, while giving a powerful sense of the individual human stories behind the immigration statistics. Their lives are safer but they are in exile from their families and friends and from the homes they have had to leave behind.

Since graduating from the Royal College of Art in 2009, Walker has become known for her ambitious and compelling paintings which explore the representation of women in different environments, from luxury villas in Palm Springs to London's proliferating nail bars. For some groups of work, Walker hires actresses and models and arranges carefully choreographed 'sets'. Each painting is then created from multiple photographs of each scene, giving a heightened sense of dramatic reality, the viewer's attention drawn to the potential symbolism of individual objects. In other paintings, such as the *Bathhouse* series, produced following a residency in Budapest in 2014, the sense of a 'constructed' image is less evident as Walker beautifully captures the relaxed, social atmosphere of this traditional activity. In 2017, Walker's paintings of nail bars, a more recent phenomenon, were exhibited at space k in Seoul. Here the encounters between women are colder and more transactional. At the same time, Walker draws attention to the visual richness of the salons with their vases of fresh flowers and shelves of nail varnish. **AN**

Wealth, status, age, sexuality, career, family, friends, body and looks all become intertwined signifiers in Walker's engineered scenarios, challenging the viewer whilst simultaneously revealing the patriarchal structures underpinning society, so many of which lead to women being held back, marginalised, disenfranchised, labelled, abused, objectified or simply overlooked, whether working for the minimum wage or leading Super-Rich lifestyles. But while Walker's subtexts are often powerful, this alone does not capture the spirit of the paintings, which are also witty, wry, playful, charming, disarming and cryptic in equal measure.
Matt Price, *Vitamin P3*, 2016

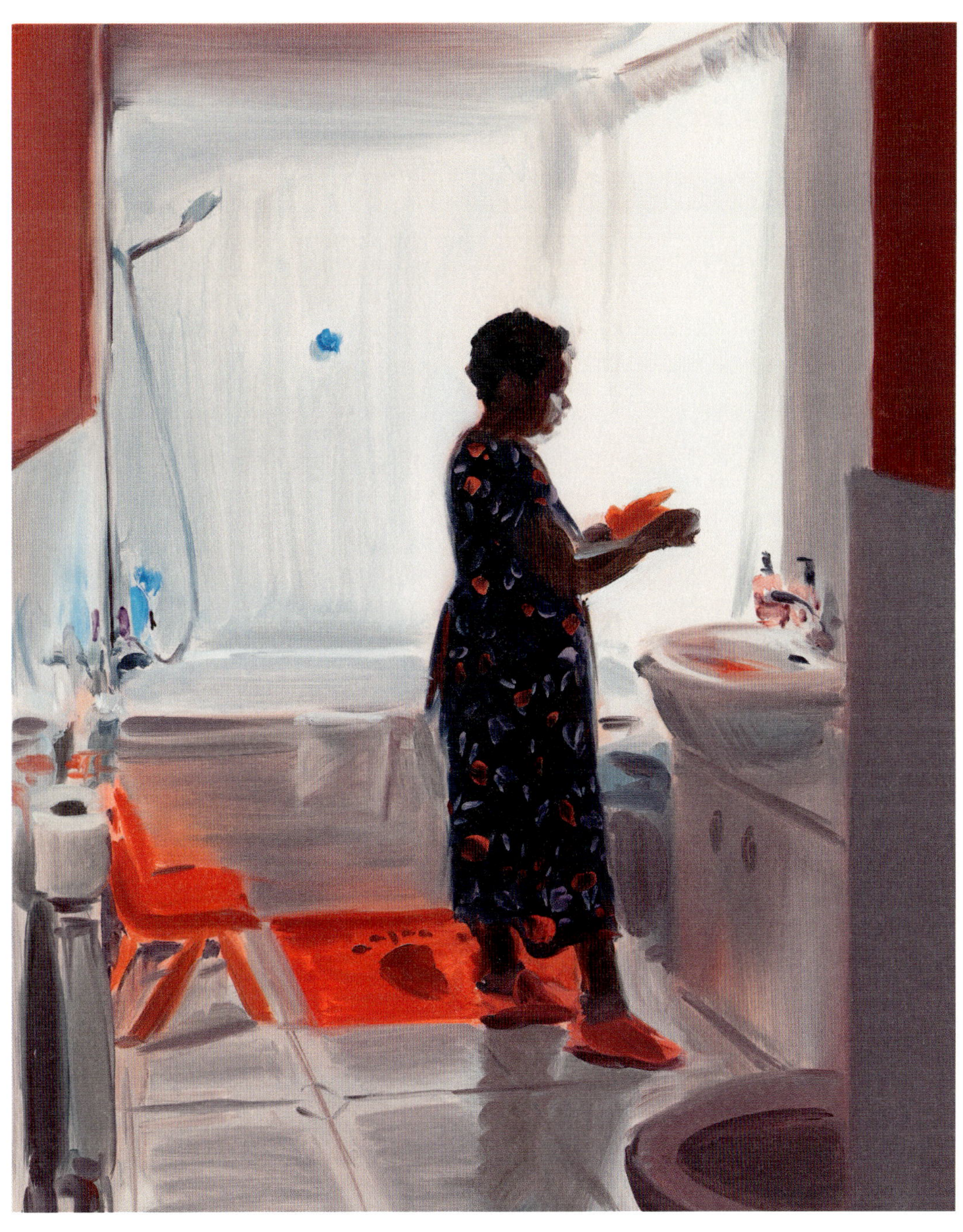

Joy, 11am, Hackney, 2017
Oil on board
430 × 305 mm

Kate Whitley

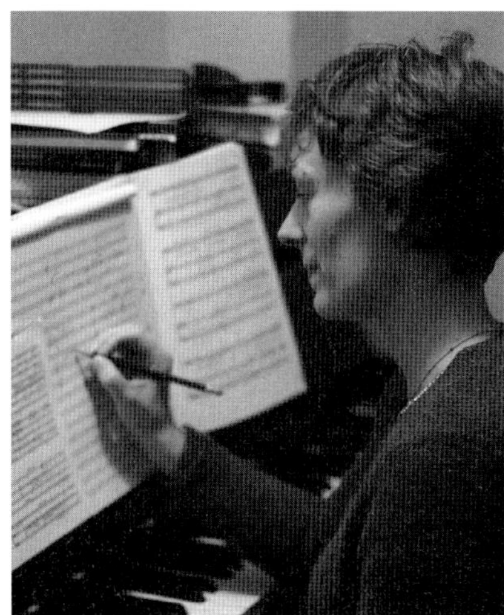

My choice of string quartet for my work for Actions *might seem surprising, as string quartet is so much seen as the epitome of abstract music making, that is removed from the world, although I don't agree with that – everything we create is part of the world.*
Kate Whitley, 2017

Born in Oxford, 1989
Lives and works in London

For *Actions*, Kate Whitley has composed a new piece for string quartet, to be performed in the House at Kettle's Yard. Whitley explains that the work draws upon the wartime correspondence between Naum Gabo and Herbert Read, "I've used *An Exchange of Letters Between Naum Gabo and Herbert Read* (1944), as an inspiration, but not directly. There are such gripping images in the letters, which I have tried to express using a musical language." *Actions* represents a continuation of Whitley's long-running relationship with Kettle's Yard: as an undergraduate at the University of Cambridge, she programmed the Kettle's Yard student lunchtime concert series, before taking up the role of Kettle's Yard 2015 New Music Programmer. She says, "It's a wonderful place to perform because the audience members are so close to you… it's a great space because it is somewhere in between a gallery, a performance space, and a house."

Whitley grew up playing piano and composing her own music, travelling to London every Saturday to attend the Junior Department at the Guildhall School of Music and Drama every Saturday. However, she always disliked the formal environment of piano exams and concert recitals, and began exploring other performance contexts, such as playing classical music with friends in local schools around Oxfordshire and staging a concert in a local pub. When studying music at university she met conductor Christopher Stark, who had been staging operas, and when they moved to London the idea for their joint initiative The Multi-Story Orchestra began. Their first performance, in a car park in Peckham in 2011, was of Igor Stravinsky's *The Rite of Spring* (1913), selected because "It was so ambitious, but also because it suited the space, which was so angular and modern."

Working with children has been a constant in her practice over the last decade, a process she says she enjoys because "Often in classical music situations, the musicians and audiences are very polite, but children are so honest. If they don't like something they will tell you. I wanted to work in this way because it's not easy – however, if you do manage to engage children then their interest is genuine and their energy and commitment is really inspiring." Whitley has also often worked collaboratively with authors: her piece *Alive* for children's choir and orchestra, which was set to words by poet Holly McNish, won a 2015 British Composers Award, while her piece *Speak Out*, set to words by Malala Yousafzai was premiered by BBC National Orchestral and Chorus of Wales on International Women's Day 2017. **SL**

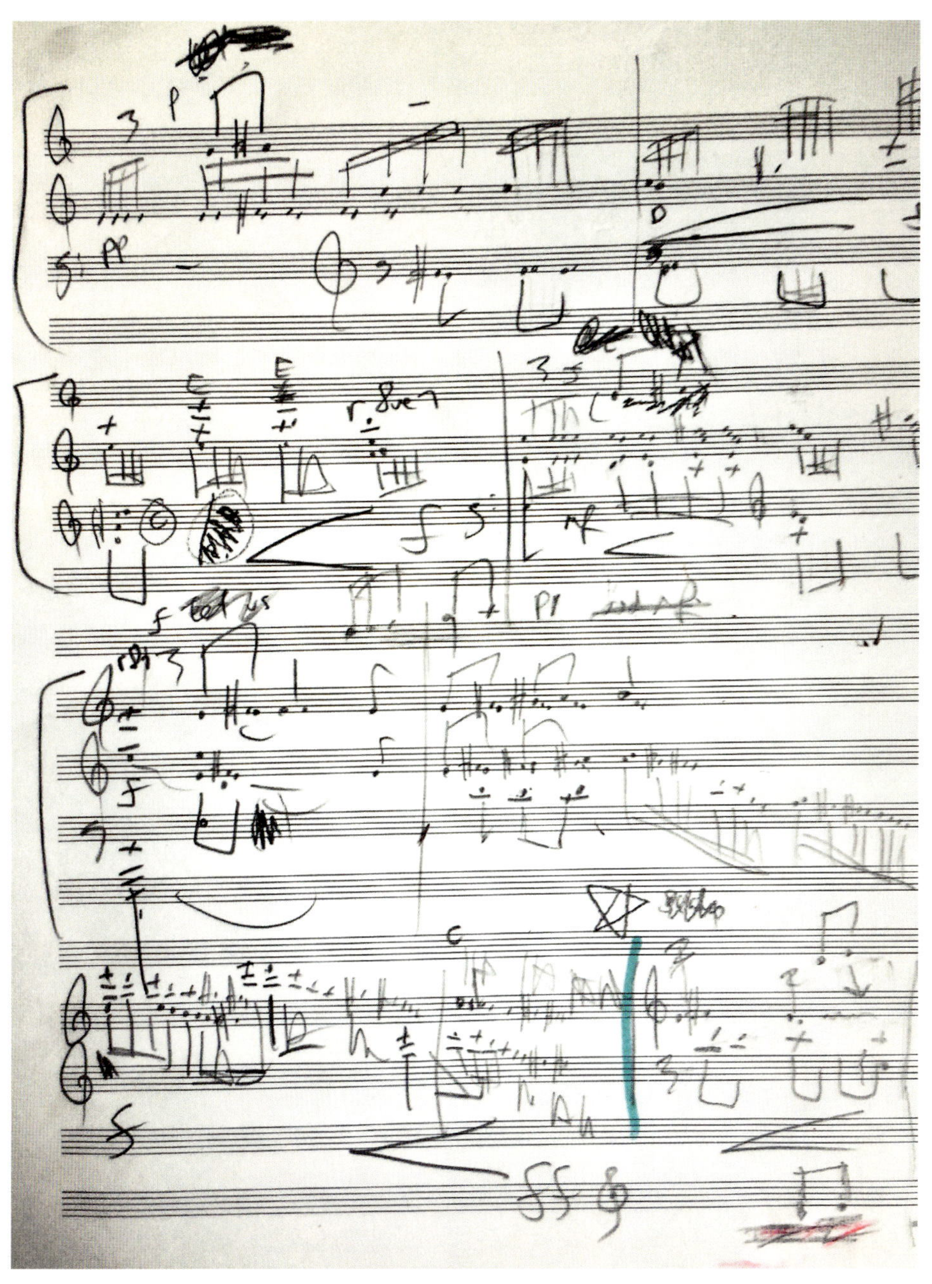

Manuscript, 2016
Pencil on paper
297 × 210 mm

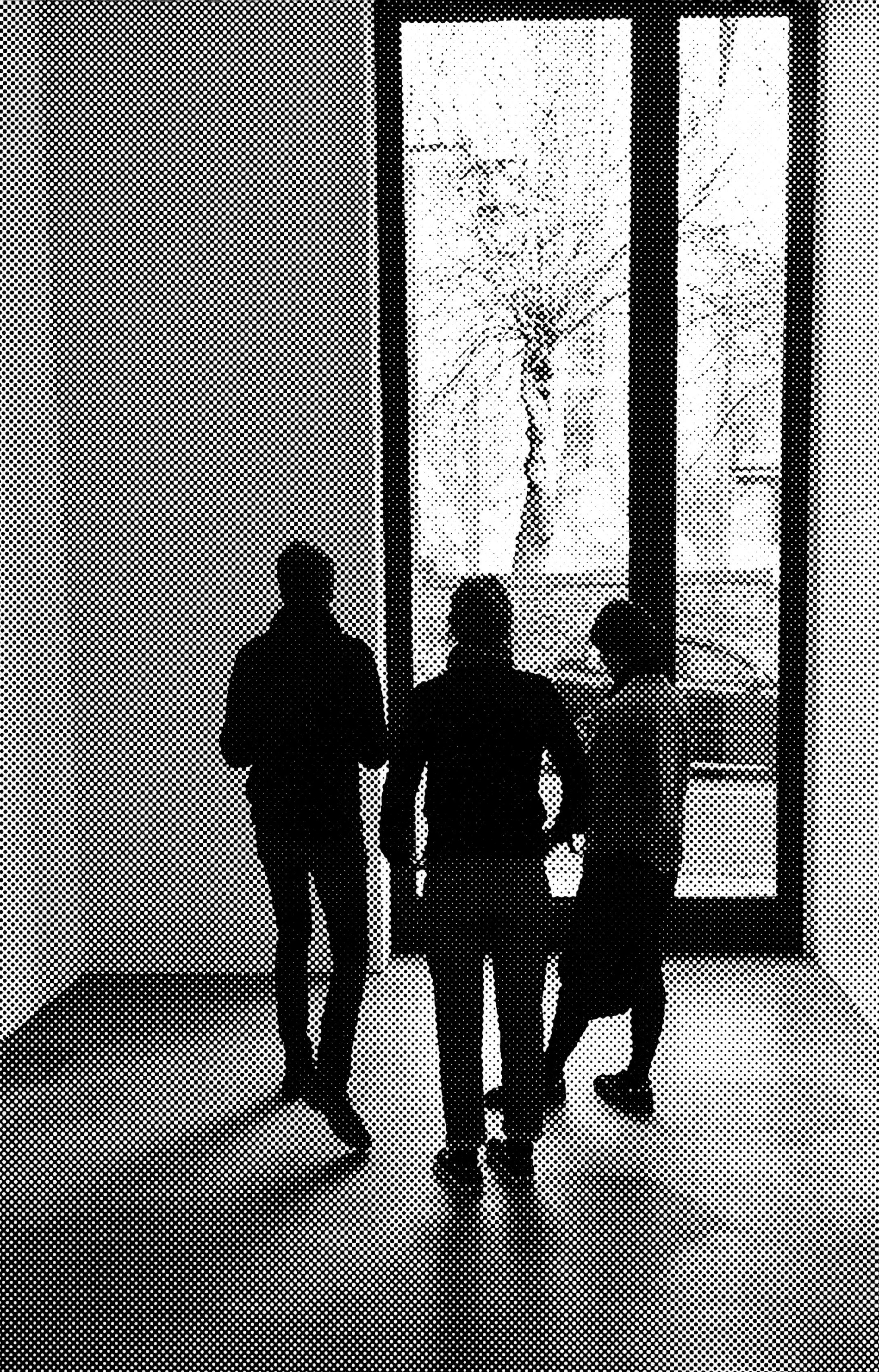

11/4–6/5/18

"I try to guard in my work the image of the morrow we left behind us in our memories and foregone aspirations and to remind us that the image of the world can be different."

Naum Gabo

A Turn With John Akomfrah On *Auto Da Fé*

Frederick Charles Moten

The greatest films are the ones that exhaust cinema, thereby taking us back into cinema's ground, its condition of possibility. That kind of cultivation is concerned neither with origin nor originality. It is a practice, rather, of incessant digging, the constant turning over of that ground, its continual erosion in the name of a fecundity that is both ancient and unprecedented. John Akomfrah isn't the first to induce mitosis in the cinematic frame and auditorium; it's just that with his audiovisual mobilization of the diptych cinema turns into a problematic of the turn rather, or in addition to, a problematic of the cut. Perspective blurs traversal as we descend, from frame to frame, into the screen's imaginal depths, point of entry become point of view's displacement. In Akomfrah's literalization of cinema's developmentally necessary deployment of fissure, as if in forensic reconstruction of a Muybridgean trace long since lost and only intermittently found, the cut allows the page to (re)turn, in ruptural loosening of fold, demanding and allowing an old practice of reading that requires the page's actual incision. Cinema cuts so that it can turn, but in its commitment to the break and its proliferation, has cinema ever really taken up the task of the break's inhabitation, that lingering, cursive enactment of version, torque, torsion, twist and turn? The turn in question, here, cannot be held in or by narrative. Though what emerges is a cinema of the open book, the verso, *el converso*, a cinema of the turn(ed); and even if there is a plot, or, deeper still, a plot's displacement; the image moves against the grain of *Bildung*, of picturing, that interplay of subjection and portraiture, and into a common place of turning out, the non-place, the murdered universality, of the refugee, the non-citizen, whose incapacity for narrative is best understood as a scarring of the story's flesh, an unmappable contour of the general wound, a disruptive complication of rounding, or worlding, a "microspherical transience." It's not an accident that arrival's ubiquitous imposition and impossibility, the terrible possibility of global positioning's extended genocidal displacement of indigeneity's essential itinerance, is Akomfrah's theme. All throughout his work it is as if the refusal of conquest's denial has become Dutch mastery's resistant animation. In *Auto Da Fé*, turn, in serrated intensification of the cut's sharpness, activates blur and thereby moves in complication of seriality, of development, as fugitivity's constantly unemancipated dissonance, its implied refusal of hard row's held tones. This exploration follows Akomfrah's engagement with Stuart Hall, the triptych of *The Unfinished Conversation*, its turning, its conversions, in the wake of *The Nine Muses* and its questioning instantiation of what Renée Green calls cinematic migration, the anticipatory counter force and counterfacticity of the forced, whose commitment to and dependence upon narrative's alternative has been Akomfrah's constant study since *Handsworth Songs*. These films combine to indicate the amazing discomposition of a massive and unprecedented water music, where the sea is doubly elemental in its roiling, its unearthing and re-earthing, its salvage and surrender in the tidal rhythm of washing up and washing out. This ubiquity of water – its cold, relentless curacy – is where the trace of crossing is brought to bear on the work of turning. Have we converted? Perhaps, then, we will have entered the history of the turn, the history of the co-presence of the turned page, of the two places at once, of post-cinematic, post-montagic, post-migratory blur, by the grace of an absolute nonlocality. Post-migratory because, at last, you can't get there from here, and no one ever really departs or arrives in this endless homelessness, this always being (re)moved. With the imperative to tell the story cinema mustn't extend the reign of narrative and portraiture. In this imperative cinema blurs the line supposedly dividing story and experiment. The cinema of the open book of the common place is a cinema of rub, feel, brush, within a general and generative amniosis. This conversive fluidity and (ab)solution is a poetics of the not in between, the cut's turn in binding, where we begin in refusal of beginning and end, immanently aesthetic in the more + less than one, inseparable in surf and rain, circling against time's seizure, fallen, damned, waiting, serving, hysterically malingering, feloniously sphering, walking, remaining, conversing, converting, burning, turning in this unbroken act of faith.

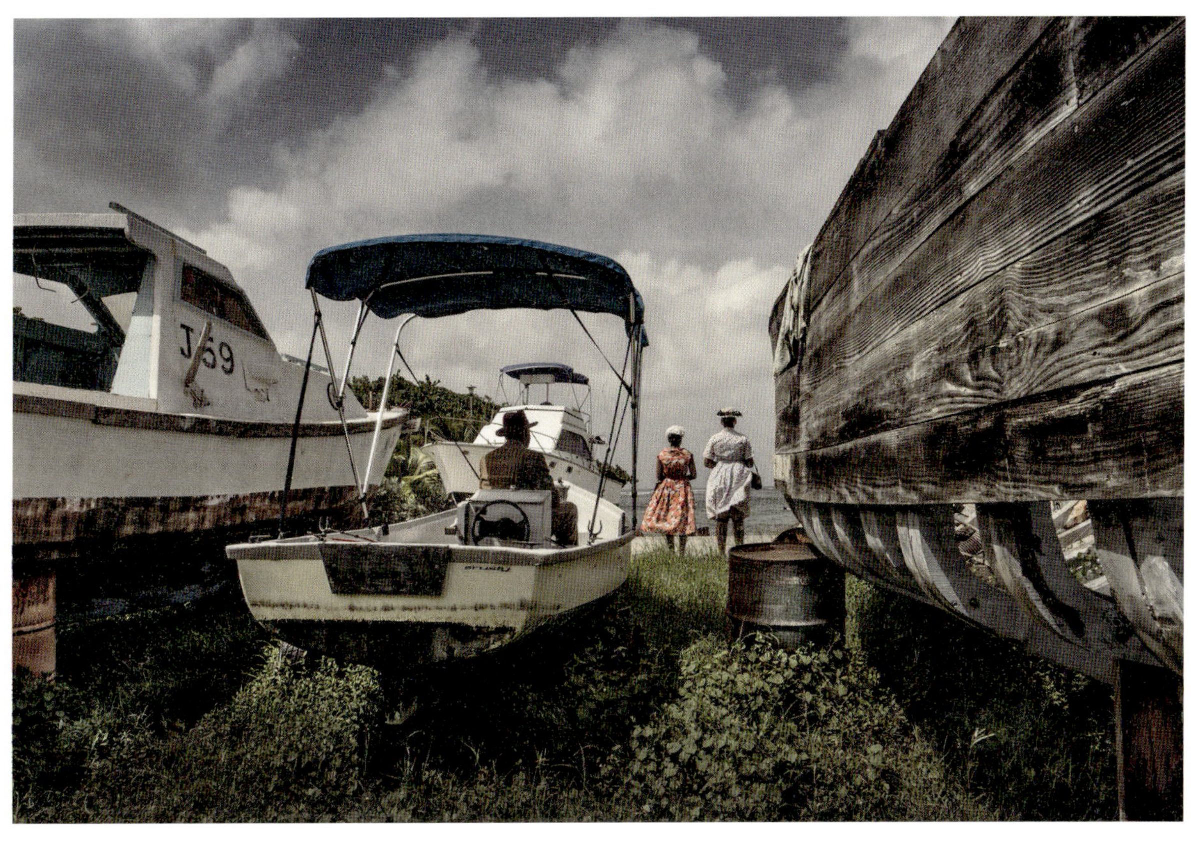

Untitled, 2016
C-print mounted on Dibond
1016 × 1524 mm

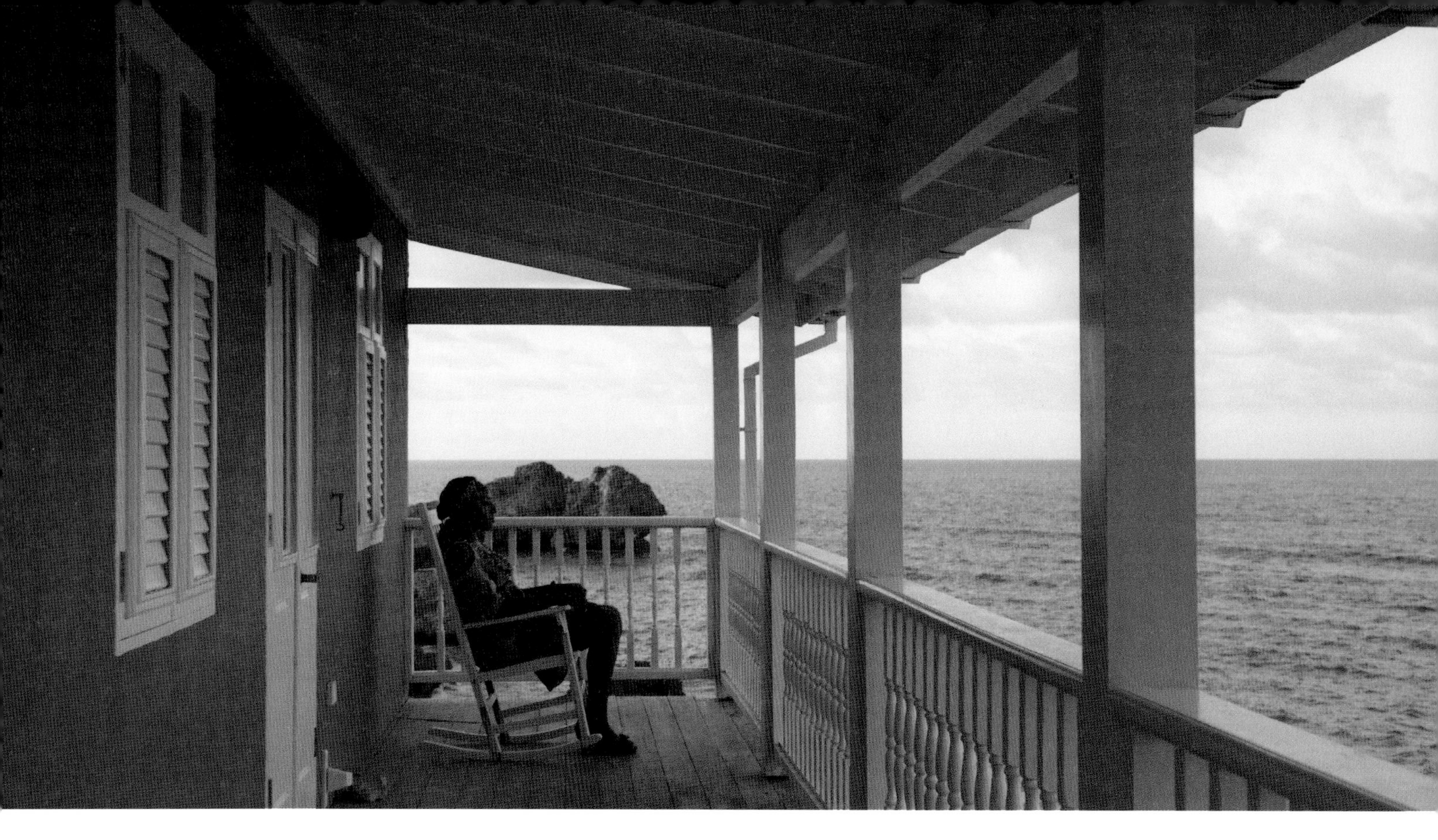

pp.104–109
Stills from *Auto Da Fé*, 2016

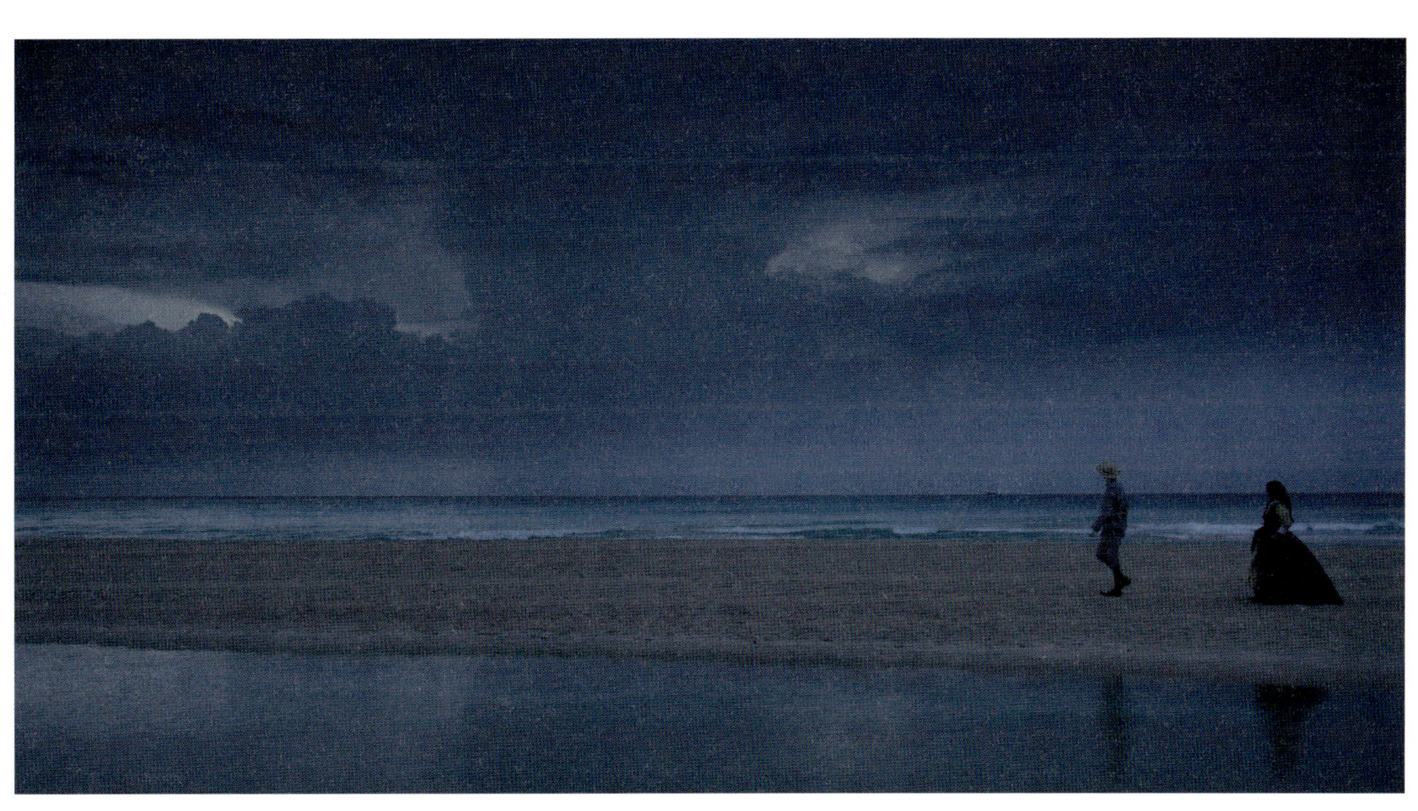

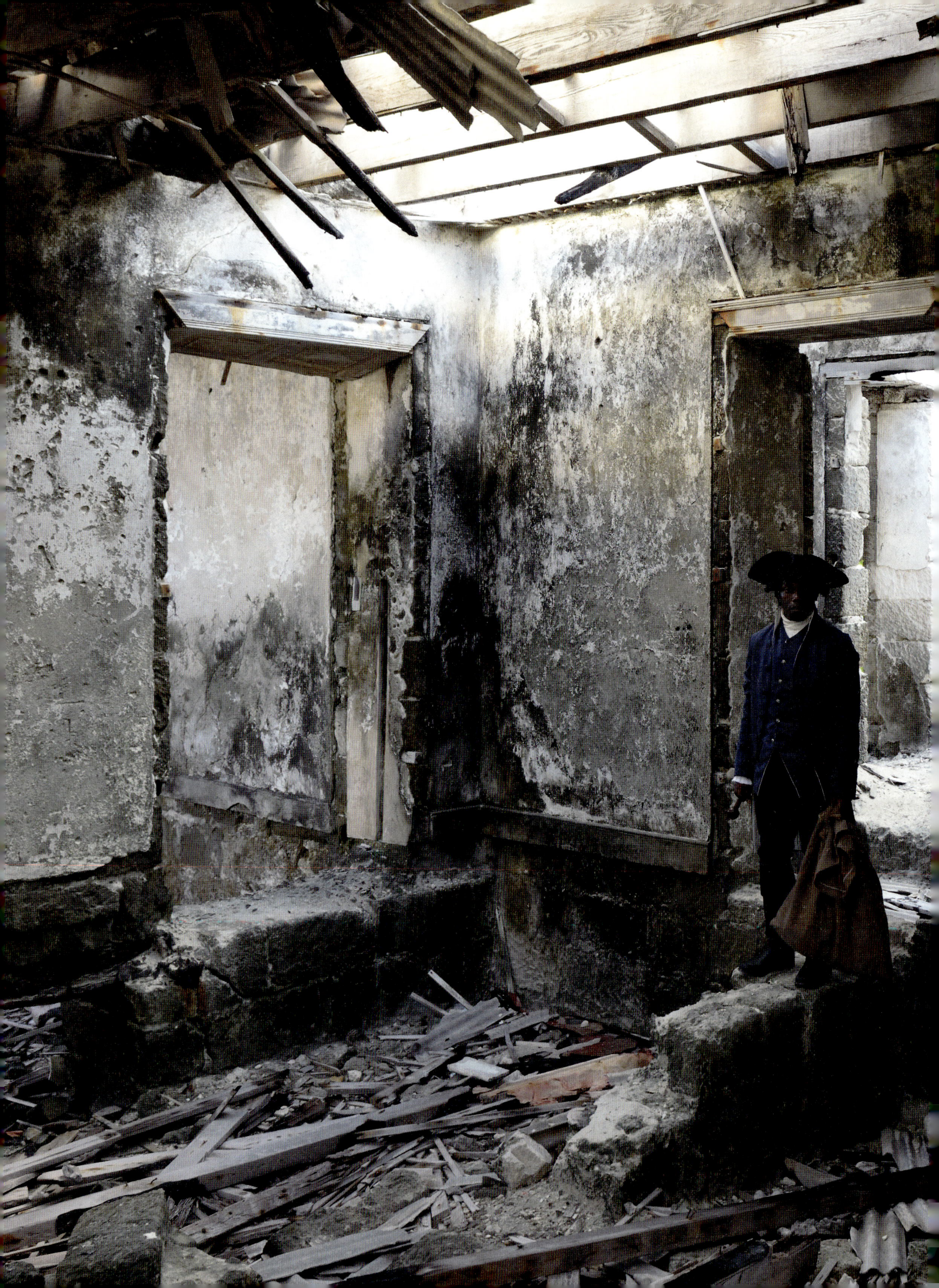

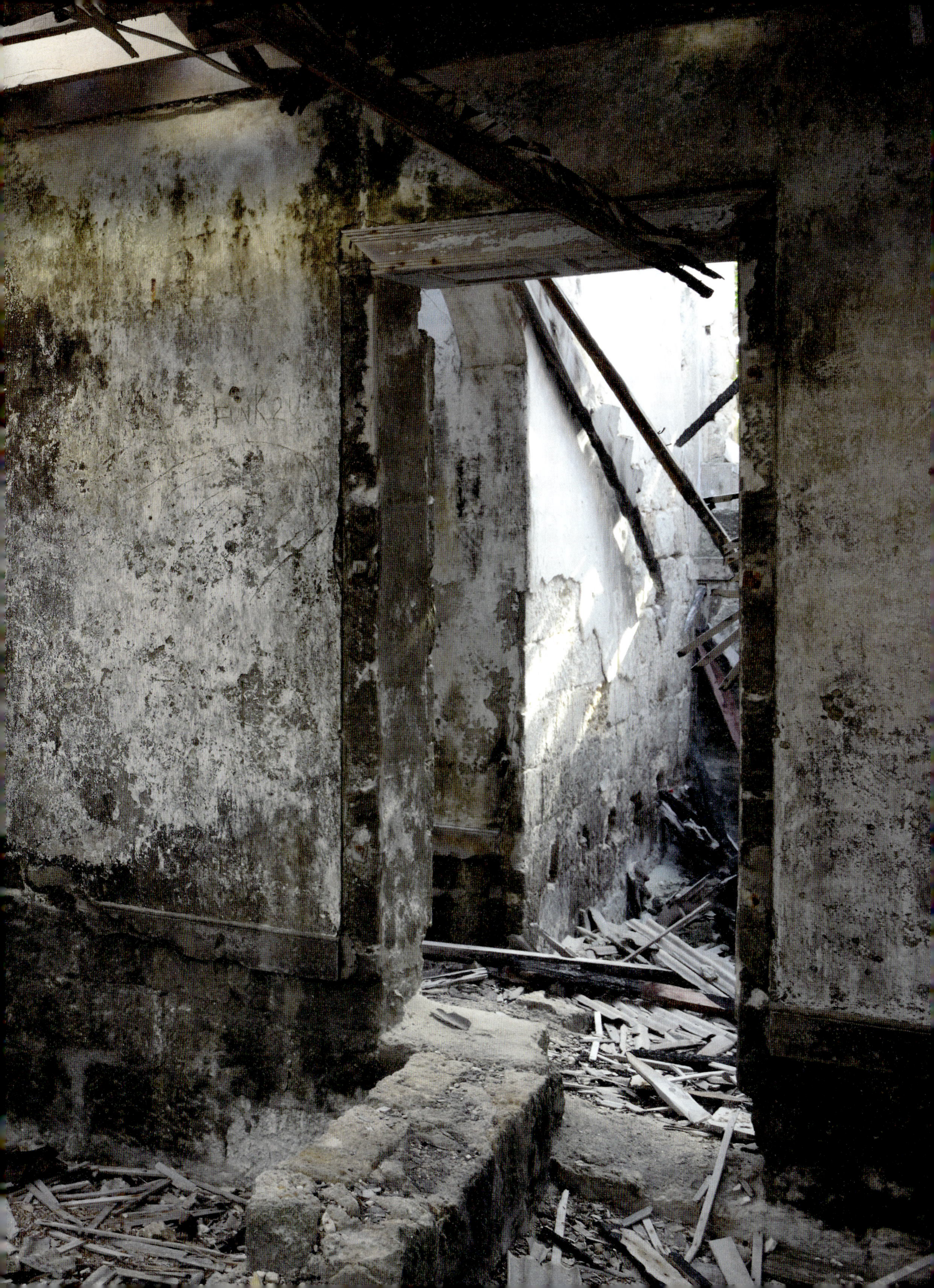

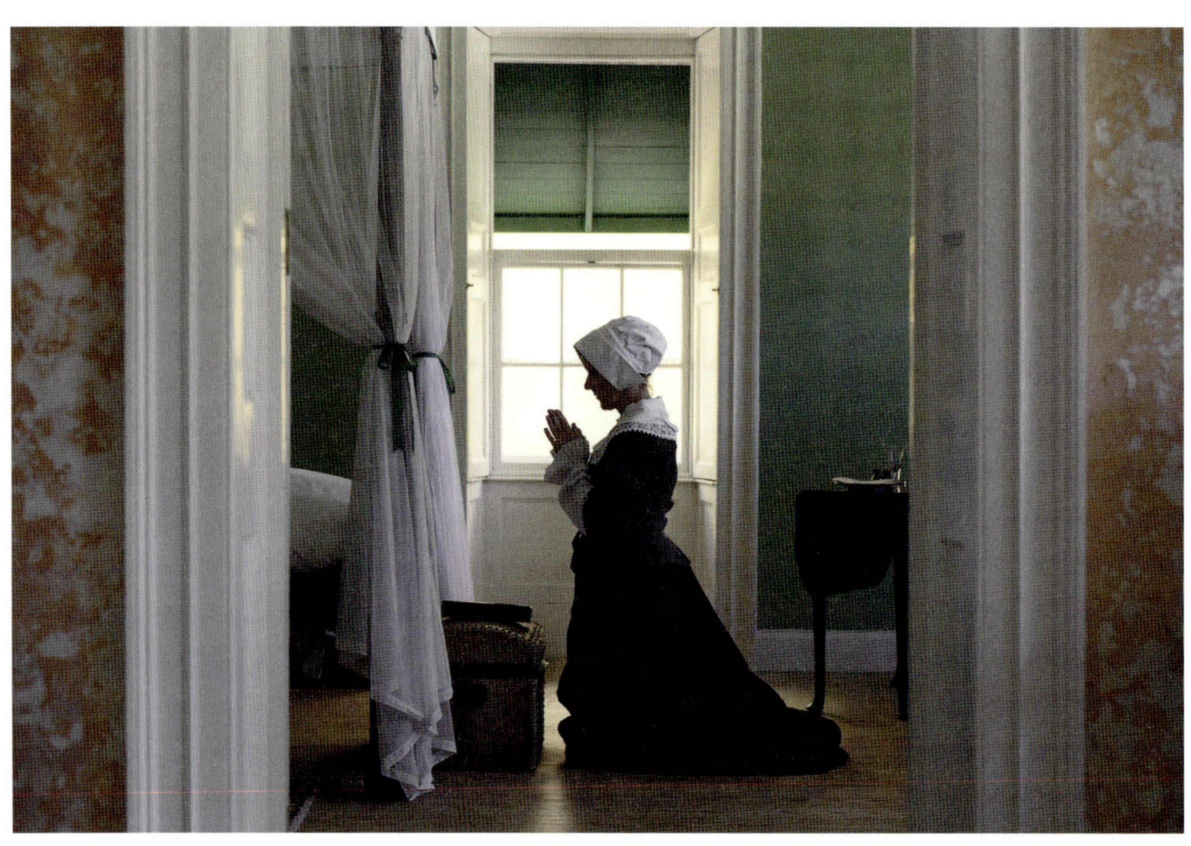

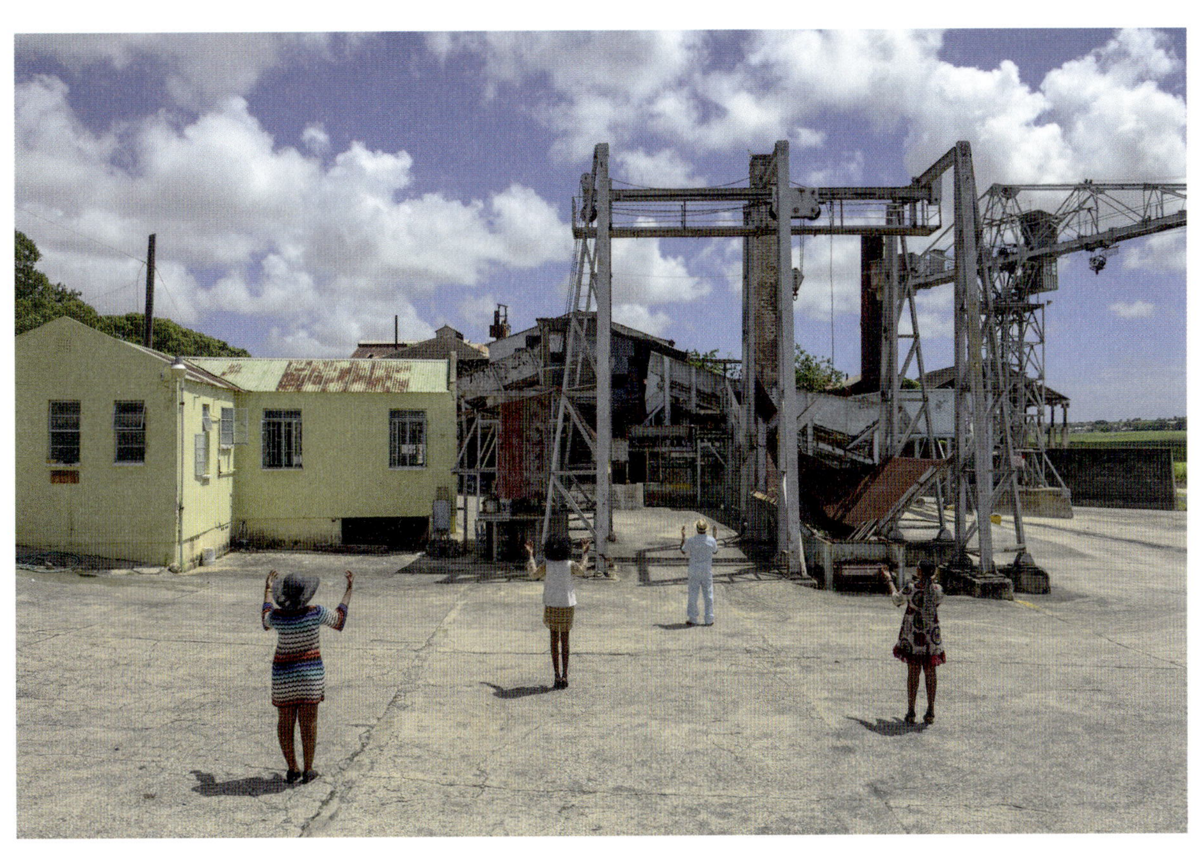

Caroline Walker in conversation with Andrew Nairne

Andrew Nairne
You are increasingly known for your richly detailed and enigmatic paintings of anonymous, often older women, in different environments. The locations or scenes, whether a luxury villa in California or a nail bar in London's Essex Road are often researched and selected by you and involve hiring and directing models. Your work has recently been described as "a complex exposé of gender inequalities and assumptions". You have also been praised for your highly skilled and sensuous use of colour and form.

Your new series *Home*, created for *Actions*, is a collaboration with the charity Women for Refugee Women and has involved meeting women in their temporary accommodation in London. In these paintings, the makeshift or impermanent is a recurring theme as the women are living in a state of limbo: sleeping on a mattress on the floor or a room on a hospital ward, with suitcases or bags nearby, and few personal possessions. To what extent are the new paintings a departure for you?

Caroline Walker
The collaboration with Women for Refugee Women has been transformative to my practice, first and foremost because it has led me to engage with the women I'm painting on a personal and specific level, to make paintings which take their individual lives as a starting point. Normally my process involves sourcing a location with particular aesthetic qualities and then finding models within a specific age range, body type and hair colour. Both the setting and the models become visual elements which I use to explore a particular theme within my wider interests of representing women's lives in contemporary society, imbuing these people and places with a narrative I have generated. In the case of *Home* I had neither met most of the women nor seen their accommodation before the visits, so the starting point for my response was coming entirely from the circumstances of these women's lives rather than anything dictated in advance by me.

Who they were as people, the environment they were in, the interior decoration of those spaces and the objects around them were all new to me. I had to think quickly about how I could use the tools I have developed for telling a story in painting to reflect in some way the experiences of these women, and my experience of meeting them. When I paint I pay much attention to which objects are included, what the lighting is, what kind of room it is and how it's decorated; all things that can tell you something about who you're looking at and why. I applied the same consideration to these works, thinking about the potential of particular objects within the paintings to tell the particular story of each woman.

When I started working in the studio with the photographs I had taken, I was concerned that the results might be slipping into the realm of traditional portraiture and that would be somehow less interesting. I suppose I'm not used to making paintings about specific 'real' people and I think that perhaps my concerns were more telling of my perception of what my subject matter is rather than how the end result actually appears. When I look around my studio there are lots of paintings which could be considered 'portraits' but because they're not paintings of real personalities, accounts of real lives, they seem to be different somehow.

I have been surprised at how much the resulting paintings in *Home* do still feel and look like my work. Like all of my work they depict women in contemporary environments, but the personal nature of these has given them an intimacy that is more intense and perhaps more questioning because they make visible the lives of people that society often wants to be invisible. I didn't want these paintings to be voyeuristic in the way that much of my work is, but I did still want there to be a slight distance from the subject which reflects my position as an outsider seeing only a snapshot of these women's lives at a particular moment.

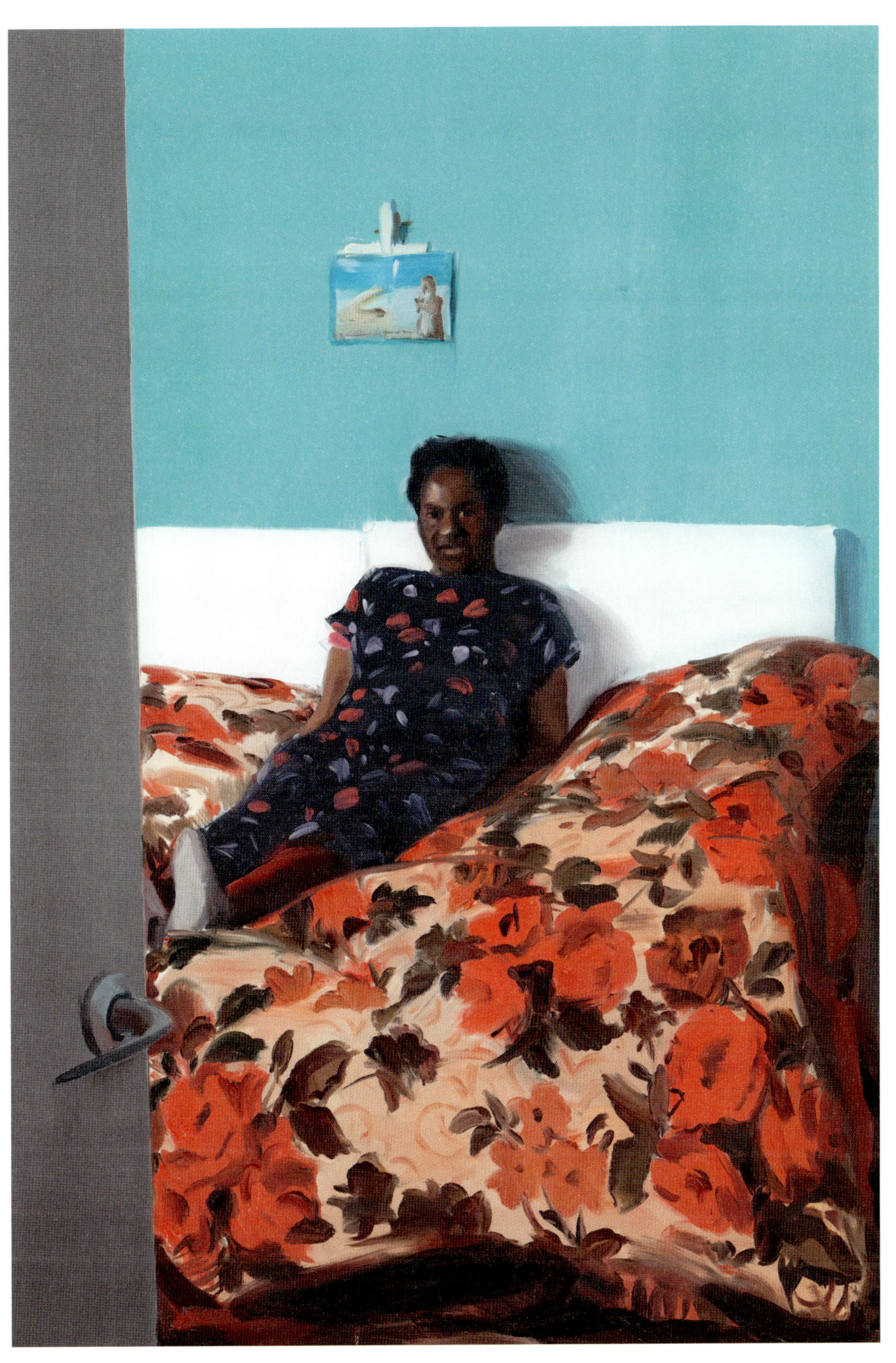

Joy, 11.30am, Hackney, 2017
Oil on linen
1480 × 1000 mm

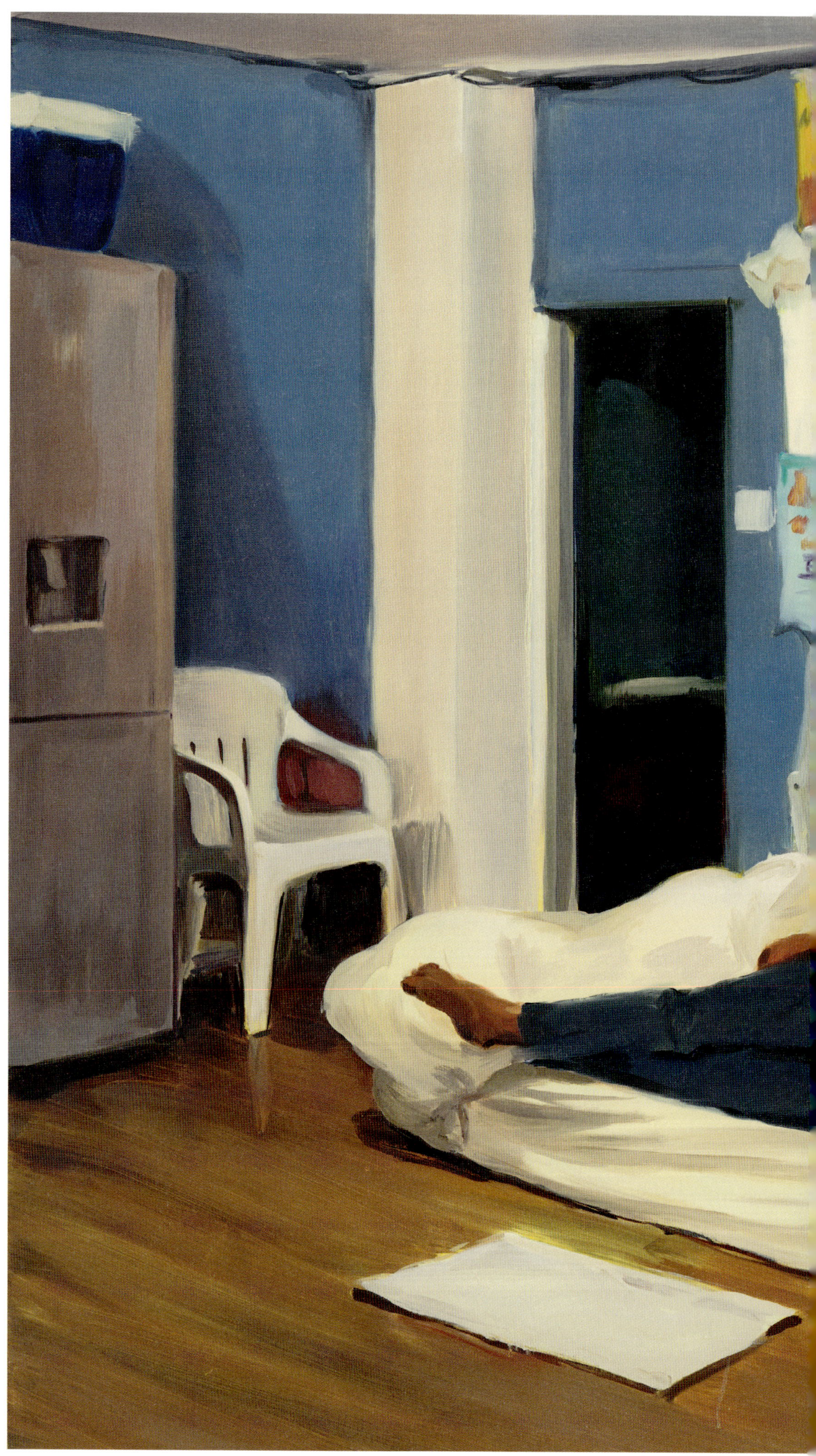

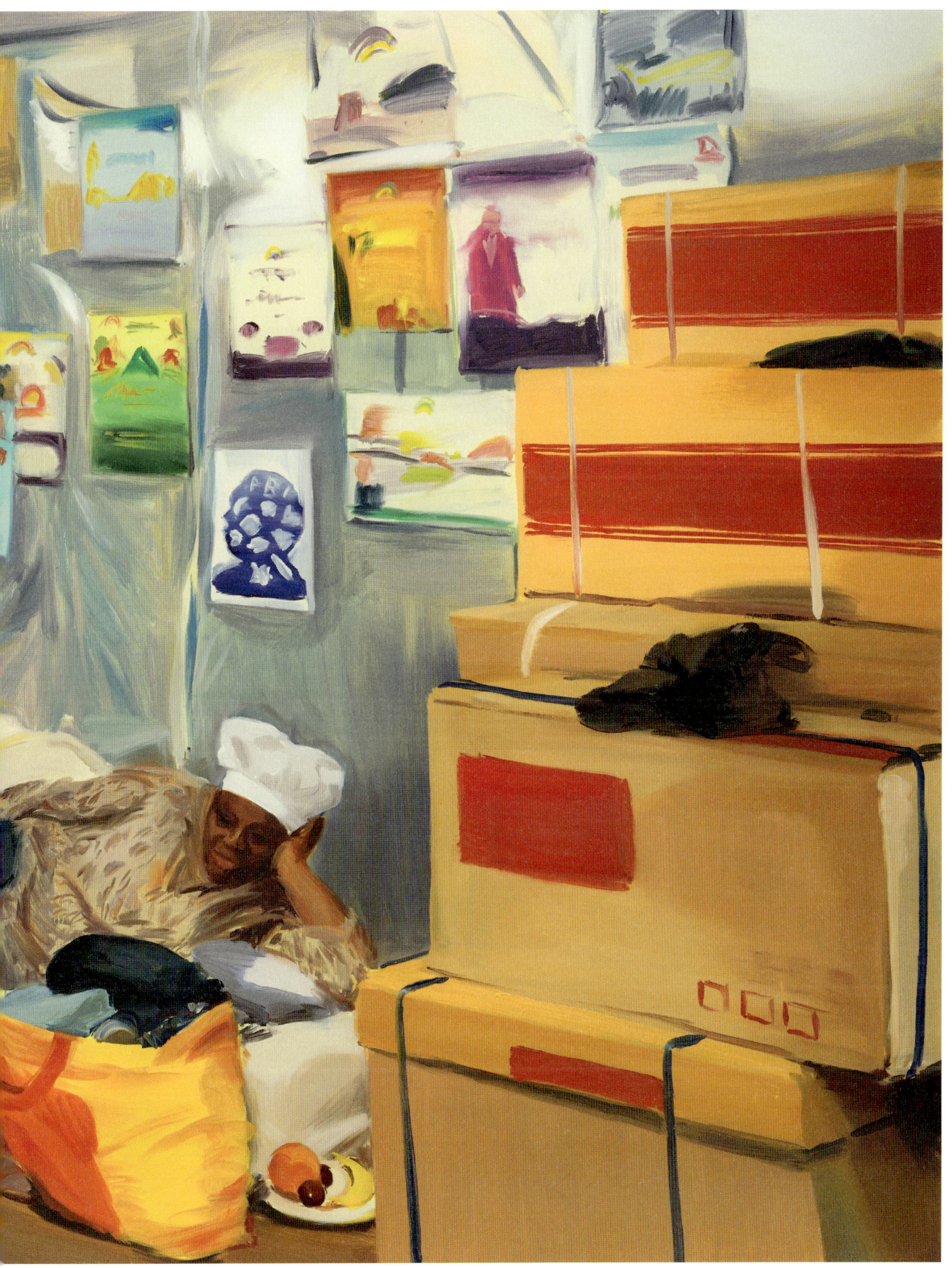

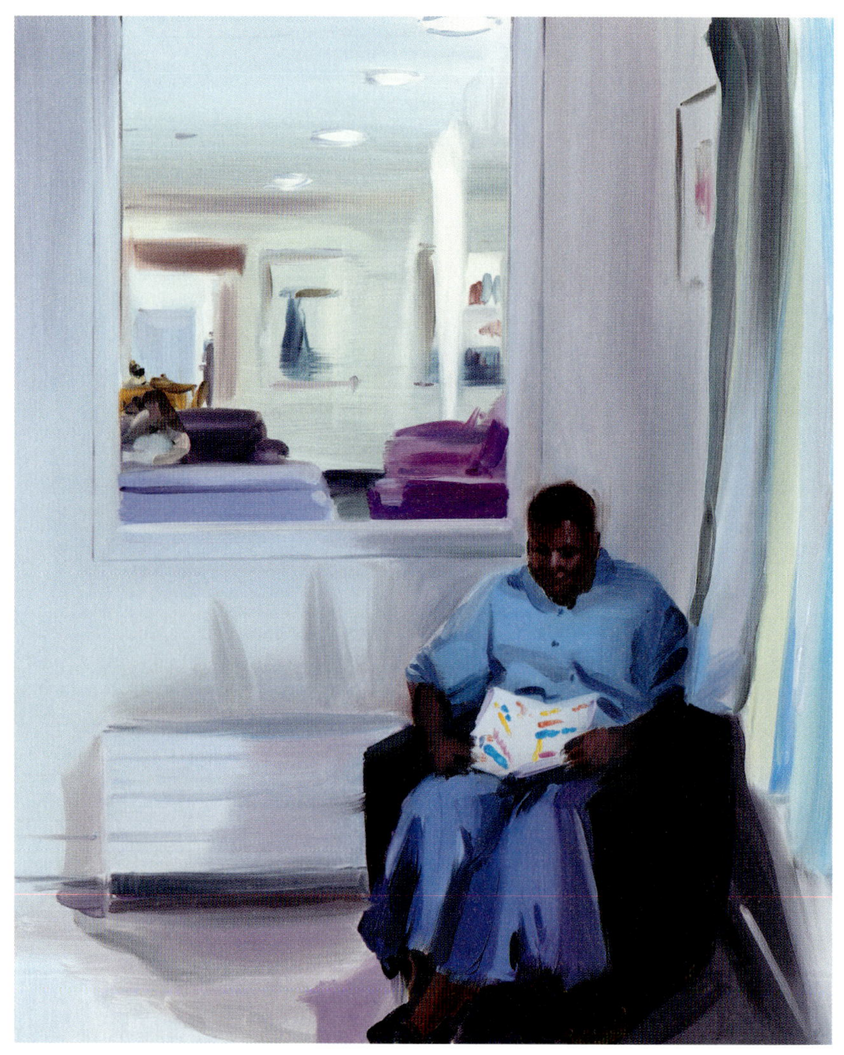

Previous spread
Abi, Midday, Brixton, 2017
Oil on linen
1760 × 2400 mm

Above
Consilia, 4.30pm, East London, 2017
Oil on board
550 × 450 mm

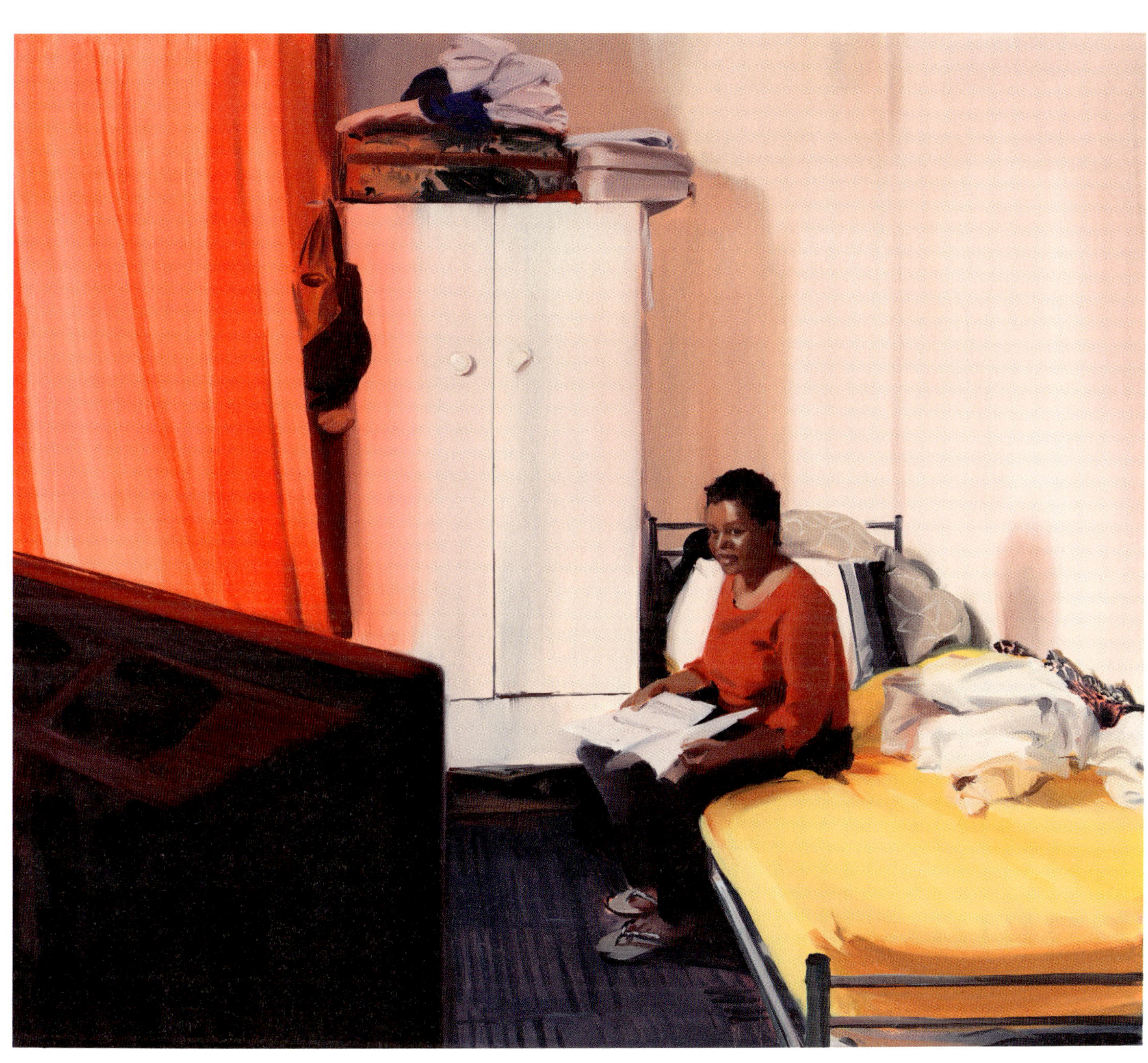

Tarh, 10.30am, Southall, 2017
Oil on linen
1750 × 2000 mm

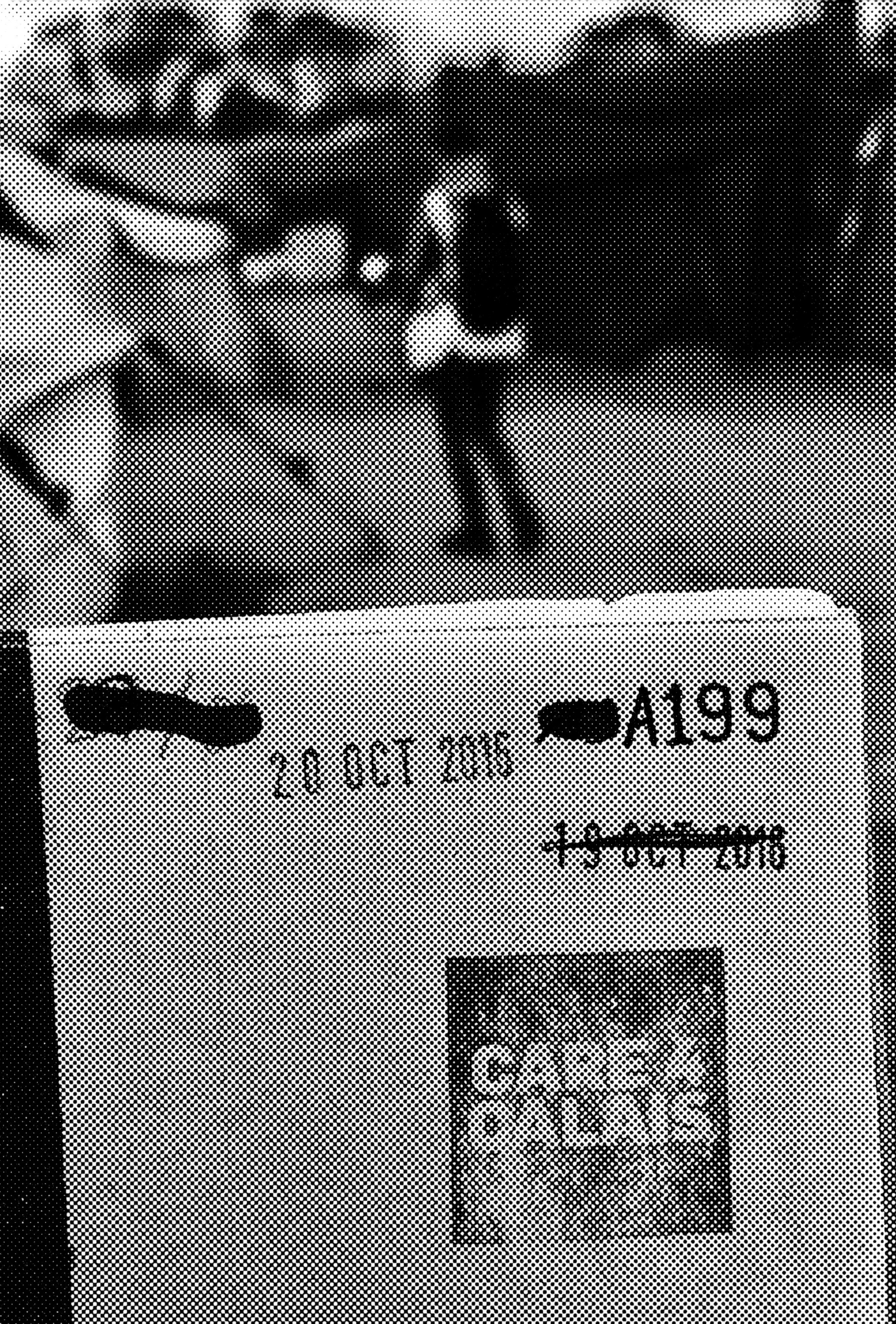
A199
20 OCT 2016
19 OCT 2016

“Looking back on the destiny of many works of art in their historical array, and having in view their relation to their own time and people as well as to posterity, I have come to the conclusion that a work of art, restricted to what the artist has put in it, is only a part of itself. It only attains full stature with what people and time make of it.”

Naum Gabo

An exchange of letters between Sarah Lowndes and Paul Goodwin

Dear PAUL,

It was good to meet you in London recently. I'm writing to you to explore further some of the ideas we talked about, in relation to the exhibition *Actions. The image of the world can be different*. As you know, the subtitle of the exhibition comes from letters exchanged between Naum Gabo and Herbert Read in 1944, which began with Gabo's letter in which he explained, "I try to guard in my work the image of the morrow we left behind us in our memories and foregone aspirations and to remind us that the image of the world can be different."[1] The ideas contained in that 1944 correspondence are the starting point for the *Actions* exhibition – which considers the purpose and relevance of art now.

As we discussed, *Actions* is an exhibition that features thirty-eight artists: the eldest, Naum Gabo, was born in 1890 while the youngest, Khadija Saye, was born in 1992. Apart from the wide historical sweep represented by the different generations of artists included in the exhibition, the artists are also of diverse nationalities: twenty-two of the artists were born in the United Kingdom, while the remaining sixteen were born in America, Bangladesh, Colombia, Cyprus, Ethiopia, France, Germany, Ghana, Guatemala, Russia, Serbia and Syria. In planning this book to accompany the exhibition, our thoughts have revolved around how best to consider the work of these thirty-eight artists. We wanted in particular, to take account of the social, political and artistic changes that had occurred in the last century and to discuss issues of translocality, post-colonialism, migration, the performative – with Kettle's Yard as the "restorative, homely yet life-changing" place where all these ideas meet.

I was very interested to read of your thoughts about the limitations of discourses around diversity – and what might happen when, for example, the artworks of Black-British artists are instead investigated in relationship to modernism. To return to one example that we briefly touched upon, how would such a discussion frame the events of John Akomfrah's life, which shaped his ongoing interest in themes of migration? Akomfrah left Ghana in 1961, and moved to London, the year before the *Commonwealth Immigration Act* (1962) restricted immigration to the UK. He later recalled, "Back in the 1960s and 1970s, it was suggested that people of colour had 'dubious' cultures which might taint Britain."[2] How would you situate the work of John Akomfrah within the framework of modernism – in particular, his film work *Auto Da Fé* (2016), which depicts a series of eight historical migrations over the last 400 years, starting with the little-known 1654 fleeing of Sephardic Jews from Catholic Brazil to Barbados?

When we met, we talked about the importance of challenging the Anglophone bias in discourse around art and design. In 1977, when Julie Mehretu was aged seven, her family fled Ethiopia, to settle in East Lansing, Michigan, where her father took up a teaching position at Michigan State University. She reflected, "Coming from this African background, you're the children of people who were there during decolonisation, when the world really fundamentally shifted and this other form of modernism emerged. Now we're all dislocated... and there's this constant negotiating of place, space, ideals, ideas."[3] I wondered if you could comment on how you would read Julie Mehretu's work within an expanded understanding of modernism, that takes account of post-colonialism?

Harold Offeh has written, "The fact that my body (black, male, queer, 40) operates as a particular cultural signifier is beyond my control. I am however invested in how my cultural identity is constructed and consumed. Its visibility is important to me, but it's never the whole story with regards to the work. Whether we make work that figures our body or cultural identity I think we should be all be concerned with the visibility or invisibility of our cultural identity. I find it deeply problematic that some cultural identities (white, male, straight, able) escape and actively allude these critical discourses."[4] Would you agree that discourses around diversity still tend to construct

"Others" (black, female, queer, disabled) without acknowledging the power relations that underpin such discussions – and how should this change?

You have written that "The actual work of black artists in terms of aesthetic and stylistic questions too often tend to be subsumed beneath 'external' or contextual issues such as 'race', diversity and cultural policy or indeed questions of nationalism in public discourse."[5] While this is certainly true, it can sometimes prove difficult to separate the consideration of the artist's work from the conditions of their life. For example, following Khadija Saye's tragic death in the Grenfell Tower fire, it is hard not to view her tintype photographs *Dwellings: in this space we breathe* (2017), through the lens of the perceived failure of provision, management and administration of social housing in this country.[6] Does thinking about Khadija Saye's work in this way rob her photographs of their "aesthetic autonomy" – or is it possible that such contextual considerations could imbue her work with even greater power?

We talked previously about how certain art forms, notably minimalism and abstraction, could be seen to transcend cultural reference points – to provide a phenomenological or transcendent experience for audiences. We discussed how the repetitive patterns and vibrant colours in Rana Begum's work are often discussed in relationship to her background, as Begum and her family left Bangladesh in 1985 to settle in St Albans in the United Kingdom, when the artist was aged eight. Begum has previously commented, "We grew up on a street where there was a lot of racism but my dad never segregated us. We were brought up to not see any kind of difference between anyone whether it's colour, religion, politics or culture. I think that's probably where Minimalism allowed me to feel that same thing... It used forms and colours that were recognised by anyone."[7] Does this idea of Minimalism as a lingua franca interest you?

While Kettle's Yard creator Jim Ede came from a position of some privilege, being privately educated, white and male, his unpublished writings reveal he may have been a closeted homosexual. Ede also suffered from health issues relating to shellshock[8] he sustained during WWI. We talked, when we met, about Ede's hospitality and his conception of Kettle's Yard as 'a living place where works of art could be enjoyed... where young people could be at home unhampered by the greater austerity of the museum or public art gallery.'[9] Would you agree that the underlying motivation of generosity that engendered (and still sustains) Kettle's Yard serves as a corrective to what Herbert Read, in his letter to Naum Gabo, identified as "the secret of the failure of our civilization"[10]: communication breakdown between people? And, could you say more about your idea of Kettle's Yard as a "dissident space" that operates differently from a conventional museum or art gallery?

We also talked about how the museum might provide a space for educational and discursive work, in which the curator acts collaboratively, with artists and audiences, to develop gradual, long-term projects. We also touched upon the legacy of Stuart Hall, who wrote, "We should perhaps learn to think of meaning less in terms of 'accuracy' and 'truth' and more in terms of effective exchange – a process of translation which facilitates cultural communication while always recognising the persistence of difference and power between different 'speakers' within the same cultural circuit."[11] Kettle's Yard has made a marked commitment to processes of "effective exchange" through the Open House residencies and outreach work, to build relationships with communities that might not feel that Kettle's Yard is available and accessible to them. What do you consider the most effective ways that museums today can facilitate cultural communication?

Yours sincerely,

SARAH.

Dear SARAH,

Thank you for your letter and kind invitation to respond to the some of the important and challenging questions that the exhibition *Actions. The image of the world can be different* raises about the practices of artists in these turbulent times. In my opinion, this exhibition and the questions it raises are just the kind of artistic intervention we need to help us to think through art's place in the ongoing, multiple crises that are currently engulfing the world. These crises range from the rise of religious and political fundamentalisms spawning death cults and terrorist atrocities, to the widening economic and social inequalities that are being produced under conditions of global neoliberal capitalism and the closing of borders and minds to unprecedented waves of human migration fuelled in part by the proliferation of never-ending military conflicts and wars. In this frightening context, I wholeheartedly concur with this exhibition's gambit of returning to the exchange of letters between Naum Gabo and Herbert Read for several reasons. First because the exchange took place during world-historical convulsions of global conflict, war and economic breakdown, conditions that while more extreme nevertheless have some parallels to our current condition. Second, the exchange contains important statements, particularly by Gabo, about how artists can position themselves in the wider culture and self-reflect on their methods and philosophies at a time of significant existential threats to society. Finally, the exchange addresses the problem of the communication of art's meanings in the face of hostility and miscomprehension by 'the masses'. It seems to me that these problematics are supremely relevant to the current predicament that all artists find themselves in.

However, in response to the specific questions you pose in your letter about artists in the exhibition from diasporic or migration backgrounds, I want to hone in on an aspect of the exchange that for me resonates very strongly with many of the curatorial and research projects I have been engaged in over the past decade or so. In his letter Gabo addresses the issue of how to respond as an artist to questions about the nature and meaning of his work, particularly in relation to its abstract nature and how it contributes to "society in general, and to our time in particular?"[12] Gabo's response is modest but clear:

"I am afraid that my ultimate answer will always lie in the work itself..."[13]

This simple understatement, part of a long tradition of artists pointing to the work itself as the crucial entry point for interpretation of artworks, struck a chord with me in my observations about the predicament that many black and non-western artists face in the exhibitionary complex of western museums and art galleries. In the curation of these artists work there is often an emphasis on their ethnicity, biography and social context to the detriment of a focus on the art they produce and the strategies they deploy to produce it.

In some ways, my own practice in exhibitions such *Migrations: Journeys Into British Art* at Tate Britain in 2012[14] – where I presented works by artists such as Keith Piper, Sonia Boyce, Donald Rodney, Rasheed Araeen and Mona Hatoum within the wider context of the theme of migration in British art – perhaps exemplifies part of the problem of the way in which black artists' works have been curated and written about over the past half century. Overdetermined and simplistic narratives around 'diversity', 'identity' and 'race' are frequently foregrounded as a given in relation to the work of these artists, even in cases where these issues are problematized by the artist or even absent from the work itself. There is often an over-contextualization and under-consideration of the work that blights discussion about black artists practices. For me it is clear that extrinsic discourses of 'diversity' are no longer able to effectively describe or account for the complexity of these artist's practices. Gabo's statement transposed into this specific context can thus speak to this dilemma and the urgency with which this problem needs to be confronted.

As a concrete recent example from my practice please allow me to briefly describe an experiment that I attempted in the exhibition I curated with Hansi Momodu-Gordon called *Untitled: Art on the conditions of our time* at New Art Exchange, Nottingham from January to March 2017.

The exhibition was a survey of current practices by twelve British artists with links to Africa and its diaspora. The curatorial move we made concerned the way in which we attempted to place the actual artworks and creative process at the *centre* of the project rather than as a *supplement* to an overarching grand curatorial thesis or argument about 'race' or diversity. This model may be seen as a kind of 'uncurating'. In the 'uncurating' model the curatorial discourse surrounding the work is radically pared down or eliminated to allow the audience to experience the work as close as possible to the way the artist intended it to be presented – at least as an entry point – in order to allow new meanings and dialogues about the work to emerge. *UNTITLED* adopted an open-ended curatorial model, where the focus was on the interplay between the artworks unmediated by a singular theme, opening up potentially new pathways for thinking about art by African diaspora artists displacing a fixed curatorial narrative, particularly narratives based around preset notions of 'diversity' or even 'black art'. The partially undefined, open nature of the exhibition made it a catalyst for the public to gain understanding of how a group of African diaspora artists were making sense of our contemporary moment, whilst also looking ahead to the future.

Having opened up this problematic in relation to Gabo's views on art that have influenced the *Actions* exhibition I now want to address the important questions that you posed in your letter about a number of artists with the above considerations very much in mind. I found your framing of these questions about some of the artists in the exhibition to be very much in accord with my own thinking especially where you reiterated the ambition of the show to investigate issues around "...translocality, postcolonialism, migration, the perfomative...". I would argue that these terms are part of an evolving language or lexicon that artists from diaspora backgrounds have been and are currently exploring in their work. I very much agree with the critic and theorist Irit Rogof in her view that we have moved on from working from "inherited knowledges" to working from the conditions of our lives such as the ones you have described, as the impetus to artistic research and production.[15] For me this means models of art criticism and curation need to significantly change and address the specificities of the kinds of conditions you described in relation to the works produced by these artists.

To read the works of John Akomfrah and Julie Mehretu in relation to modernism for example might mean looking at how those works articulate conditions of translocality and migration by working both within and against modernist tropes and strategies. In Akomfrah's *Auto Da Fé* I find it fascinating the way he extracts the maximum from use of the classic (literary) epic form while juxtaposing tableaux imagery and narratives of migration drawn from multiple 'localities' over time (Brazil, Barbados etc.) using the very modernist trope of bricolage. The effect of these multiple and seemingly contradictory spatio-temporal strategies effectively historicises the apparently 'contemporary' condition of the translocal enabling the viewer to better understand the historical continuities and breaks in the ways migration shapes the 'local'.

You asked me to consider Julie Mehretu's work in relation to "an expanded understanding of Modernism, that takes account of post-colonialism". It's interesting to think about this question in relation to her seminal work *Mogamma: A Painting in Four Parts* (2012) which in some senses is similar in ambition to Akomfrah's *Auto Da Fé* in its amalgam of epic scale and elements of modernist techniques such as abstraction. The painting brings post-colonial sites of uprising such as Tahrir Square (Mogamma is the name of Cairo's main government building) into relation with other sites of protest across time and space including Tiananmen Square, Place de le Bastille and Zuccotti Park in New York where the Occupy movement evolved. Although there are glimpses of recognisable places and sites in the work these fleeting images are overlain and merged with myriad marks, lines and shapes making it impossible for the viewer to have a coherent 'total' view. Mehretu has often spoken of this visual complexity as opening up a 'third space' between what's happening on the canvas in the paintings themselves and the viewer's space of vision of the works which itself evolves the longer one sits with the paintings. It is arguably in this 'third space' where dislocation and the constant need to negotiate 'place, space, ideals, ideas', evoke the 'other modernisms' that are required in order for the viewer to visually navigate in an age of migration and constant flux.

The questions you asked around the work of Harold Offeh and Khadija Saye relate to crucial issues of how dominant power structures in the art world and at large can often obscure and deny the artistic integrity of works by these artists. In Offeh's case I would argue that it is not just 'cultural diversity' that constructs 'others' while concealing the power relations underpinning how it relates to these same 'others'. As Offeh actually hints at in the quote you cited there is a question of 'whiteness' and white privilege that often dares not speak its name while at the same time using its structural invisibility to maintain control and order. I would again refer to Gabo's call to focus on the work itself for ways to undo the invisibility of whiteness and therefore render it less powerful. An early video and performance work by Offeh opened up a potential pathway to address this. In *Four Ways to Feel Amazing* (2002) Offeh plays an everyman figure attempting to construct a better life through a four-step plan drawing on the language of self-help magazines and manuals. Although this work makes no overt reference to 'race' it could be argued that the work subtly evokes the possibility of blackness achieving the same conditions of universality within western culture as a generic form of whiteness; or fail while trying. The understatement and lack of didacticism in the work can provide some inspirational pointers for artists looking to deconstruct hegemonic constructions of identity in the sphere of the everyday.

It is perhaps tempting but wrong in my view to read Khadija Saye's powerful photographic series *Dwellings: in this space we breathe* directly in relation to the systemic failures of social housing identified after the Grenfell fire. It is not so much that thinking about her work in this way robs the work of its aesthetic autonomy. This would be to return to unproductive formalist arguments about the autonomy of the artwork that have been rehearsed and debunked many years ago. However, I would argue that the problem with such arguments is that they can reduce and instrumentalise the work to narrow interpretations based on political logics that impede multiple other readings arguably present in the work itself. In *Dwellings* concerns around how the artist engages with her long held interests in traditional Gambian spiritual practices and the deep-rooted urge to find solace within a higher power are effectively muted by readings that seek to tie the work uniquely to the politics around the terrible conditions of the artist's demise.

Your question about my interest in minimalism as a lingua franca in relation to the colour-saturated installations, sculptures and works on paper by Rana Begum relates to much of my current concerns and research. I'm really intrigued by the way that some artists are revisiting recent art historical movements much as Minimalism not so much as a form of accepted 'inherited knowledge' which they merely regurgitate and reproduce. I believe they are often responding to the specific conditions in which they live and finding new solutions that speak to the demands of the present. In Begum's *No. 700 Reflectors* (2016) an installation of 30,000 coloured and striped reflectors in a square near Kings Cross in London the artist opens up questions about the nature of public space and how cities are being reshaped. The question she seems to be asking is: in whose image is the city being reshaped?

So finally, I want to close with a response to your final questions that relate to the space where the artistic dialogue in *Actions* takes place: in Kettle's Yard. You asked me first about my comment that Kettle's Yard is a "dissident space" and second how can museums today facilitate "cultural communication". In my view, the first question can help to answer the second one. Museums today are under assault in my opinion from hostile, homogenising forces of neoliberal globalisation and commodification which are transforming the way they relate to audiences. There is a growing conformism in museum and gallery spaces that seeks to turn visitors into consumers and provide a flattened series of spectacular 'experiences'. At the same time, many museums are showing the same artists in the same stale white cube gallery spaces. Kettle's Yard through the pioneering work of Jim Ede has always cultivated a very non-conformist and singular, if at times eccentric vision, of what a gallery and a collection could be. The singularity of the spaces – decidedly non-white cube – and the often marginal, 'under the radar' location of Kettle's Yard within the social ecology of the University of Cambridge has arguably made it a 'dissident space' where 'minor' discourses and practices can settle. Kettle's Yard's perceived anachronism, singular vision and focus on the materiality of the domestic setting as a legitimate space to view and contemplate works of art does, it seems to me, provide a 'safe space' in which Gabo's vision of thinking about how the "image of the world can be different" can flourish away from the conformism of many contemporary museums.

Yours sincerely,

PAUL.

[1] "An Exchange of Letters Between Naum Gabo and Herbert Read", *Horizon*, vol. X, No. 53 (July 1944).

[2] Hannah Ellis-Petersen, "John Akomfrah: 'I haven't destroyed this country. There's no reason other immigrants would'", *The Guardian*, 7 January 2016. https://www.theguardian.com/artanddesign/2016/jan/07/john-akomfrah-vertical-sea-arnolfini-bristol-lisson-gallery-london-migration

[3] Jason Farago, "Julie Mehretu paints chaos with chaos – from Tahrir Square to Zuccotti Park", *The Guardian*, 20 June 2013. https://www.theguardian.com/artanddesign/2013/jun/20/painting-art

[4] Harold Offeh, Interview with Andrew Nairne, October 2017.

[5] Jelle Bouwhuis and Paul Goodwin, "A Conversation on the Work of Iris Kensmil", *Iris Kensmil* (Breda, NL: Club Solo, 2015), p. 2.

[6] Harriet Sherwood, "Grenfell Tower: local people should be on inquiry panel, bishop says", *The Guardian*, 4 August 2017. https://www.theguardian.com/uk-news/2017/aug/04/grenfell-tower-consultation-period-deadline-approaches

[7] Harriet Fitch Little, "Rana Begum on form, colour and light", *Financial Times*, p.17 March 2017. https://www.ft.com/content/2f5a18ac-fe7f-11e6-8d8e-a5e3738f9ae4

[8] There are marked similarities between the 'shellshock' suffered by First World War veterans, the 'combat fatigue' or 'gross-stress reaction' manifested in Second World War troops and the syndrome known post-Vietnam War as Post-Traumatic Stress Disorder (PTSD), which was first included in the third, 1980 edition of *The Diagnostic and Statistical Manual of Mental Disorders* (DSM). Early analysis of shellshock and its symptoms can be found in Elliot Smith and T.H. Pear, *Shell-Shock and Its Lessons* (London: Longmans Green, 1917) and W.H.R. Rivers, *Instinct and the Unconscious: A contribution to a Biolological Theory of the Psycho-Neuroses* (Cambridge: Cambridge University Press, 1922).

[9] "History", Kettle's Yard. http://www.kettlesyard.co.uk/collection/history/

[10] "An Exchange of Letters Between Naum Gabo and Herbert Read".

[11] Stuart Hall, "Introduction", *Representation* (1997), second edition, Stuart Hall, Jessica Evans and Sean Nixon, eds. (Sage: London, 2013), xxvi.

[12] "An Exchange of Letters Between Naum Gabo and Herbert Read".

[13] *Ibid*

[14] *Migrations: Journeys into British Art*, Tate Britain, 31 January–12 August 2012. Paul Goodwin was one of six co-curators on this exhibition where he curated the section "New Diasporic Voices" with the artists mentioned.

[15] See Irit Rogoff lecture at the University of the Fine Arts Hamburg, 22 November 2016. Retrieved from http://www.aesthetikendesvirtuellen.de/en/events/irit-rogoff-the-way-we-work-now

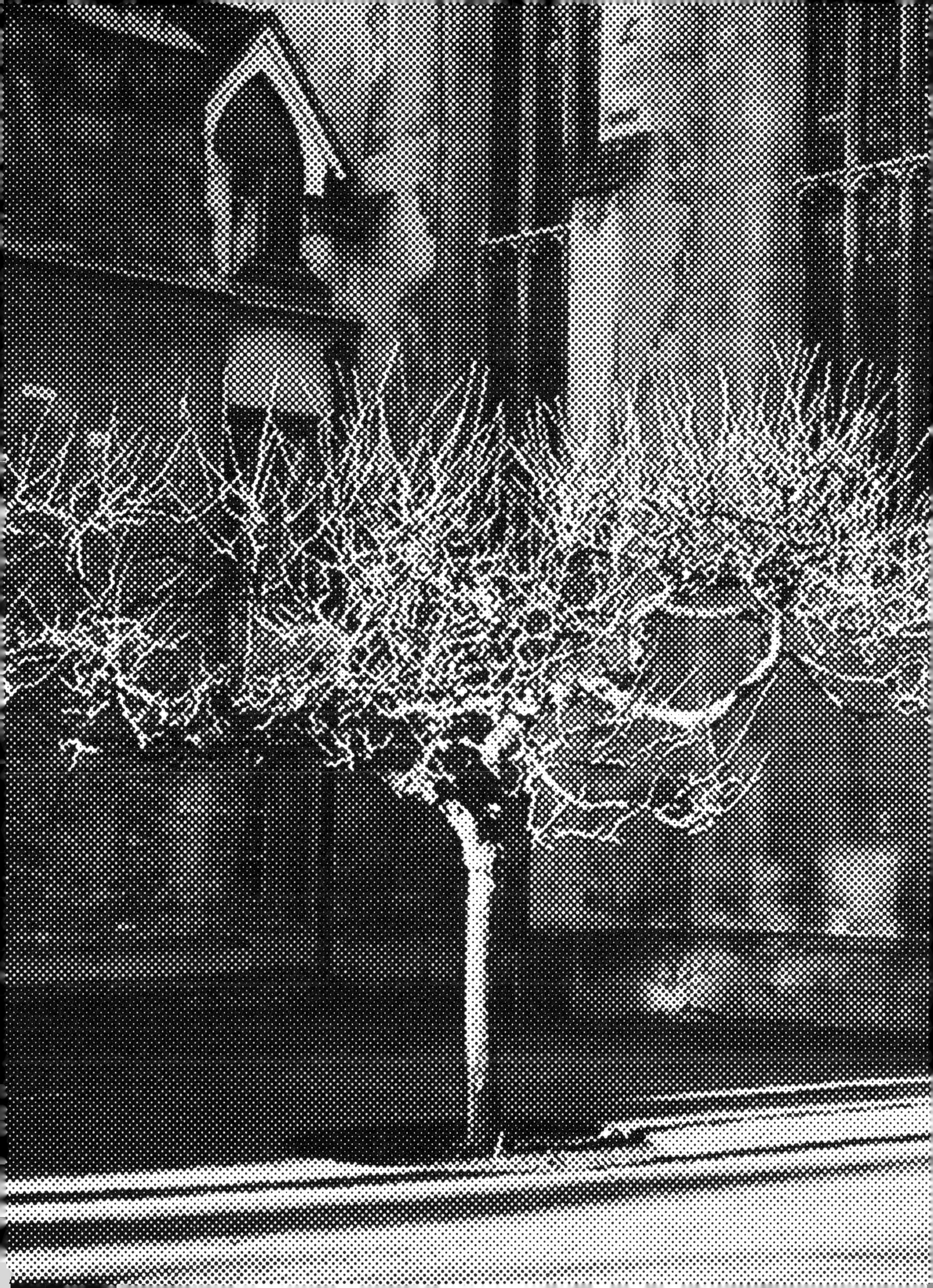

Actions Timeline
Sarah Lowndes

1910 **Henri Gaudier-Brzeska** leaves his native France to pursue a career as an artist in London, with his companion the writer Sophie Brzeska. In London, Gaudier-Brzeska becomes part of the Vorticism movement of Ezra Pound and Wyndham Lewis, and also a founding member of the London Group.

1914–16 Outbreak of the First World War. **Jim Ede**, then a student of painting at Newlyn Art School, is commissioned in September 1914 as an officer with the South Wales Borderers. On 5 June 1915, **Henri Gaudier-Brzeska** is killed fighting for the French army in the trenches at Neuville-Saint-Vaast. Jim Ede serves on the Western Front, until 1916, when he is invalided out suffering from trench gastritis, jaundice and stress of active service. Persistent neurasthenia (shell shock) keeps Ede from returning to the front, and he is posted back to England, to recruit and train officer cadets at Trinity College, Cambridge. While there he hosted social evenings for his men three nights a week.

1917 Two revolutions in Russia dismantle the Tsarist autocracy and lead to the rise of the communist state of the Soviet Union.

Naum Gabo and his brother, Antoine Pevsner (who have been living in Copenhagen and Oslo) return to Moscow, to work alongside Vladimir Tatlin, Wassily Kandinsky and Alexander Rodchenko. In 1922 Gabo moves on again, this time to Berlin.

1918 In October, Arab troops led by Emir Feisal, and supported by British forces, capture Damascus, ending 400 years of Ottoman rule. The First World War Armistice is signed on 11 November. In the United Kingdom, the Representation of the People Act grants women over thirty the right to vote.

1921 Young artist **Barbara Hepworth**, who was born in Wakefield, Yorkshire, wins a county scholarship to the Royal College of Art, London and studies there, alongside Henry Moore and John Skeaping.

After leaving his studies at London's Slade School of Art, **Jim Ede** takes up a post at the National Gallery (later called Tate Gallery) in 1921, where he will work as a curator until 1936. He begins collecting the work of notable and emerging artists from the British and European avant-garde, beginning with his acquisition of much of the estate of **Henri Gaudier-Brzeska**. In the years ahead, Ede will also acquire works by Constantin Brancusi, **Naum Gabo**, Henry Moore, **Ben Nicholson** and **Barbara Hepworth** for his own collection.

1932–34 **Ben Nicholson** lives in London from 1932 to 1939, making several trips to Paris in 1932 and 1933 with **Barbara Hepworth**, where they visit the studios of Hans Arp, Constantin Brancusi, Georges Braque, Piet Mondrian and Pablo Picasso. In 1933, Nicholson and Hepworth co-found the Unit One art movement with artist Paul Nash, the critic Herbert Read and the architect Wells Coates, which seeks to unite Surrealism and Abstraction in British art. Nicholson produces his first geometric and abstract reliefs.

1935–36 Having first met in the 1920s, **Naum Gabo** and **Jim Ede** meet again in Paris in 1935. Ede then provides Gabo with the introductions he needs to move to London later that year, where he meets British artists including **Barbara Hepworth** and **Ben Nicholson** – who begin making Constructivist-influenced works such as Nicholson's *1936 (white relief), second version, 1957* (1957). In 1936, Jim Ede resigns from his post at the Tate and with his wife Helen, goes to live in a modernist house called Whitestone they have commissioned to be built outside Tangier, Morocco.

1937 *Circle: International Survey of Constructive Art*, edited by **Naum Gabo** and **Ben Nicholson** with Leslie Martin is published, promoting internationalism and art with modern ambition.

Meanwhile, in Germany, Adolf Hitler's National Socialist Party party stage a public exhibition of *Degenerate Art*, a derogatory demonstration of modern artworks deemed to be of "insult to German feeling".

1939 Outbreak of the Second World War.

Gustav Metzger (born to Polish-Jewish parents in Nuremberg, Germany) arrives in Britain with his brother as a refugee under the auspices of the Kindertransport: the remainder of his immediate family, including his parents, will be murdered in the Holocaust. In September, as London becomes increasingly dangerous, newly-weds **Ben Nicholson** and **Barbara Hepworth** relocate to Carbis Bay, Cornwall, where they are joined soon afterwards by **Naum Gabo** and his wife Miriam. The notable colony of artists working in West Cornwall during the Second World War and the years afterwards includes potter Bernard Leach and painters Patrick Heron and Peter Lanyon.

1943 **Helen and Jim Ede** return to the United Kingdom where they carry out hospital visits and lectures for servicemen in support of the war effort.

Joseph Beuys (then aged twenty-two) is a radio operator and gunner on board a Luftwaffe Stuka German plane which crashes on the Crimean front, killing the pilot. According to Beuys, he only survives because some Tartars find him unconscious in the snow and take him back to their tents, where they cover his body in fat and wrap him in felt to keep him warm: a myth which is later disproved.

1944 **Naum Gabo**, who is still living and working in St Ives, Cornwall exchanges letters with the writer Herbert Read, which are published in *Horizon* magazine in July. In his letter, Gabo sets out a vision for art as a force for changing how we see the world and act within it, insisting "the image of the world can be different". Gabo's *Linear Construction in Space, No. 1* (1944–5) is created around the time that the letters are published.

1945 Germany surrenders to the Soviet Union and the Western Allies. The full scale of the Holocaust begins to be discovered by the Allied forces. In the United Kingdon, a Labour government is elected, led by Prime Minister Clement Atlee – wartime leader Winston Churchill and his Conservative party is rejected.

Helen and Jim Ede return to Tangier.

1946 **Helen and Jim Ede** begin offering weekend retreats for servicemen on leave from Gibraltar at their house, a scheme that continues until 1947.

1948 The Jewish state known as Israel is declared, but from the beginning there are violent clashes with neighbouring Arab states over the allocation of lands to Israel. In the United Kingdom, the British Nationality Act gives British citizenship to all people living in Commonwealth countries, and full rights of entry and settlement in Britain. In June, the arrival of the SS Empire Windrush at Tilbury Dock, Essex, bearing passengers from Jamaica, marks the beginning of post-war mass migration from the West Indies to the United Kingdom and the beginning of modern British multicultural society.

1949 **Barbara Hepworth** buys Trewyn Studio, St Ives, where she lives following her 1951 divorce from **Ben Nicholson** until her death in 1975. Previously, Hepworth's accommodation had restricted her towards producing modestly sized objects and paintings such as *Two Figures, Yellow and Brown* (1947) but after moving to Trewyn, the scale and ambition of her work increase dramatically. Hepworth is commissioned to make two sculptures for the South Bank site of the Festival of Britain (1951) and has a retrospective in her hometown of Wakefield (1951).

1953–54 **Naum Gabo** becomes a US citizen in 1952 and is Professor at the Graduate School of Architecture at Harvard University between 1953 and 1954. His works during this period include *Linear Construction in Space No. 2* (conceived 1949).

1956–58 **Helen and Jim Ede** come to Cambridge to create "a living place where works of art could be enjoyed... where young people could be at home unhampered by the greater austerity of the museum or public art gallery." With the help of architect Roland Aldridge, they convert four small cottages close to St Peter's Churchyard into one idiosyncratic house and a place to display Ede's collection of twentieth-century art. Kettle's Yard is originally conceived with students in mind and after the renovations are completed, in 1957, Jim Ede keeps "open house" every afternoon of term, personally guiding his visitors around his home.

1957 Ghanaian autonomy is declared. **John Akomfrah** is born in Accra, Ghana. Kwame Nkrumah, first Prime Minister of Ghana is the first African head of state to promote the concept of Pan-Africanism, which he had been introduced to during his studies in the United States, at the time when Marcus Garvey was promoting his "Back to Africa" movement.

1959 **Gustav Metzger** was amongst the group of leading writers, musicians, artists and others who formed the Campaign for Nuclear Disarmament (CND) in 1958. Metzger publishes his manifesto *Auto-Destructive Art*, informed by his experience of twentieth-century society's destructive capabilities and articulating his intention to use art to "confront society".

1961 **John Akomfrah** relocates to London.

1964 **Helen Frankenthaler**'s work is included in the exhibition *Post-Painterly Abstraction*, curated by Clement Greenberg, for the Los Angeles County Museum of Art. The exhibition introduces a new generation of abstract painting, distinct from Abstract Expressionism, that comes to be known as Colour Field painting. Frankenthaler's *Mountains and Sea* (1952) remains perhaps her best-known painting, however her technique undergoes further refinements visible in works such as *Abstract* (1960–61).

1965 America begins military intervention in Vietnam.

Gustav Metzger begins making works such as *Liquid Crystal Environment*, which combine his interest in technology and science with the concept of auto-creative art. He presents the lecture "The Chemical Revolution in Art" at the University of Cambridge. The following year, Metzger's psychedelic light projections are used on stage at London's Roundhouse during performances by rock bands Cream, The Move and The Who and the artist, with John Sharkey, also initiates the Destruction in Art Symposium.

1966 **Jim Ede** gives the House at Kettle's Yard and its contents to the University of Cambridge – although he and his wife Helen continue to live in the house for another seven years, during which time they extend the House and add an exhibition gallery, both to the design of the architects Sir Leslie Martin and David Owers. In March, Harold Wilson's Labour Party wins a majority of ninety-six seats in UK general election.

1967 By the end of 1966, 6,000 Americans had been killed in action in Vietnam and there are many direct-action protests against the Military Selective Service Act of 1967 and America's continued involvement in the war, notably the Spring Mobilization to End the War held in New York in April in which over 400,000 protestors march. In June, the Six Day War is fought between Israel and the neighbouring states of Egypt, Jordan and Syria. Israel seize the Golan Heights from Syria and occupy Palestinian lands in the West Bank, including East Jerusalem and the Gaza Strip: hundreds of thousands of Palestinians flee to neighbouring countries as refugees. In England and Wales, the Sexual Offences Act is passed, which decriminalises homosexual acts in private between two men, if both are over the age of twenty-one.

Richard Long is a student at St Martin's School of Art, London, being taught by Anthony Caro and Phillip King – when he makes *A Line Made by Walking* (1967).

1968 In May a period of civil unrest breaks out in France, punctuated by demonstrations and massive general strikes as well as the occupation of universities and factories across the country. The slogan *Egalité! Liberté! Sexualité!* resonates across Europe. Enoch Powell delivers his infamous "Rivers of Blood" speech to the Conservative Association in Birmingham advocating "stopping further inflow and promoting the maximum outflow" of immigrants to the United Kingdom.

1971 **Zoran Popović** works within the group of conceptual artists around the Students' Cultural Centre (SKC), Belgrade, which includes Era Milivojević, Raša Todosijević, Marina Abramović, Neša Paripović and Gera Urkom. Popović's work *Axioms* (1971–73) is one of the earliest actions realised before an audience in the former Yugoslavia.

1973 Britain enters the European Economic Community (EEC) – which is incorporated into the European Union (EU) in 1993.

Helen and Jim Ede retire to Edinburgh.

1975 In the United Kingdom, the Sex Discrimination Act and Equal Pay Act are introduced, aiming to end discrimination over offers of work and pay to men and women.

Mary Kelly works collaboratively with the Berwick Street Film Collective on the documentary *Nightcleaners* (1970–75) and produces *Post-Partum Document* (1973–79).

1976 In the United Kingdom, the Race Relations Act makes it unlawful to discriminate on grounds of race, colour, nationality or ethnic origins.

1977 **Linder**'s collage of a naked woman with an iron for a head appears on the sleeve of the first Buzzcocks single *Orgasm Addict* (1977). The Ethiopian "Red Terror" or Qey Shibir begins and lasts until 1978. **Julie Mehretu** is aged 7, her family flee Ethiopia, to settle in East Lansing, Michigan, where her father takes up a teaching position at Michigan State University.

1979 Conservative party leader Margaret Thatcher is elected Prime Minister of the United Kingdom – the first woman to hold the office. Thatcher's term of office (1979–90), coincides with the presidency of Ronald Reagan (1981–89), representing a marked swing to the right on both sides of the Atlantic.

Vicken Parsons is studying painting at the Slade. Working in 'the Abstract Studio', she is inspired by her tutor John Hoyland, using vibrant colours to begin exploring interior space and an acknowledgment of the flatness of the picture plane. Parsons meets artist Antony Gormley the same year. They travel across America together.

1980 Five years after **Barbara Hepworth**'s death, and according to her wishes, her home, studio and garden at Trewyn Studio, St Ives, are opened to the public – and much of her work is given to the nation, in the care of the Tate Gallery.

1981 Aged seventeen, **Edmund de Waal** defers his entry into Trinity Hall, University of Cambridge to read English, opting instead to undertake a two-year apprenticeship with potter Geoffrey Whiting (a student of Bernard Leach) – during which time de Waal makes hundreds of pots, including casseroles and honey pots.

1982 For *Documenta 7*, **Joseph Beuys** proposes the project *7000 Oak Trees*, in which said trees would be planted throughout the city of Kassel, each paired with a basalt stone. The project, seen locally as a gesture towards green urban renewal, takes five years to complete and subsequently spreads to other cities around the world. In November that same year, **Linder** takes to the stage of the Haçienda in Manchester with her band Ludus, wearing a dress made of raw chicken sewn onto layers of black net – with a large black dildo underneath which she reveals to the audience as a finale. **John Akomfrah** had found the influential Black Audio Film Collective, one of the first groups to challenge how the black British community were represented on screen and in the media, with the artists David Lawson and Lina Gopaul in London in 1982.

1983 **Basel Abbas** is born in Nicosia, Cyprus, in the same year that a separate Turkish Cypriot state in the north of the island of Cyprus is established by unilateral declaration: a move widely condemned by the international community and which continues to be an ongoing dispute today. Meanwhile, in America, in the city of Boston, his future artistic collaborator, **Ruanne Abou-Rahme** is born.

1984 The inaugural year of Britain's biggest art prize, the Turner Prize, established by the Tate Gallery to stimulate debate around contemporary art, which is won by expatriate painter Malcolm Morley.

1985 In March, Mikhail S. Gorbachev is elected the new leader of the Union of Soviet Socialist Republics (USSR), ushering in a new era of Perestroika and Glasnost (reforms to bestow more rights and freedoms upon the Soviet people).

Issam Kourbaj leaves his native Syria to study in Leningrad, after a display of his work at the Soviet Cultural Centre earns him a scholarship. **Rana Begum** and her family leave Bangladesh to settle in St Albans in the United Kingdom, when the artist is aged eight. Meanwhile, in Glasgow, David Harding is appointed Head of the new Environmental Art Department at Glasgow School of Art, where students including Christine Borland, Claire Barclay, Douglas Gordon, **Nathan Coley** and Martin Boyce are encouraged to produce art outside studios and galleries ("with or through people") in the post-industrial city's derelict buildings and empty shop units.

1986 The Black Audio Film Collective's first film, *Handsworth Songs* (1986) explore the events surrounding the 1985 race riots in Birmingham and London through a charged combination of archive footage, still photos and newsreel, woven into a reflective, multi-stranded narrative with a mosaic-like soundtrack.

1988 As warehouse parties around Britain spread rave music subculture, **Anya Gallaccio** exhibits in the *Freeze* warehouse exhibition in London's Docklands, organized by Damien Hirst, along with seventeen fellow Goldsmiths students, including Hirst, Angela Bulloch, Sarah Lucas and Gary Hume, several of whom had been taught by tutor Michael Craig-Martin, marking the beginning of the YBA (young British artist) phenomenon.

1989 A revolutionary wave of civil resistance sweeps Central and Eastern Europe, resulting in the end of communist rule in Poland, Hungary, East Germany, Bulgaria, Czechoslovakia and Romania. The end of the Cold War is symbolised by the fall of the Berlin Wall on 9 November.

After being nominated for the Turner Prize four times (in 1984, 1987, 1988 and 1989) **Richard Long** finally wins the award and creates *White Water Line* (1989) in the Tate's Duveen galleries, a work that is created by pouring liquid pigment in one continuous snake-like movement. Painter **Callum Innes** participates in the group exhibition *Scatter* at the Third Eye Centre in Glasgow, which features works by Graeme Todd, Wendy McMurdo, Louise Scullion and Kevin Henderson, amongst others. The work in the exhibition, curated by Andrew Nairne, is presented as "contemplative, open-ended and responsive", in contrast to the work of the earlier generation of figurative painters.

1990 After eleven years in power, Margaret Thatcher resigns in the wake of the Poll Tax Riots, and is replaced by John Major.

Kettle's Yard founder **Jim Ede** dies in Edinburgh. A memorial stone is laid in St Peter's Church, Cambridge inscribed, "Jim Ede 1895-1990, who created Kettle's Yard and helped preserve this church."

In London, choreographer and film-maker Darshan Singh Buller persuades Celeste Dandeker to dance from her wheelchair for the award-winning dance film *The Fall* (1990). Soon afterwards, Dandeker meets painter and dancer Adam Benjamin and the two begin teaching integrated workshops at London's Aspire Centre for Spinal Injury, out of which, they develop **Candoco Dance Company** (established in 1991), a professional dance company focused on the integration of disabled and non-disabled artists.

1991 The first Gulf War leaves a legacy of instability in the Middle East – increasing numbers of refugees fleeing war zones and rising incidence of terrorist attacks on the West will become the two biggest social and political challenges of the years ahead.

Cornelia Parker presents *Cold Dark Matter: An Exploded View* at the Chisenhale Gallery in London.

1992 **Callum Innes**, who has been exhibiting since the mid-1980s, has two major exhibitions, at the ICA, London and the Scottish National Gallery of Modern Art, Edinburgh, which showcase his series of works entitled *Identified Forms,* in which Innes applies his working process of 'de-painting'.

Michael Harrison is appointed Director of Kettle's Yard, a post he holds until 2011.

1993 In June, Tate St Ives opens, the second regional Tate after Tate Liverpool. The new galleries are intended to showcase artists associated with Cornwall, especially those already held in the Tate collection, such as Bernard Leach, **Barbara Hepworth**, Patrick Heron and Peter Lanyon.

1995 **Oscar Murillo**'s family leave Colombia to settle in Hackney in the East End of London, when Murillo is aged nine. **Anya Gallaccio** exhibits in the fourth instalment of Hayward Touring survey exhibition *British Art Show*, which brings the work of both the YBAs and emerging neo-conceptual artists from Glasgow to British audiences outside London. Gallaccio's piece *Head Over Heals* consists of 365 orange gerbera daisies strung together in looping chains crisscrossing an entire room and left to fade and wither as the exhibition progresses.

1997 Tony Blair leads the Labour Party to election victory in the United Kingdom with the party's highest ever number of parliamentary seats. In the general election, an unprecedented number of women are elected to the House of Commons. 101 of the 120 new women MPs are Labour candidates, who are dubbed "Blair's Babes" by the tabloid press.

Cornelia Parker is part of the first all-women Turner Prize shortlist, alongside Christine Borland, Angela Bulloch and Gillian Wearing (who wins the prize).

1999 The report *Guatemala: Memory of Silence* (1999) written by the UN-backed Commission for Historical Clarification confirms that more than 200,000 people were killed during the Guatemalan Civil War (1960-96). **Regina José Galindo** writes the pieces that become part of her book *Personal and Intransmisible* (2000) and which lead to her first performances, such as *Lo voy a gritar al viento* (1999), in which the artist hangs from the arch extending across the street in a heavily trafficked area of downtown Guatemala City and reads her poems without a microphone, alluding to the way that women's voices are often ignored.

2000 German artist **Melanie Manchot** receives critical acclaim for her series of C-prints, *Liminal Portraits* (1999-2000) after her semi-nude portraits of her mother appear on billboards in the UK and USA.

2001 9/11 terrorist attacks by the Islamic terrorist group al-Qaeda on the United States result in military repercussions in Afghanistan, where al-Qaeda leader Osama Bin Laden is rumoured to be in hiding.

Ghanaian born, British-raised artist **Harold Offeh** graduates from the photography MA course at the Royal College of Art – and wins acclaim for his single-shot performance to camera work *Smile* (2001). The work depicts Offeh in close up, maintaining a part grimace, part smile to a soundtrack of Nat King Cole's *The Smile Song*, "That's the time you must keep on trying/Smile – what's the use in crying?" As an Artangel commission, **Jeremy Deller** stages an ambitious re-enactment, of *The Battle of Orgreave* from the 1984 Miners' Strike, working with 800 historical re-enactors and 200 former miners who had been part of the original conflict.

2003 America leads the invasion of Iraq, which ousts dictator Saddam Hussein but leads to a conflict that will last for the next decade. On 15 February, two million people march in anti-war demonstrations across the United Kingdom, with a further eight million attending anti-war rallies worldwide, making this the biggest peace rally ever held.

Issam Kourbaj, now resident in Cambridge, creates the wall installation *Sound Palimpsest* (2003), in response to the invasion of Iraq. The work is made up of recycled pages, overlaid with fragments of Arabic songs, scraps of graffiti and X-rays. Meanwhile, **Nathan Coley** sets out on a series of expeditions, from Los Angeles to Death Valley, from Rio de Janeiro to Amazonas, from Edinburgh to Rannoch Moor, to explore the places where urban space meets the wilderness. His reflections on preconceived notions of frontiers are published the following year by Bookworks under the title *Urban/Wild*. The same year, **Harold Offeh** presents *Haroldinho* (2003), a video work documenting a persona created and performed by Offeh during a two-month residency in Rio de Janiero. The work reflects Offeh's transition from private performances to his subsequent practice, in which he often also uses collaboration and conversation to develop projects that respond to specific places. **Regina José Galindo** carries out her most celebrated work, *Quién puede borrar las huellas? (Who Can Erase the Traces?)* (2003).

2004 Architect **Jamie Fobert** is commissioned to make an extension for Kettle's Yard, a commission that he follows with an extension to Tate St Ives and the creation of Garage, a new Centre for Contemporary Culture in Moscow, housed within a 1920s bus depot. He explains, "We have an interest in making spaces which are perceptually rich. We want to create buildings which have volume, material and light."

Idris Khan graduates with a Masters from the Royal College of Art, and attracts praise for a single image he produces by scanning in every page from the Qur'an.

2005 There are fifty-two deaths and hundreds of injuries in London after an attack by Islamic fundamentalist terrorists. Angela Merkel of the Christian Democratic Union (CDU) is elected Chancellor of Germany. Merkel wins praise from the international community for her drive towards renewable energy and her enlightened stance on immigration.

2007 **Edmund de Waal** makes an installation at Kettle's Yard, returning to a place he often visited while studying English at Trinity Hall in the mid 1980s. In London, **Katie Paterson** graduates from Master's studies at The Slade with a graduation exhibition *Vatnajökull (the sound of)*, which highlights the environmental impact of global warming.

2008 **Alice Channer** graduates in sculpture from London's Royal College of Art, and soon draws critical interest for her sculptures and textile works that dress the architecture of a given space – such as *Inhale, Exhale*, at the iconic Mackintosh Museum at Glasgow School of Art (2010) for which the dark wooden beams of the museum are draped with engineered loops of pale fabric. **Melanie Manchot** begins filming her daughter Billie, aged eleven, with a Super-8 camera for a minute every month.

2009 Democrat Barack Obama is elected the first black President of the United States. Obama ends US military involvement in the Iraq War, increases US troop levels in Afghanistan, orders US military involvement in Libya and orders the military operation that results in the death of Osama bin Laden.

At Hallowe'en, **Linder** carries out a performance piece called *Allentide* at Tate St Ives, and while in Cornwall she makes a tactile connection with the works of **Barbara Hepworth**. She recalls, "I was invited to visit her sculpture garden at night. It was a beautiful night, when the veils between the worlds are very thin. We were encouraged to feel our way around on this damp, dark, wet night. I made a connection with her and her work through feeling rather than seeing. It was a kind of belated epiphany."

2010 The coalition government formed in the United Kingdom by Conservative leader David Cameron and Liberal Democrat leader Nick Clegg in 2010 promotes the free market economy while enforcing "austerity measures" in the form of cuts to public spending, notably in the areas of welfare (health care, social housing and benefits), in education and in the arts. More than 4.6 million Palestinians are refugees and many are living in camps in the West Bank, Gaza Strip, Syria, Jordan and Lebanon.

Basel Abbas and Ruanne Abou Rahme begin exhibiting mixed media works that utilise the remix techniques of the drum and bass scene to respond to the contradictions of the Palestine and the Arab world. In *Contingency* (2010), Abbas and Abou Rahme explore the sonic particularities of the Qalandia checkpoint, the portal between Jerusalem and Ramallah in the West Bank (where the artists live), which often features in news reportage. **Katie Paterson** asks experts in nanotechnology to help her realise *Inside this desert lies the tiniest grain of sand* (2010). In the same year, **Anna Brownsted** graduates from the Central School of Speech and Drama, in London and establishes her own company Unclaimed Creatures, to design and direct immersive theatrical experiences, which consider audience-of-one performance structures that 'produce' the participant as a protagonist, for example *Object 27* (2010), a site-responsive live installation and encounter commissioned by the British Museum to take place in amongst their permanent collection.

2011 The Tunisian Revolution leads to the Arab Spring, as popular protests and demand for reform, begin in Tunisia but spread within weeks to Egypt, Yemen, Bahrain, Libya and Syria.

In Cambridge, Michael Harrison retires after nineteen years as Director of Kettle's Yard – his successor, Andrew Nairne is appointed to take forward an ambitious redevelopment plan including the creation of an education wing. Nairne says, "One of my absolute commitments is to build relationships with communities that don't feel Kettle's Yard is available and accessible to them."

The Tunisian Revolution inspires French-Tunisian Parisian street artist **eL Seed** to create his first large-scale mural, which he realises in 2012 in the Tunisian city of Kairouan. The mural features a calligraphic representation of passage by Tunisian poet Abu al-Qasim al-Husayfi dedicated to those struggling against tyranny and injustice. **Kate Whitley**, a composer and pianist who lives in South London, starts running The Multi-Story Orchestra with conductor Christopher Stark. In the same year, **Emma Smith** develops *The Playback Project* over the course of a year with The Showroom, London, working with students from Quintin Kynaston School, day visitors to sixty Penfold Street, The Barnabus Group and members of the public "to tell and share stories relating to experiences of the local area. The stories span eighty years of local experiences over different time frames: first arrivals to life-long experiences." The Hepworth Wakefield opens in the hometown of **Barbara Hepworth** – to house works donated by Hepworth's family and temporary exhibitions of new art, alongside works by Hepworth's contemporaries Henry Moore and **Ben Nicholson**.

2012 In America, Barack Obama is re-elected and orders further American military intervention in Iraq in response to the growing power of the Islamic State following the 2011 US withdrawal from Iraq – while continuing to withdraw American troops from Afghanistan.

Idris Khan is commissioned to make a wall drawing for the British Museum exhibition, *Hajj: Journey to the Heart of Islam*. **Julie Mehretu** presents *Mogamma: A Painting in Four Parts* (2012) at Documenta 13. Mehretu's work draws upon the concept of the public square, which references not only Tahrir Square in Cairo but also other politically charged public plazas such as Tiananmen Square and the Place de la Bastille and Zuccotti Park in Manhattan, where the Occupy Wall Street movement began. **John Akomfrah** completes the three-screen installation *The Unfinished Conversation* (2012), a moving portrait of the cultural theorist Stuart Hall's life and work. This work interweaves Hall's biography with key national and international events, such as the attack on the working class in Britain and the Suez Crisis, thereby linking the personal with the historical, through use of archival footage and original interviews. Completed two years before Hall's death in 2014, the installation is a testament to a thinker who is widely revered as the godfather of multiculturalism.

2013

British-born artist **Khadija Saye** graduates from UCA Farnham, presenting as her final project a series which reflects upon her Gambian heritage, entitled Crowned which documents Afro-Caribbean hairstyles and was shot in a home-studio in her twentieth floor apartment in Grenfell Tower, West London. The following year these works were exhibited as part of The Discerning Eye exhibition at the Mall Galleries, London. **Alice Channer** has a solo exhibition at Hepworth Wakefield of a new body of figurative work collectively entitled *Invertebrates*, which includes casts of Channer's fingers, stretched using three-dimensional technology, which are slotted into a low aluminium structure inspired by the horizontal, curving skeletons of snakes and other reptiles. **Linder** is appointed the first artist in residence at Tate St Ives, and moves to Cornwall for a year. She works in the same studio, number 5, previously used by **Ben Nicholson** and produces a new body of work referencing **Barbara Hepworth**'s love of dance and her engagement with nature for a solo exhibition, also at Hepworth Wakefield.

2014

Rana Begum, inspired by the basket weaving of her childhood, creates the installation *No. 473 Baskets* at the Dhaka Art Summit in Bangladesh. **Katie Paterson** produces a series of *Campo del Cielo* meteorites.

New paintings by **Vicken Parsons** are displayed amongst the permanent collection at Kettle's Yard, alongside paintings, sculptures and drawings by **Ben Nicholson**, **Barbara Hepworth** and **Henri Gaudier-Brzeska**.

2015 At the general election in May, David Cameron is re-elected as Prime Minister, giving the Conservatives a surprise parliamentary majority for the first time since 1992. In September, backbench MP and anti-war campaigner Jeremy Corbyn is elected as Labour leader; he says people are "fed up with the injustice and the inequality" of Britain. In October, a series of Islamic fundamentalist terrorist attacks by jihadists radicalized by the conflicts in Syria and elsewhere in the Middle East and North Africa begin, when an airbus flying from Sharm el-Sheik in Egypt to St Petersburg is bombed, killing 224 people. In Paris on 13 November, 132 people are killed and 350 wounded in a co-ordinated city-wide campaign of terrorist attacks, attributed to jihadist group Isis. Figures released in 2015 by the UN High Commissioner for Refugees (UNHCR) show there were almost sixty million people forcibly displaced globally and 19.5 million refugees (persons fleeing armed conflict or persecution) worldwide at the end of 2014.

In June, Kettle's Yard temporarily closes for redevelopment by **Jamie Fobert Architects**, who describe the planned changes "as a series of gentle additions that will offer greatly improved support services for visitors to Kettle's Yard House and Gallery", including a four-floor education wing, improved exhibition galleries, a new entrance area and a café. Fobert writes, "The entire spatial sequence will feel extended continuity will be achieved by sensitivity to the domestic scale and calm aesthetic of the original House." After the building closes, Kettle's Yard commission a number of projects, as part of Open House, a creative programme in partnership with communities in North Cambridge, which includes **Emma Smith**'s *Variations on a Weekend Theme* (2015). In London, **Issam Kourbaj** presents *Another Day Lost* (2015), a series of installations inspired by and based on the ongoing Syrian conflict.

In May, **Oscar Murillo** debuts his ongoing long-term project *Frequencies*, with a large-scale installation of canvases shown as part of the 56th Venice Biennale: All the World's Futures. *Frequencies* is created in collaboration with members of Murillo's family and political scientist Clara Dublanc, and is realised through canvases that have been temporarily affixed to classroom desks in selected schools across the globe.

2016 In a UK referendum on the 23 June 51.9 per cent (of those who participate) vote to leave. David Cameron resigns and is replaced by Theresa May. Labour MP Sadiq Khan is elected Mayor of London – the city's first ethnic minority mayor and the first Muslim to become the mayor of a major Western capital. Donald Trump is elected forty fifth president of the USA.

On 1 July, **Jeremy Deller**'s *We're Here Because We're Here* is enacted in train stations, car parks and shopping centres across the UK – as 1,400 volunteer participants dressed in First World War uniforms perform a living memorial to those lost in the Battle of the Somme.

In October, Andrew Nairne, Director of Kettle's Yard and artist **Caroline Walker** volunteer with Care4Calais in the "Jungle" at the French port, where at least 7,000 people, mostly migrants, mainly from Africa and the Middle East, are living in squalid conditions as they await opportunities to board lorries bound for the UK, clashing with drivers and police.

2017 On 29 March the British government invoke Article 50 of the Treaty on the European Union. Seeking a mandate to continue Brexit negotiations, Theresa May calls for a snap election – resulting in a hung parliament – May remains as Prime Minister, with support from the Northern Irish Democratic Unionist Party (DUP). Throughout the spring, the UK is rocked by a series of Islamic fundamentalist terrorist attacks – in London, on 22 March, in Manchester on 22 May and in London on 3 June.

In May, **Khadija Saye** exhibits her work, *Dwelling: in this space we breathe* (2017), as part of the Diaspora Pavilion presented at the 57th Venice Biennale. Her work greatly impresses Kettle's Yard Director Andrew Nairne who subsequently meets with the artist and invites her to exhibit her work as part of the *Actions* exhibition at Kettle's Yard in 2018. On 14 June, **Khadija Saye** (then aged twenty-four) dies, along with seventy others, in the Grenfell Tower fire in West London, leading to calls for a public inquiry.

2018

The three-year long redevelopment of Kettle's Yard buildings at Castle Street, realised by **Jamie Fobert Architects** opens to the public. The major exhibition *Actions. The image of the world can be different*, curated by Andrew Nairne, opens at Kettle's Yard on 10 February, occupying numerous spaces including the new galleries, in the House amongst the collection, in St Peter's Church and outdoors in north Cambridge. The exhibition programme also includes new performances developed by **Anna Brownsted**, **Candoco Dance Company** with choreographer **Laila Diallo**, **Harold Offeh**, **Emma Smith** and **Kate Whitley**.

“I believe art to be the most immediate and most effective of all means of communication between human beings.”

Naum Gabo